AF522360

Logistics and Distribution Management

Logistics and Distribution Management

Farhan Ali Khan

RANDOM PUBLICATIONS
NEW DELHI (INDIA)

Logistics and Distribution Management

ISBN 978-93-5111-227-3

Published in 2014 in India by

RANDOM PUBLICATIONS

4376-A/4B, Gali Murari Lal, Ansari Road
New Delhi-110 002
Phone : +91-11-43580356, +91-11-23289044
e-mail: randomexports@gmail.com, sales@randompublications.com, info@randompublications.com

Reprint 2021

Type Setting by : Keystoneprintads, Delhi-110051

Digitally Printed at : Replika Press Pvt. Ltd.

Preface

Uncertainty is certain. So are increased complexity, competition, and compliance. Third-party logistics (3PL), port-based logistics, and specialized services are on the rise. With the new normal forcing logistics service providers (LSPs) to focus on their business models, today's imperatives are filling service gaps, cutting carbons, and organic growth. Future success, however, begins with strategies and services that resonate the needs and demands of tomorrow's global enterprises. Keeping businesses in motion will require mastering the verticals you serve, becoming the customer's brand custodian, and sharing risk - while collaborating efficiently with 3PL players to maximize possibilities on the move.

Agreed, the worst of the economic slowdown is over, but companies are still grappling with reduced demand and ever-increasing fuel prices. Many carriers sold their equipment during the slowdown. When the economy gets healthy and stays there, capacity could be an issue - is there enough fleet strength to hit the roads? With 80% of the world's population - and rising - in emerging economies, a truckload of potential awaits by expanding to new geographies. But for overcoming infrastructure issues and network roadblocks to get huge volumes of cargo to the right place at the right time, enterprises need re-engineering of business processes and technology platforms. When the margin for error is narrow and customer loyalties shift unexpectedly, understanding the competition inside out can help you stay ahead. It's much easier to compete to win, when you play to your strengths and your competitors' weaknesses. A strategic market plan augmented by business intelligence and mobility systems and solutions can aid boardroom decisions and frontline operations.

We blend our expertise in consulting, technology, and sourcing to help our clients solve complex business challenges and unlock their value levers by creating outcomes in three key areas: business transformation, accelerating innovation, and efficient operations. This book will help in logistics manager's quest to improve service and reduce cost, as well as keeping them aware of the many different facets of logistics and the supply chain. It should be of interest to practicing managers and supervisors, to candidates undertaking examinations for the various professional institutes, and to students who are reading for degrees in logistics distribution and supply chain management.

I thank all members of my team who have helped in the preparation of the book. My special thanks go to "Random Publications" who have published the book.

– Farhan Ali Khan

Contents

1

Introduction

LOGISTICS AND DISTRIBUTION

The key components of logistics have been an important feature of industrial and economic life for countless years, but it is only in the relatively recent past that logistics has been recognized as a major function in its own right. The main reason for this has probably been the nature of logistics itself. It is a function made up of many sub-functions and many sub-systems, each of which has been, and may still be, treated as a distinct management operation. Both the academic and the business world now accept that there is a need to adopt a more holistic view of these operations in order to take into account how they interrelate and interact with one another. The appreciation of the scope and importance of logistics and the supply chain has led to a more scientific approach being adopted towards the subject. This approach has been aimed at the overall concept of the logistics function as a whole and also at the individual sub-systems. Much of this approach has addressed the need for, and means of, planning logistics and the supply chain, but has also considered some of the major operational issues.

SCOPE AND DEFINITION

Parallel to the growth in the importance of distribution, logistics and the supply chain has been the growth in the number of associated names and different definitions that are used. Some of the different names that have been applied to distribution and logistics include:

- Physical distribution;
- Logistics;
- Business logistics;
- Materials management;
- Procurement and supply;
- Product flow;
- Marketing logistics;
- Supply chain management;

- Demand chain management; and
- There are several more.

There is, realistically, no 'true' name or 'true' definition that should be pedantically applied, because products differ, companies differ and systems differ. Logistics is a diverse and dynamic function that has to be flexible and has to change according to the various constraints and demands imposed upon it and with respect to the environment in which it works. These many terms are used, oft en interchangeably, in literature and in the business world. One quite widely accepted definition that uses some of these terms also helps to describe one of the key relationships. This is as follows:

- Logistics = Materials management + Distribution

An extension to this idea helps to illustrate that the supply chain covers an even broader scope of the business area. This includes the supply of raw materials and components as well as the delivery of products to the final customer. Thus:

- Supply Chain = Suppliers + Logistics + Customers

Logistics and the supply chain are concerned with physical and information flows and storage from raw material through to the final distribution of the finished product. Th us, supply and materials management represents the storage and flows into and through the production process, while distribution represents the storage and flows from the final production point through to the customer or end user. Major emphasis is now placed on the importance of information as well as physical flows and storage, and an additional and very relevant factor is that of reverse logistics – the flow of used products and returnable packaging back through the system.

The question of the most appropriate definition of logistics and its associated namesakes is always an interesting one. There are a multitude of definitions to be found in textbooks and on the internet. A selected few are:

- Logistics is... the management of all activities which facilitate movement and the coordination of supply and demand in the creation of time and place utility.
- Logistics is the art and science of managing and controlling the flow of goods, energy, information and other resources.
- Logistics management is... the planning, implementation and control of the efficient, effective forward and reverse flow and storage of goods, services and related information between the point of origin and the point of consumption in order to meet customer requirements.
- Logistics is... the positioning of resource at the right time, in the right place, at the right cost, at the right quality.

It is interesting to detect the different biases – military, economic, academic, etc. An appropriate modern definition that applies to most industry might be that logistics concerns *the efficient transfer of goods from the source of supply through the place of manufacture to the point of consumption in a cost-effective way whilst providing an acceptable service to the customer.* This focus on cost-effectiveness and customer service will be a point of emphasis throughout this book. For most organizations it is possible to draw up a familiar list of key areas rep resenting the major components of distribution and logistics. These will include transport, warehousing, inventory, packaging and information. This list can be 'exploded' once again to reveal the detailed aspects within the different components. All of these functions and sub-functions need to be planned in a systematic way, in terms both of their own local environment and of the wider scope of the distribution system as a whole. A number of questions need to be asked and decisions made.

HISTORICAL PERSPECTIVE

The elements of logistics and the supply chain have, of course, always been fundamental to the manufacturing, storage and movement of goods and products. It is only relatively recently, however, that they have come to be recognized as vital functions within the business and economic environment. The role of logistics has changed in that it now plays a major part in the success of many different operations and organizations. In essence, the underlying concepts and rationale for logistics are not new. They have evolved through several stages of development, but still use the basic ideas such as trade-off analysis, value chains and systems theory together with their associated techniques. There have been several distinct stages in the development of distribution and logistics.

1950S AND EARLY 1960S

In this period, distribution systems were unplanned and unformulated. Manufacturers manufactured, retailers retailed, and in some way or other the goods reached the shops. Distribution was broadly represented by the haulage industry and manufacturers' own-account fleets. There was little positive control and no real liaison between the various distribution-related functions.

1960S AND EARLY 1970S

In the 1960s and 1970s the concept of *physical distribution* was developed with the gradual realization that the 'dark continent' was indeed a valid area for managerial involvement. This consisted of the recognition that there was a series of interrelated physical activities such as transport, storage, materials handling and packaging that could be linked together and managed more effectively. In particular, there was recognition of a relationship between the various functions, which enabled a systems approach and total cost perspective to be used. Under the auspices of a physical distribution manager, a number of distribution trade-offs could be planned and managed to provide both improved service and reduced cost. Initially the benefits were recognized by manufacturers who developed distribution operations to reflect the flow of their product through the supply chain.

1970S

This was an important decade in the development of the distribution concept. One major change was the recognition by some companies of the need to include distribution in the functional management structure of an organization. The decade also saw a change in the structure and control of the distribution chain. There was a decline in the power of the manufacturers and suppliers, and a marked increase in that of the major retailers. The larger retail chains developed their own distribution structures, based initially on the concept of regional or local distribution depots to supply their stores.

1980S

Fairly rapid cost increases and the clearer definition of the true costs of distribution contributed to a significant increase in professionalism within distribution. With this professionalism came a move towards longer-term planning and attempts to identify and pursue cost-saving measures. These measures included centralized distribution, severe reductions in stock-holding and the use of the computer to pro vide improved information and control. The growth of the third-party distribution service industry was also of major significance, with these companies spearheading developments in information and equipment technology. The concept of and need for integrated logistics systems were recognized by forward-looking companies that participated in distribution activities.

LATE 1980S AND EARLY 1990S

In the late 1980s and early 1990s, and linked very much to advances in information technology, organizations began to broaden their perspectives in terms of the functions that could be integrated. In short, this covered the combining of materials management (the inbound side) with physical distribution (the outbound side). The term 'logistics' was used to describe this concept. Once again this led to additional opportunities to improve customer service and reduce the associated costs. One major emphasis made during this period was that informational aspects were as important as physical aspects in securing an effective logistics strategy.

1990S

In the 1990s the process was developed even further to encompass not only the key functions within an organization's own boundaries but also those functions outside that also contribute to the provision of a product to a final customer. This is known as *supply chain management.* The supply chain concept gave credence to the fact that there may be several different organizations involved in getting a product to the marketplace. Thus, for example, manufacturers and retailers should act together in partnership to help create a logistics pipeline that enables an efficient and effective flow of the right products through to the final customer. These partnerships or alliances should also include other intermediaries within the supply chain, such as third-party contractors.

2000 TO 2010

Business organizations faced many challenges as they endeavored to maintain or improve their position against their competitors, bring new products to market and increase the profitability of their operations. This led to the development of many new ideas for improvement, specifically recognized in the redefinition of business goals and the re-engineering of entire systems. Logistics and the supply chain finally became recognized as an area that was key to overall business success. Indeed, for many organizations, changes in logistics have provided the catalyst for major enhancements to their business. Leading organizations recognized that there was a positive 'value added' role that logistics could offer, rather than the traditional view that the various functions within logistics were merely a cost burden that had to be minimized regardless of any other implications. Thus, the role and importance of logistics continued to be recognized as a key enabler for business improvement.

IMPORTANCE OF LOGISTICS AND DISTRIBUTION

It is useful, at this point, to consider logistics in the context of business and the economy as a whole. Logistics is an important activity making extensive use of the human and material resources that affect a national economy. Several investigations have been undertaken to try to estimate the extent of the impact of logistics on the economy.

IMPORTANCE IN THE ECONOMY

One such study indicated that about 30 per cent of the working population in the UK are associated with work that is related to logistics. Another study undertaken by Armstrong and Associ ates (2007) found that, for the main European and North American economies, logistics represents between about 8 per cent and 11 per cent of the gross domestic product of each country. For developing countries this range is higher at around 12 per cent to 21 per cent – with India at about 17 per cent and China at 21 per cent. These numbers represent some very substantial costs, and serve to illustrate how important it is to understand the nature of logistics costs and to identify means of keeping these costs to a minimum. Countries with the lowest costs are those where there has been a longer recognition of the importance of logistics. It is to be expected that the logistics costs of developing countries will decrease over the next few years. About 25 years ago, if the same statistics had been available, these percentage elements would undoubtedly have been a lot higher in all of these countries. In the UK, records go back for 25 years, and logistics costs were then around the 18 to 20 per cent mark.

IMPORTANCE OF KEY COMPONENTS

The breakdown of the costs of the different elements within logistics has also been addressed in various surveys. One survey of US logistics costs undertaken by Establish/Herbert Davis (2008) indicated that transport was the most important element at 50 per cent, followed by inventory carrying cost (20 per cent), storage/warehousing (also at 20 per cent) customer service/order entry (7 per cent) and administration (3 per cent). This survey also produced a pan-European cost breakdown. This placed transport at about 40 per cent, warehousing at about 32 per cent, inventory carrying cost at about 18 per cent, customer service/order entry at about 5 per cent and administration at about 5 per cent of overall costs. In both studies the transport cost element of distribution was the major constituent part, particularly due to high fuel costs. US transport costs are especially affected by this due to long distances travelled.

IMPORTANCE BY INDUSTRY SECTOR

The relative make-up of these costs can vary quite significantly between different companies and, particularly, between different industries. There are some quite major differences amongst the results from the various companies. One of the main reasons for these cost differences is that logistics structures can and do differ quite dramatically between one company and another, and one industry and another. Channels can be short (ie very direct) or long (ie have many intermediate stocking points). Also, channels may be operated by manufacturers, retailers or, as is now becoming increasingly common, specialist third-party distribution companies. The relative importance of logistics is, of course, measured in relationship to the overall value of the particular products in question. Cement is a low-cost product (as well as being a very bulky one!), so the relative costs of its logistics are very high. Spirits (whisky, gin, etc) are very high-value products, so the relative logistics costs appear very low. A series of studies undertaken by Datamonitor (2008) indicate that the global logistics market (including all in-house and outsourced logistics operations) is dominated by retail logistics services (63.9 per cent). This applies globally and is reflected in all key markets. The retail sector has been at the forefront of some of the most advanced and innovative developments in logistics and supply chain thinking.

LOGISTICS AND SUPPLY CHAIN STRUCTURE

The fundamental characteristics of a physical distribution structure could be considered as the flow of material or product, interspersed at various points by periods when the material or product is stationary. This flow is usually some form of transportation of the product. The stationary periods are usually for storage or to allow some change to the product to take place – manufacture, assembly, packing, break-bulk, etc. The different types of transport (primary, local delivery, etc) and stationary functions (production, finished goods inventory, etc) are shown. There is also, of course, a cost incurred to enable the distribution operation to take place. The importance of this distribution or logistical cost to the final cost of the product has already been highlighted. As has been noted, it can vary according to the sophistication of the distribution system used and the intrinsic value of the product itself. One idea that has been put forward in recent years is that these different elements of logistics are providing an 'added value' to a product as it is made available to the final user – rather than just imposing an additional cost. This is a more positive view of logistics and is a useful way of assessing the real contribution and importance of logistics and distribution services. The added value element varies considerably from one product to another.

2

The Wholesaling Structure

NATURE OF WHOLESALING

Practically all important newspapers and many trade publications regularly carry comments on wholesale trade. The volume, status, and trend of such trade have long been regarded as significant barometers of general business conditions. Yet, as will be seen from the following discussion, no clear definition or conception of wholesaling was evolved until the results of the first Census of Wholesale Distribution were presented in 1932. Even today, considerable confusion exists as to the meaning of wholesaling and the fundamental distinction between wholesaling and retailing. As a result, wholesaling transactions are often misconstrued as being synonymous with the sales made by wholesale establishments or, more narrowly, with the business done by so-called merchant wholesalers or, in an even more restricted manner, with the sales of *regular* wholesalers made to retailers for the purpose of resale as distinct from their sales to industrial or business consumers.

Importance of Distinguishing Between Wholesaling and Retailing

The term *wholesaling* must be properly defined and differentiated from *retailing* for the sake of understanding the essence of wholesaling and the manifold problems peculiar to it. The importance of such a distinction arises out of both theoretical and practical considerations. It is essential to the quantitative measurement of each of these segments of our economy. No census enumeration can be made without such a distinction, nor can changes or trends in wholesaling and retailing be properly and respectively gauged without it. Certainly, no analytical study can be made of each of these parts of our marketing system without clear cut definitions.

Practical considerations are sometimes even more vital. One of the most important of these relates to certain types of taxes. Many states and some cities impose a tax on *retail* sales. The question immediately arises: What is a retail sale? The same is true of many state taxes on inventories or gross receipts. The amount or rate of such taxes may differ in a particular state, depending upon whether they are imposed upon wholesalers or retailers, higher rates generally being levied upon retail inventories or receipts. Furthermore, a number of states impose a chain store tax that applies only to retail establishments. Another practical consideration concerns federal wage and hour administration. The Fair Labour Standards Act of 1938 set up minimum hourly wages and a maximum work week of 40 hours without overtime pay. This law has been amended on several subsequent occasions to raise the minimum hourly wage and to broaden somewhat the scope of coverage. In general, however, the law has not applied to local retail stores and service establishments. To be exempt from its provisions, an organization must prove that its business is that of a retail, not a wholesale, establishment.

For purposes of complying with the provisions of the Robinson Patman Act, a seller may have to distinguish clearly between wholesalers and retailers and between wholesale and retail transactions of customers. For example, assume that a manufacturer decides to give wholesalers who buy from him a so-called functional discount of 20 per cent as compensation for wholesaling services, with this discount to be deducted from the price charged to retailers for the same goods. Such a manufacturer is then confronted with two problems: first, of determining who is and who is not a wholesaler; and second, in the event of a *split-function* establishment (i.e., one that operates partly at wholesale and partly at retail), on how much of the total volume of purchases may such a discount be allowed. In such cases, the Federal Trade Commission has held that such a wholesaler is entitled to the functional discount referred to above only on that part of his purchases which he resells in a wholesale manner. That position obviously raises many complications and insurmountable practical difficulties, especially when similar or identical goods are bought from a variety of sources and it is impossible to determine whose products were sold at retail and how much. The foregoing considerations are merely a few examples of the need for clarification of concepts, but they are deemed adequate to demonstrate that both the student of marketing and the marketing executive encounter many analytical and practical business management problems which call for clear definitions of wholesaling.

BASES FOR DEFINING WHOLESALING TRANSACTIONS

Before a correct concept of wholesaling can be formulated, it is essential to understand the nature of a wholesaling *transaction,* for the composite of such transactions makes up the total of wholesaling or wholesale trade. In attempts to define such a transaction several bases have been used, the more pertinent of which are:

- Price
- The quantity of goods involved in the transaction
- Method of operation of the selling concern
- Status or motive of the purchaser

Price

It is often assumed that there are more or less normal retail prices for goods purchased by ultimate consumers and that the sale of a given commodity at a price substantially lower than the so-called normal retail price is probably "wholesale." While retail prices are *usually* higher than wholesale prices, this is not universally true and cannot be determinative in ascertaining the basic nature of a transaction. Loss leaders featured by price-cutting retailers are illustrative. Advertised bargains are sometimes sold to ultimate consumers at prices below those quoted by wholesalers to their regular retail customers. Similarly, clearance sales not infrequently feature some items at a price less than the actual wholesale cost to the store. Despite such lower prices, there is no doubt about the retail character of these transactions.

Quantity Sold

The term *wholesale,* or sale in *whole* rather than in small quantities, suggests a definition based upon the quantity of the merchandise involved in the transaction; hence a wholesaler is commonly thought of as one who buys and sells in large quantities, while a retail store is characterized by numerous small sales. Actual practice, however, vitiates this basis for distinction as it is not uncommon for a druggist, for example, to buy from his wholesaler one-twelfth of a dozen of an item or some other very small quantity. No one would argue that this is a retail transaction. The federal courts, too, have declared time and again that "Whether a buyer is a wholesaler or not does not depend upon the quantity he buys. It is not the character of his buying but the character of his selling which marks him as a wholesaler. Nevertheless, the quantity in a transaction, especially when viewed in the light of normal experience in a given line of trade, tends to indicate the nature of the transaction—whether wholesale or retail—but is by no means determinative.

Seller's Method of Operation

The method of doing business of the selling concern throws some light on the nature of the business. There are certain principal attributes of a wholesale establishment, just as there are such attributes that characterize a retail store. A wholesale establishment usually employs outside salesmen, does not normally make sales over the counter to any substantial degree, and is not open to the general consuming public. In addition, its credit operations as judged both by procedure and services used are different from those employed by retailers. Wholesalers also belong to different local, sectional, and national trade associations or other groups. But it must be remembered that not all sales even by bona fide regular wholesalers are at wholesale, for to some extent many of them also sell to ultimate consumers for personal or household consumption. Similarly, it is not unusual to find a retail store selling merchandise to another retail store for purposes of resale or selling in substantial amounts to firms purchasing for business or industrial use. Consequently, this criterion of method of operation, while *generally* indicative of the nature of transactions, is, like the quantity involved in the transaction, far from being determinative.

Purchaser's Status or Motive of the Purchaser

The clearest distinction between wholesaling and retailing transactions is that based upon the status or motive of the purchaser.

Theoretical Approach

On the basis of this criterion, all sales made to ultimate or individual consumers who buy the goods for their own use or for the use of their family constitute retail sales. It is equally clear that all goods, regardless of quantity involved, that are purchased by a customer for resale to his customers are sold at wholesale. Thus, when a service station operator buys a single tire for resale to a customer, the transaction is wholesale. But a problem arises when goods are purchased, not for resale, but for further processing or as machinery and equipment to be used by a manufacturer, a retailer, a restaurant, or a builder of homes. While the purchased product in such cases is not to be resold in the same identical form, it becomes part of the cost structure of the buyer and must be recovered by him, either immediately or eventually, in the prices received for the products or services that he sells, if he is to continue operation on a sound business basis and contribute to the production of economic values. Business purchasers, whether they buy for resale or for business use, occupy a position in the productive process and expect to add some value by virtue of making the purchase. Ultimate consumers or purchasers at retail, on the other hand, are clearly set apart by virtue of status or motive, inasmuch as their objective is to use up or derive personal satisfaction from the economic values previously contributed.*Wholesaling,* then, according to the clearest distinction that can be made, *includes all marketing transactions in which the purchaser is actuated by a profit or business motive in making the purchase, whether the goods are purchased for resale in the same form or for use in the business or industrial process.*

Practical Modification

The above approach, while theoretically sound, under certain conditions presents insurmountable difficulties in a practical attempt to classify business transactions according to their wholesale or retail character. Such difficulties arise especially in connection with the purchase of goods for business use, when such goods are bought in an establishment operated essentially as a retail store (i.e., one that is open to the public and is so generally recognized) and are purchased in small quantities and perhaps also at the regular retail price. In instances of this kind, it would be exceedingly difficult to distinguish the business purchaser from the ordinary consumer and, indeed, in most instances there may be little practical reason for attempting to do so. In the light of this problem, it is appropriate to modify the foregoing definition of wholesaling so that it is more workable under the stated conditions. *Wholesaling*, from such a viewpoint, *includes all transactions in which the purchaser is actuated by a profit or business motive in making the purchase, except for transactions that involve a small quantity of goods purchased from a retail establishment for business use, which transactions are considered as retail.* This means that the following types of sales generally fall within the province of wholesaling:

- Sales by manufacturers or their sales branches to wholesalers and other types of wholesale middlemen
- Sales to retailers of all kinds
- Sales to restaurants and hotels
- Sales to manufacturers, mines, oil well companies, fisheries, railroads, public utilities, and government departments
- Sales to barbers in the form of supplies and equipment; the same applies to all sales of equipment and supplies by all so-called supply houses, so long as such equipment and supplies are not purchasd by ultimate consumers for their own personal use
- Sales of laboratory or office equipment and supplies to professional men such as doctors and dentists
- Sales of building materials to contractors, except when they act as agents of the home owners
- All operations and activities of middlemen who in some way aid in the transfer of title to goods when such goods are not sold to ultimate or individual consumers; in this group are naturally included brokers, resident buyers, purchasing agents, selling agents, manufacturers' agents, and the like.
- All purchases of farm products for resale to others than individual consumers, irrespective of whether such purchases are made directly from middlemen

The following types of transactions, while within the theoretical framework of wholesaling, are *illustrative* of sales that, for practical reasons under certain conditions, are considered as retail.

- Purchase of one set (four or five) of tires by a retail grocer from a gasoline service station or a tire company's retail outlet, to be mounted on the grocer's delivery truck
- Purchase of miscellaneous office supplies by a lawyer in the stationery department of a department store
- Purchase of several items of upholstered furniture from a retail furniture store, by a manufacturing company, to furnish a reception room for visitors to the plant

CONCEPTS OF WHOLESALING OR WHOLESALE TRADE

The various criteria which have been used, correctly or incorrectly, to define or indicate the nature of a wholesaling transaction have given rise to three main concepts concerning the totality of wholesaling which are identified with the following:

- All wholesaling transactions, no matter by whom performed
- The operations of wholesalers
- The operations of all wholesale establishments

Broad Conception

From a broad but entirely proper viewpoint, wholesaling embraces all wholesaling transactions, regardless of the character of the institution performing the wholesaling functions. It includes, therefore, all sales by agricultural producers, producers in the extractive industries, factories and processing establishments, except such sales as may be made by them to ultimate consumers; it includes, obviously, the sales of all wholesalers and other establishments operating in a wholesale manner, except for the retail sales of split-function concerns; it includes, moreover, all sales by retailers to other retailers who buy for resale and sales by them to business users when such users are readily distinguished from ultimate consumers because the quantity purchased is more than an ultimate consumer would ordinarily buy.

A broad conception of wholesaling, moreover, might well include the marketing of various kinds of business services. Some types of services are marketed to other business organizations for purposes of resale, as illustrated by certain types of automotive repair services which are sold by an automotive dealer and billed to the consumer by him, but where the work is actually done by a specialist (e.g., automotive glass shop or air-conditioning establishment) who regards his relationship with the automotive dealer as being of a wholesale nature.

Business services which are not resold to the consumer in the same form as rendered become part of the cost structure of the buyer in the same manner as the purchase of industrial goods and are therefore of the same economic significance and import, and differentiated from the marketing of consumer goods and services.

The Narrow Conception

In ridiculous contrast to the broad concept is the narrow viewpoint, commonly held by laymen, that wholesaling is confined to the operations of regular wholesalers or of those who call themselves wholesalers, and even then it may be limited to their sales to retailers for resale to ultimate consumers. The unrealistic nature of the narrow concept is demonstrated by the fact that very few wholesalers sell exclusively to retailers but number among their customers various business users and institutional buyers. The view is misleading, furthermore, because it fails to reflect the operations of thousands of specialized establishments that do business primarily in a wholesale manner, often just like regular wholesalers, but are not owned or operated by wholesalers.

The Middle View—Wholesaling in Terms of Establishments

While the narrow view of wholesaling is utterly preposterous, there are practical reasons for considering wholesaling in a somewhat less comprehensive view than the broad concept explained above. A middle and a very valuable conception is one based on the *institutional structure of business establishments primarily engaged in wholesale trade.* This view includes all transactions of such establishments, regardless of whether they are owned and operated by wholesalers, other wholesale middlemen, retailers, farmers, or manufacturers. It does not include, however, the wholesaling activities of manufacturers or retailers who do not maintain separate establishments for such purpose. It is this concept that forms the basis for the discussion of our wholesaling *structure,* and it is this concept that underlies the various data collected and presented by the Censuses of Business and by the U.S. Department of Commerce.For purposes of this book, however, when the term *wholesaling* is used without direct reference to the structure, it refers to the broader conception and embraces all transactions conducted on a wholesale basis, regardless of who performs them. Just as there is a difference between *retail sales* (which may be made by farmers and manufacturers as well as by retailers) and *retail store sales* (which are made by retail establishments as reported by the Census), so there is a difference between the total of *all wholesaling transactions* no matter who performs them and the *wholesale trade of wholesale establishments.*

Regardless of viewpoint, it is essential that the terms *wholesale establishment* and *wholesale transaction or sale* be carefully defined, for each figures in every concept of wholesaling or wholesale trade. Each of these two terms defies simple and categorical definition. This has already been shown in part in the preceding discussion of wholesale *transactions.* The meaning of the term *wholesale establishment* also has given rise to considerable controversy and calls for at least a brief discussion at this juncture.

What Is a Wholesale Establishment?

A wholesale establishment may be defined as a *recognizable place of business that is primarily engaged in performing marketing functions, including the functions of exchange, on the wholesale level of distribution.* Such an establishment may be owned and operated by a bona fide wholesaler who takes title to the goods, by a wholesale middleman like a broker or commission man who does not take title to the goods in which he deals, by a manufacturer, by a farmer or group of farmers, or by a retailer. This is the general sense in which the term has been used by the Bureau of the Census and by other federal agencies, and this is the sense in which the courts have so far ruled that the term should be generally taken.But the very definition just given implies possibilities for friction and difference of opinion on several scores. Among the most controversial questions are the following:

- What is an establishment?
- Is *ownership* of an establishment pertinent to its classification as a *wholesale* establishment?
- How is primary emphasis upon marketing activities to be determined?
- What proportion of the total business of an establishment must be done in a wholesale manner for it to be classified as a wholesale establishment?

The term *establishment* refers to a *single* place of business. It is not synonymous with a company, a corporation, an organization, or an enterprise, unless such company, corporation, organization, or enterprise is coextensive with the single physical place of business. The place of business need not be an entire building but may be only part of a building, store, office, warehouse, or even part of a home from which business is regularly transacted. Under certain situations, a physically separated place of business may consist of more than one building. For example, lumber yards and petroleum bulk stations usually consist of fenced yards or grounds enclosing a number of structures and various types of physical facilities, but all are occupied and operated as a single business establishment. All physical places of business operated by a single organization cannot, however, be considered as consisting of a single establishment.

This has been made emphatically clear in important federal court decisions relating to chain store organizations. In a case where a defendant was seeking exemption from the provisions of the Fair Labour Standards Act, it was claimed that the company consisting of 2,300 retail stores, 11 warehouses, a main office, and several manufacturing plants was, in the aggregate, a retail establishment. The court denied most vigorously this assertion in stating that to regard the entire business of a chain organization of this kind as a single establishment "would do indescribable violence to the word 'establishment.'"

The question as to whether *ownership* of a place of business is determinant in establishing its wholesale character has usually concerned the treatment to be given chain store and department store warehouses. Places of business owned by manufacturers and by farmers' marketing organizations, if operated in a wholesale manner, have been regularly considered as wholesale establishments. It has often been claimed, however, that warehouses operated by chain store organizations for the purpose of supplying the retail units of the organization are but part of the retail business of the enterprise. Even the Bureau of the Census has succumbed to this untenable view by failing to include the sales of such establishments in the Censuses of Wholesale Trade for 1935 and thereafter, despite authoritative protestations and contrary to the treatment in the Censuses for 1929 and 1933.

To say that chain store warehouses are retail establishments because they are part of a retail organization makes no more sense than to say that a wholesale establishment operated by a manufacturing company is a manufacturing establishment, or that a wholesale place of business operated by a group of farmers is but a part of farming. Whether a given place of business is a wholesale establishment is purely a matter of what it does, how it functions, and whether it operates basically in a wholesale manner. The *functional* basis rather than the ownership basis of distinction has been consistently followed in judicial interpretations. For example, the court ruled as follows: We hold... that the warehouse and central office of petitioner's chain store system cannot properly be considered a retail establishment....A warehouse and a central office such as petitioner maintains are vital factors in this integration of the retail and wholesale functions. They are necessary instruments for the successful performance of the wholesale aspects of a multifunction business of this type....

The disappearance of the independent middleman, together with his separate operations and charges, does not mean, however, that his essential intermediary or wholesale function of moving goods from producer to retailer has been abolished. In this instance it has only been taken over by the retailer, acting through its own distinct wholesale units...

In line with the reasoning advanced in this discussion, the authors have taken the position that wholesale warehouses operated by multiunit retailing organizations must logically be considered as an integral part of wholesaling. They have, accordingly, made appropriate adjustments in the wholesale census data presented in order that the totals shown include the sales and billings of such warehouses. The question as to whether an establishment is *primarily engaged in marketing functions* arises in various kinds of borderline cases in which it appears that a place of business might be considered either as a manufacturing or as a wholesaling establishment. Manufacturing is concerned with the creation of form utility and many wholesaling organizations are engaged in this, at least to some extent. Illustrative are wholesale grocers who roast and grind coffee or grade and package tea or spices, glass jobbers who cut window or plate glass to order and grind or polish edges, and industrial wholesalers who cut and thread pipe or fittings to the specifications of customers.

When such manufacturing or processing activities are merely incidental to the performance of wholesaling functions, the establishment is regarded as wholesaling in character. On the other hand, there are many places of business that make wholesale sales but in which the primary function is that of manufacturing. Examples include flour mills, food canning plants, automobile assembly factories, and paper mills. Such establishments usually exist basically for the purpose of giving useful form to the product, and thus they are enumerated as manufacturing establishments or factories and are outside the scope of the wholesaling structure, as conceived in the middle or establishment viewpoint.

Between these two rather clear-cut categories are a number of places of business of more doubtful status, and even the best informed persons find it difficult to effect a definite classification. An example is afforded by milk-bottling plants, which were included in the 1948 Census of Business as wholesaling establishments, because the preponderance of opinion at that time was that they were primarily engaged *in marketing* milk products. By the time of the 1954 Census, however, such plants were classified among the manufacturing industries, because it was considered that they were primarily engaged in form utility creation, including the separation of milk and cream, pasteurization, homogenization, and bottling of milk, and often the processing of related products such as butter, cottage cheese, and ice cream.

The question pertaining to the *proportion of wholesale business* required for classification as a wholesale establishment arises only in cases involving single places of business that operate both in a retail and in a wholesale manner. There are varying viewpoints on the matter. The most logical requirement is that followed by the Bureau of the Census in which the majority, or over 50 per cent, of the business, in dollar volume, is governing. Thus establishments are placed in retailing or in wholesaling categories according to their major activity. For purposes of the wage and hour provisions of the Fair Labour Standards Act, a broader rule was adopted. If more than 25 per cent of the sales are wholesale, the establishment is recognized as wholesale and forced to comply with the provisions of the Act. Such a ruling undoubtedly has stemmed from the position repeatedly taken in U.S. Supreme Court decisions that for purposes of exemption a law should be construed narrowly and for purposes of coverage it should be interpreted broadly.

VOLUME OF WHOLESALE TRADE AND MAJOR TYPES OF INSTITUTIONS

The total volume of wholesale trade is generally an unknown quantity because data for all wholesaling transactions, as viewed from the truest and broadest concept discussed above, are not collected and published. For practical reasons already indicated, the measurement of wholesale trade is restricted to the volume of business transacted by wholesale establishments as recognized by the Bureau of the Census, and it is the operations of such establishments that constitute the basis for all quantitative data presented in this discussion.

Volume of Trade: Wholesaling Structure

The volume of trade transacted by wholesale establishments has fluctuated with changes in business conditions. In Census of Business years prior to World War II, actual volume in current prices declined from a high of $69 billion in the prosperous year 1929 to a low of $31 billion in the depth of the depression in 1933, and by 1939, a recovery year, volume increased to $58 billion. In the highly prosperous postwar year 1948, which was marked by a then unprecedented level of industrial production and business activity, wholesale trade approximated $190 billion and it increased to $300 billion for 1958. A substantial part of these fluctuations is explained by price changes growing out of changing economic conditions. In order to obtain a more revealing picture of the trend in the physical volume of goods distributed by the wholesaling system, it is necessary to adjust sales in current dollars by means of a price index and thus arrive at a *physical-volume equivalent* expressed in constant dollar values. The results of such a deflation are shown below:

Year **at Current Prices** **(in billions)** **Wholesale Prices** **(1958 = 100)** **in 1958 Prices** **(in billions)**		**Actual Volume** **Index of** **Physical Volume**	
1929	$69.0	51.9	$132.9
1933	31.4	35.9	87.6
1935	44.7	43.6	102.5
1939	57.8	42.0	137.6
1948	189.7	87.6	216.5
1954	246.5	92.5	266.5
1958	299.2	100.0	299.2

A comparison of the physical volume equivalents reveals that sales volume data at current prices often convey a misleading impression. During the depression years of the 1930's, the *quantity* of goods distributed at wholesale did not decline as substantially as indicated by the actual volume in current dollars. While current dollar volume was less in 1939 than in 1929, physical Volume was actually somewhat greater. Again, although the 1948 sales volume was some 2.9 times the 1929 level, much of this is explained by a higher level of wholesale prices. The physical volume of trade in 1948 was actually only 1.8 times that of 1929. Between 1948 and 1958, the dollar volume at current prices increased by 58 per cent, but in terms of physical volume the increase was only 38 per cent.

Major Segments of Wholesaling Structure

Based upon *types* of establishments, the wholesaling structure consists of six major segments. Four of these are classes which are distinguished according to the ownership and method of operation of establishments, as follows:

- Wholesalers: merchant establishments operated by concerns that are primarily engaged in buying, taking title to, usually storing and physically handling goods in large quantities, and reselling the goods, usually in smaller quantities, to retailers or to industrial or business users.

- Manufacturers' sales branches: establishments that are maintained by manufacturers *apart from manufacturing plants* and which are operated by them primarily for the marketing of their own products at wholesale. Some of these have warehousing facilities where stocks of goods are maintained, whereas others are merely sales offices. Many of them also wholesale allied and supplementary lines purchased from other manufacturers.
- Agents and brokers: functional middlemen who do not, for all or most of their business, take title to the goods in which they deal but who negotiate sales (or purchases) for clients or principals. They are compensated in the form of commissions on sales or purchases.
- Chain store warehouses: establishments that are operated by retail multiunit organizations primarily for the purpose of assembling and distributing goods and performing other wholesale functions for the stores of such organizations.

Two additional classes are distinguished, not on the basis of ownership, but because of the unusual character of their physical facilities or method of operation. These are:

- Petroleum bulk stations: places of business engaged primarily in the storage and wholesale distribution of gasoline, oil, or other bulk petroleum products. These may be independent like wholesalers, or owned and operated by petroleum refining companies like manufacturers' sales branches, or by chains of gasoline service stations like chain store warehouses. They are segregated from wholesalers, manufacturers' sales branches, and chain store warehouses, because of the peculiar nature of their physical facilities, unique method of operation, and dealings basically in the same types of rather distinctive products, regardless of differences in ownership.
- Assemblers: establishments engaged primarily in purchasing farm products or sea foods in growers' markets or producing regions. They usually purchase in relatively small quantities, concentrate large supplies, and thus assemble economical shipments for movement into major wholesale market centers. Such establishments may be owned and operated by merchant wholesaling firms and hence are really part of the wholesale merchant classification; by manufacturers such as food canners or packers and to that extent they are really manufacturers' buying branches; by chain retailing companies and hence are not unlike chain store warehouses with emphasis on buying; or by farmers' marketing organizations.

There has been a consistent trend for the total number of wholesale establishments to increase. Whereas there were about 170,000 such establishments in 1929, there were more than 290,018 in 1958. Such a rate of increase has not, however, characterized each of the individual segments. Establishments operated by wholesale merchants are the most numerous type. They have increased in number substantially and have consistently accounted for about 41 per cent of an increasing physical volume of wholesale trade. Manufacturers' sales branches rank second in terms of sales volume, and have increased somewhat in importance in recent decades. While outranked numerically by three of the six major segments, they account for 29 per cent of total wholesale trade. Agents and brokers are third in volume of business, and while they have been increasing numerically, they have lost ground in relative volume importance. They transact about 15 per cent of the total volume. These three segments, collectively, account for about 85 per cent of total wholesale trade.

Study of the major components of the structure, based, reveals that fundamental changes in the general character of the wholesaling system are not to be expected over a relatively short period of time. While the total dollar amounts of trade volume and even of the physical volume of goods distributed change drastically with business conditions, the relative *proportions* allocated by the competitive economy among the various segments tend to remain fairly stable except where certain general upward or downward *trends* are discernible over an extended period of years.

Retail and Wholesale Trade Compared

Most laymen, if asked to speculate about the relationship between total volume of retail and wholesale trade, would likely reason that retail trade is ordinarily considerably larger. Two logical arguments might be advanced in support of such a conclusion. First, it may be reasoned that sales at retail usually involve a higher price and that, therefore, retail sales should naturally be higher by the amount of the retailer's margin.

Second, it might be stated that many retailers do not purchase all of their goods from wholesale establishments and that such purchases, while wholesale in nature, are not included in the data for the wholesaling structure. Sales to retailers direct from factories not maintaining branches or sales offices, or sales to retailers direct from agricultural producers not operating specialized wholesale assembly establishments are not covered in enumerations of wholesale trade as reported by the Bureau of the Census. Such arguments, while logically tenable, are responsible for a widely prevalent misconception regarding relative wholesale trade volume. Actually, the total volume of business of wholesale establishments is usually 40 to 50 per cent greater than the total volume of retail store sales. This is shown as follows:

Year Sales (in billions) Establishments (in billions)	Retail Store Sales of Wholesale Wholesale Sales as % of Retail Sales		
1929	$ 47.8	$ 69.0	144.3
1939	41.4	57.8	139.5
1948	128.8	189.7	147.2
1954	170.0	246.5	145.0
1958	199.6	299.2	149.9

In order to provide an explanation for this relationship, it is necessary to consider the various classes of customers served by wholesale establishments and the relative importance of each.

Customers Served by Wholesale Establishments

An analysis by classes of customers reveals that sales by all wholesale establishments to retailers for purposes of resale account for only 38 per cent of the total wholesale trade. Even wholesalers sell less than half their volume to retailers. Some 62 per cent of wholesale trade is either never reflected in retail store sales statistics because the goods are not sold again in the same form, or involves duplication in sales before the goods reach the retail level of distribution.

The second most important class of customers consists of industrial or business users. Sales of installations, equipment, semi-manufactured goods, parts, supplies, or raw materials account for 36 per cent of the total. This includes not only the sale of industrial goods to factories, but the purchase by retailers, wholesalers, and service establishments of goods that are used up or consumed in the business process. Considerable duplication exists in the wholesale field because of the large amount of business transacted by one wholesale establishment with another wholesale establishment in selling goods for resale. Manufacturers' sales branches, for example, sell some goods to wholesalers and these same goods are sold again by the wholesalers to retailers. In fact, many wholesale merchants sell to other smaller wholesalers who then resell to retailers. Duplication of this kind accounts for 20 per cent of total wholesale trade.

A small proportion of the business transacted by wholesale establishments represents export business, and another small per cent is accounted for by sales directly to household consumers and farmers. Careful study of the should serve to dispel certain misconceptions. They reveal clearly why the total volume of wholesale business is considerably larger than the total volume of retail store sales. Data for each type of operation show some important variations within the wholesale structure. For example, it is often assumed that sales made through agents and brokers represent duplications in the wholesaling process. Few people realise the extent to which such functional middlemen are used to serve retailers and industrial consumers, rather than operating completely between the form-utility producer and the wholesaler.

It has also often been assumed that manufacturers' sales branches with stocks are employed primarily as a substitute for wholesalers, that is, as a device whereby the manufacturer assumes the wholesaler's functions when circumventing him in the channel of distribution by selling direct to retailers. Actually the bulk of the sales made by such branches represents sales to industrial users or to other wholesale establishments purchasing for resale. Wholesalers are popularly viewed as agencies engaged in the distribution of consumer goods. While retailers constitute the most important class of customers for wholesalers, almost one-third of their business represents sales to industrial or business users. Information of this kind, when carefully studied and analyzed, gives one a better picture and a keener appreciation of the complexities of the wholesaling structure.

Geographic Concentration of Wholesale Trade

Unlike retail trade, the wholesale trade structure tends to be heavily concentrated in major wholesale trading centers. This is shown by the following data:

	Wholesale	
Establishments		
(per cent of total)	Sales of Whole-	
sale Establishments		
(per cent of total)		
24 largest metropolitan areas		
with population of		
U +00A0more than 1	41.7	59.0
million each		
165 metropolitan areas		
with population of less		
than 1 million each	26.2	25.9
Remainder of country	32.1	15.1

Some 59 per cent of wholesale trade is concentrated in the 24 largest metropolitan areas. These same areas account for only 38.7 per cent of retail trade and only 34.7 per cent of the population. The number of wholesale establishments is not so highly concentrated as is sales volume, indicating that those of unusually large sales volume size tend to be located in the largest trading centers. The degree of geographic concentration of sales volume varies considerably among different classes of wholesale establishments. For wholesalers, the pattern is very similar to that for all wholesale establishments.

Manufacturers' sales branches and offices reflect the highest degree of concentration in large cities. This is explained largely by substantial sales to industrial users and other wholesale establishments buying for resale, which customers are heavily concentrated in major areas. The operations of agents and brokers are also concentrated in the largest wholesale centers to an extraordinary degree. Petroleum bulk plants, which sell primarily to retail gasoline service stations, are dispersed very widely, correlating closely with the distribution of population. Assemblers are to be found chiefly in local growing regions for agricultural commodities. Consequently, their operations are also widely dispersed.

3

Wholesalers

Up to this point, the wholesaling structure has been examined from a broad perspective and consideration has been given to the special circumstances encountered in the wholesaling of industrial products. Three major institutional arrangements for wholesaling:

- Wholesalers,
- Wholesaling activities integrated with retailing and manufacturing,
- Functional middlemen. Since the ownership of wholesalers is generally distinct from that of their sources of supply and of their customers, the wholesaler's role in the channel of distribution differs in some important ways from the performance of wholesaling functions by integrated establishments or divisions of retailing or manufacturing companies. As a *merchant* middleman, the wholesaler buys and sells on his own account and at his own risk, thus providing also a distinct contrast with the wholesaling activities of various kinds of functional or agent middlemen.

Quantitative Position of Wholesalers

The importance of wholesalers is not well understood. Indeed, many regard such institutions as antiquated marketing agencies and hold the opinion that wholesalers have steadily declined in importance. Even among informed economists and businessmen, opinions are often expressed to the effect that "the wholesaler is doomed." Such opinions are doubtless based on a somewhat reduced role of wholesalers in a few industries. In dry goods, for example, wholesalers are not as important as they were prior to the 1920's, primarily because of the growth of direct-buying chain organizations in the general merchandise and apparel fields. Also, directto-retailer selling by manufacturers has increased in some lines of durable goods, notably automobiles and certain major household appliances. In spite of these developments, wholesalers in most lines of trade have held their own or improved their position. Wholesalers, moreover, have played a very significant role in various newer industries which have experienced rapid growth in modern times. Illustrative of kinds-of-business classifications in which wholesalers have made striking gains are automotive parts, electrical equipment and electronics, refrigeration and air conditioning, sporting goods, paper and paper products, and aircraft parts and supplies.

The significance of wholesalers is reflected by the number of business establishments they operate. For the year 1958 the Census of Business reported 189,728 *wholesaler* establishments (exclusive of those separately classified with assemblers and petroleum bulk plants), as compared with 79,784 in 1929—an increase of 138 per cent. In fact, the total number of *wholesaler*-operated establishments in 1958 was considerably greater than the total number of all kinds and types of wholesale establishments in operation in 1929.

From the standpoint of sales volume, the record of wholesalers is also impressive. As previously indicated, they account for more than 40 per cent of the total sales volume of all wholesale establishments, and the volume of goods distributed by them has increased markedly, as shown in the following tabulation:

	Sales Volume in 1958 Dollars				
(in billions)				**Per Cent Increase**	
	1939	1948	1958	1939-58	1948-58
Wholesalers	$51.9	$ 87.4	$121.7	134	39
Retail stores	92.5	147.8	199.6	116	35

The physical volume of goods marketed by wholesalers increased by 139 per cent over the 1939-58 period and by 39 per cent in the 1948-58 decade. In both instances the increase is significantly higher than that experienced by the retail trade structure, thus providing convincing evidence that the wholesaler has not only maintained his competitive position in modern times, but has actually improved it.

Ownership and Legal Organization

The nature of the wholesaler's segment of the wholesaling structure is indicated by selected data pertaining to the ownership, legal organization, and scale of operations within this segment. About one-half of all wholesaler establishments are proprietorships or partnerships, and this group accounts for about one-fourth of total sales of wholesalers. Corporations, cooperative associations, and other forms of legal organization, while accounting for about one-half of the establishments, do three fourths of the sales.

Single-unit independent organizations dominate the field, with over 87 per cent of the establishments owned by wholesalers and some 70 per cent of wholesalers' sales. Multiunit wholesalers with ten or more establishments per company account for only about 11 per cent of the total sales of wholesalers. The competitive position of large versus small scale wholesalers and of single-unit versus chain organizations is characterized by essentially the same attributes as developed in the analysis of these factors as applied to retailers.

REGULAR OR FULL-FUNCTION WHOLESALERS

All the functions normally associated with the term "wholesaler" are performed by *regular* wholesalers, often called *full-function* or *service* wholesalers. They buy merchan-dise on their own account, operate from warehouses which serve as headquarters and for the maintenance of stock, sell usually through salesmen who call on the trade regularly, extend credit, make delivery, and assume risks incident to their business, including the risks of ownership of inventory and receivables. Nearly 180,000 establishments are operated by regular wholesalers, and they account for about 96 per cent of the sales of all wholesalers.

Since wholesalers have been able to survive changes in business in modern times and have been able to maintain and even improve their competitive position in spite of spirited rivalry with direct-selling manufacturers on the one hand and large, direct-buying retailers on the other, it must be inferred that they perform valuable economic services.

Wholesalers of Consumer Goods

Some 45 per cent of the sales volume of all wholesalers represents sales of consumer goods to retailers although, of course, this type of sale is predominant or practically the only kind in many firms. The character of the wholesaler's productive services in consumer goods marketing may be studied, first, from the viewpoint of the wholesaler's customers and, second, from that of his sources of supply. From such an analysis, it will be apparent that distribution through wholesalers is not only desirable or absolutely essential under certain conditions, but that it also results in lower marketing costs to society than would be possible under any known alternative method of marketing.

Services to Retailers

Services rendered by wholesalers to retailers are of greatest significance when viewed in the light of the *typical* retail store. From the discussion in the preceding part of this book, it will be recalled that such a store is a relatively small, independent business, operated by an owner-manager, without benefit of numerous specialized employees, and handling a variety of merchandise manufactured by a number of firms located in different regions of the country often far removed from the store.

One of the regular wholesaler's most important functions is to *plan for and to anticipate the requirements of his customers.* Most retailers do not find it feasible or convenient to keep track of sales by individual items of merchandise and are unable to determine their needs for merchandise except for short periods. Because the wholesaler operates on a large scale, it is possible for him to maintain careful stock control records and thus determine in advance the quantities of various items that will be needed to satisfy the requirements of his trade. Moreover, he constantly studies the offerings of manufacturers to determine whether the customers in his territory will be able to sell the offered merchandise in profitable quantities. This customer-mindedness involves both searching for new merchandise and dropping old items before they become obsolete.

A second vital function is that of *assembling an assortment of numerous merchandise items from many manufacturers* or other suppliers. A clear idea of the wholesaler's assembly job is gained by considering the number of items carried in retail stores. An average retail grocer is said to handle from 2,000 to 3,000 items made by hundreds of manufacturers, and supermarkets carry 6,000 or more. Hardware merchants with 3,000 to 8,000 items and retail druggists whose stock may contain 12,000 items are keenly appreciative of the economic significance of the assembly function of the wholesaler. They know that they could not possibly undertake the task of assembling the variety of goods which they need to satisfy the requirements of their customers, if this had to be done on a direct-buying basis. They count on the wholesaler to bring together thousands of items from hundreds or thousands of sources so that all can be purchased from a single source of supply, in the simplified pattern of relationships and contacts.

Third, the wholesaler brings merchandise to his customers at lower costs than would otherwise be possible, partly because he *buys in large quantities.* In many lines of trade, the typical quantity of an item purchased by a wholesaler is several hundred times as great as the typical quantity of the same item as resold by the wholesaler to retailers. In some trades, such as groceries, hardware, alcoholic beverages, and plumbing supplies, the quantity purchased by the wholesaler is often in carload or truckload lots. This results in two kinds of economies. First, the manufacturer is able to sell to the wholesaler at a much lower price than he would have to obtain from retailers. Sales and handling costs are relatively much lower on large orders, and such differentials are reflected in the pricing schedules offered to wholesale buyers. Second, transportation costs on large shipments are relatively much less. Retailers buying in less-than-carload or less-than-truckload quantities would have to pay two or three times the carload or truckload rates paid by wholesalers, and even more than this when buying in quantities of less than 100 pounds from a given manufacturer. These combined economies are often greater than the wholesaler's cost of doing business, with the consequence that goods are made available by wholesalers in local markets at prices lower than those which would otherwise prevail.

Fourth, the wholesaler produces time and place utility by *maintaining a reservoir of goods near the point of ultimate demand.* In the absence of wholesalers, retailers would be forced to carry much larger inventories in order to be able to meet consumer demand. The wholesaler enables the retailer to operate with a minimum inventory, since the latter can draw upon the stock maintained by the former, for quick replenishment at frequent intervals, thus speeding stock turnover, reducing capital requirements, and minimizing risks of inventory ownership in the retail establishment. The wholesaler can generally store merchandise much more economically than retailers could.

One reason is that when a single reserve stock replaces several hundred stocks otherwise carried on the shelves of as many retailers, it can be much smaller in size and still meet the demands, for fluctuating demand from individual retailers is subjected to the law of averages when it is supplied from wholesale warehouses. Inventories of seasonally produced but regularly consumed products can be carried by wholesalers more conveniently and at less cost than by the average retailer, because wholesalers are as a class better able to secure loans from bankers to finance their merchandise stocks. The physical warehousing is carried by wholesalers at less expense than would be incurred on stocks carried by retailers, for they are specialists and have effective storage space available. Many items must be stored under proper temperature and moisture control conditions and must be protected from vermin. Most retailers do not have facilities for rendering such special services and hence are glad to recognize storage as a proper function of the wholesaler.

Fifth, wholesalers serve retailers by *providing prompt delivery service.* In metropolitan areas orders are usually delivered to retail stores the day after they are placed with the wholesaler's salesmen. In other communities and rural sections, deliveries are made once or twice a week under normal conditions. Retailers can normally get much faster delivery from wholesalers than could be provided by manufacturers, owing to the wholesalers' other functions of anticipating demand, assembling merchandise and storing it near to the customer clientele and, in addition, to the common utilization of the most expeditious methods of facilitating the movement of goods from wholesaler's warehouse to retail store. A sixth important customer service is *financial assistance through the extension of trade credit.* Without such assistance from wholesalers many merchants who possess real merchandising ability could not enter the retailing business, and many others would find it impossible to continue. Neither manufacturers nor regular financial institutions are as well equipped as the wholesaler with respect to providing this service.

In the case of the average independent retailer, credit granting by the manufacturer would be uneconomical because of the distance separating him from his customers and the relative difficulty and cost of securing accurate credit information and in collecting overdue accounts. In the second place, it is doubtful whether the manufacturer would grant the retailer terms favorable enough to allow him to continue in business. A single retailer with his relatively small order is not important to a manufacturer of a limited number of items, but he is a vital element in the success of the wholesaler from whom he buys the products of hundreds of manufacturers. Hence he can be thoroughly and competently investigated and financed if the results would seem to justify such action.

Commercial banks and other financial institutions are a source of capital to many retail organizations, but they are unable to supply the total of the outside financing needed by most stores. In fact, many independent retailers operate with such a small amount of equity capital that they cannot qualify for any bank financing. This is especially true of the smallest retailers, many of whom operate without adequate accounting controls and are unable to furnish accurate financial statements. The banker, moreover, lacks the constant contact with retailers which is available to the wholesaler through the continuing calls of his salesmen, who are able to detect changes in the status of a retailer's business and report such changes to the wholesaler's credit manager.

Because of their favorable position in this respect, regular wholesalers have found it desirable or necessary to extend credit to their customers, thus allowing the retailer to purchase merchandise and pay for it at a later date from funds derived from the sale of the same merchandise to the ultimate consumer. In this manner wholesalers supply a large amount of the capital needed by independent retailers for the purpose of carrying an adequate inventory.

A significant and expanding area of customer service is that of *providing information and assistance on retail store* merchandising and operating problems. Progressive wholesalers realise that their prosperity depends in the last analysis, upon the success of their customers. This has led to numerous attempts to strengthen working relations between wholesaler and retailer. As a consequence, wholesalers have provided various kinds of services which were at one time regarded as the sole function of the retailer.

In the drug trade, for example, it is not uncommon for service wholesale druggists to provide retailers with programs of assistance in the following areas: sales promotion counsel and aids, sales training for store employees, information about other druggists' promotions, advice and assistance on display arrangements, advice on getting special displays, advice on store layout and arrangement, information on sources of items not stocked by the wholesaler, and managerial advice. Technological and merchandising changes have called forth new forms of assistance of an informational or promotional character. Changes in pharmaceutical lines have made it difficult or impossible for the retail druggist to keep abreast of a continuing flow of new products. Consequently, many wholesalers have adopted special-service departments staffed by trained pharmacists employed for the express purpose of giving the retailer technical information. Such experts are equipped with files of special information and answer retailers' questions by telephone, as well as handle emergency orders for new or unusual prescription items not normally carried by the retailer.

In many instances the provision of additional services to the retailer has been accompanied by some modification of wholesalers' selling methods. In the grocery trade, for example, the use of preprinted order forms has become common. The wholesaler's entire stock is listed on such forms which are published as booklets. This enables the retailer to make up a weekly order at a time of his own choosing, and it usually results in more carefully considered buying, since use of the order form serves as a careful check on the total stock. The wholesaler's sales representative is saved much time that would otherwise be spent in routine order taking, and he is thus in a position to call on regular customers less frequently, spend more time in each store on his visits, and provide retailers with helpful merchandising assistance.

Some wholesalers have developed rather extensive programs of accounting assistance for their customers, particularly in trades where it is feasible for the retailer to concentrate most of his purchases with one major supplier. Among the various financial and accounting services available from some wholesalers are the preparation of income tax returns, analysis of insurance needs, preparation of financial and operating statements, comparative analysis of accounting statements based on ratios derived from a group of stores, and special analyses for particular situations, that is, new location or expansion.

Wholesalers often provide store engineering and architectural service for the planning of new stores or the modernization of existing operations, financial aid for new stores, store equipment, stamp and other premium plans, and even aid in the selection of new sites. Such aids are found in varying degrees in many lines, including groceries, hardware, drugs, plumbing and heating, dry goods, and variety type merchandise.

Services to Sources of Supply

The wholesaler, under certain conditions, performs a variety of marketing functions much more efficiently and economically than can be done by the manufacturer or other source of supply. This is based on the assumption, which is in line with established facts, that the average manufacturer is not a powerful business organization with unlimited capital and credit, far-flung branch houses, multitudes of trained salesmen, credit managers, advertising and other executives. While a few of the best-known manufacturing companies are of this character, the typical concern is a small unit in the business world.

Often it is handicapped by a lack of capital. The executives are frequently lacking in sales or marketing experience. Most of their time and energy is devoted to manufacturing problems, and they are glad to allow wholesalers to assume the functions of contacting and servicing retailers. Particularly is this true when only a single commodity or only a narrow line of products is manufactured. Under such circumstances the typical sale to the retailer is small and hence would be very costly if made direct.

One service that many wholesalers provide to suppliers is that of *advising on marketing problems* from the point of view of a distribution specialist. Because of intimate contacts with retailers, wholesalers can evaluate trends in demand and suggest desirable modifications in product lines. Most manufacturers are usually too far removed from ultimate consumers to do this effectively and count upon the wholesaler to estimate demand, provide help in preparing for it, and furnish warnings about changing consumer preferences that may be indicative of declining sales. Such details as the size of the unit, the type of package most in demand, and variations in quality are a part of his normal advice to the manufacturer. In the absence of the wholesaler, every manufacturer would be forced to conduct extensive market surveys to determine his potential market, its location, and characteristics. Second, wholesalers *establish connections with the whole field of retail outlets.* The wholesaler provides his suppliers with a definite clientele of relatively permanent customers who have been cultivated by his sales force, attracted by his service, and pleased with the quality of the merchandise he has recommended in the past.

It was shown that retailers would find it both difficult and time consuming to make direct contact with all of the manufacturers whose goods they stock. It is equally difficult for most manufacturers to make direct contact with all retailers that sell the kind of product made by them. A manufacturer of food products, for example, might wish to eliminate the wholesaler and organize his own sales force to call on retailers. He would be confronted with the problem of contacting about 260,000 grocery stores, not to mention general stores or restaurants which are good customers for many kinds of such products. The problems of hiring, training, and maintaining a sales force adequate to make such contacts are so tremendous that they can be intelligently considered only by a very few of the largest manufacturers.

Typical manufacturers with national distribution find that they have problems enough in attempting to sell to full-line grocery wholesalers who, by way of comparison, are only about one per cent as numerous as grocery stores.

Similarly, the manufacturer of a drug product would face the problem of contacting some 56,000 retail drug and proprietary stores if it were not for the wholesaler. By selling through a reasonable proportion of the 311 full-line establishments operated by drug wholesalers, he is, however, able to reach all these retail outlets. Again, the manufacturer of an item sold through hardware stores would be forced to contact about 35,000 such retail establishments, plus many more thousands of building supply stores, lumber yards, and other retailers handling such merchandise, instead of only 425 general-line establishments operated by hardware wholesalers. It is the wholesaler's function to establish connections with retailers even where there are unusual local or regional problems to be resolved. For example, in the state of Ohio, where distilled alcoholic beverages are distributed through state liquor stores, beer and wine are sold through regular licensed retail outlets. Over 11,000 retail stores sell wine for off-premises consumption, and about 20,000 restaurants, bars, taverns and others sell it by the drink or package.

For most such outlets, wine is only a small part of the total business, and the dealer has such limited capital and storage space that he is forced to buy in small quantities. By selling through some 20 to 30 wholesalers located in different trading centers throughout the state, wine producers are able to obtain distribution contacts with all the thousands of retail trade outlets. Seeking to present his products to the retail trade, a manufacturer faces an almost insurmountable task unless he produces a very wide line of related products, or unless he finds it expedient to confine sales to retailers who are able to buy in unusually large quantities. Because most retail business is local and is done by small stores, a manufacturer who omits the typical merchant from his salesmen's routes eliminates a large portion of his market potential.

The wholesaler, on the other hand, is able to cultivate his entire territory of operation. Because of the large number of different items that he carries, he is able to consolidate products of different manufacturers into a single order, thus obtaining a sale of sufficient value to justify sales calls on the smallest merchants, even those located in tiny villages and at remote points not regularly served by our transportation system.

Third, the wholesaler *reduces the manufacturer's cost of physical distribution.* Since wholesalers ordinarily buy in economical quantities, a few large shipments from manufacturers to wholesalers are substituted for the more numerous small shipments to retailers that would be necessary in direct selling. This greatly reduces transportation costs between the point of manufacture and local markets, enabling the manufacturer to present his merchandise to the consumer at a lower price than would otherwise be possible. While the storage function of the wholesaler is of value to the retailer, it is just as valuable to the manufacturer. Because of specialized facilities and the fact that goods come to the wholesaler from a variety of manufacturers many of whom have seasonal peaks, though not all at the same time, the wholesaler can store more cheaply than can the manufacturer or retailer. As the space devoted to storing the products of one manufacturer is released by declining seasonal sales it can be utilized for another line just coming into seasonal demand. Partly for this reason, most manufacturers cannot use storage space as efficiently as does the wholesaler.

Some full-line manufacturers can approach this efficiency and do so in warehouses located both at manufacturing plants and in the leading distributing centers. The great mass of manufacturers, however, must depend on the wholesaler for economical storage. Additional savings in the cost of physical distribution are made by the wholesaler through simplification of order filling procedures, packing, checking, and shipping, in warehousing facilities especially designed for these important functions. By consolidating many items from different manufacturers for delivery to retail stores, the cost of handling and delivering an order is spread over all of the items on the order, and thus the cost per unit is minimized for each item. Fourth, *wholesalers reduce the capital requirements of manufacturers.* Because of quantity sales to wholesalers and comparatively low selling expense, the manufacturer can operate on less capital than would be required in direct selling to retailers. When the wholesaler stores for the manufacturer, he reduces the latter's investments in finished stock inventory which otherwise would be necessary. Wholesalers as a class pay bills promptly, another factor making for lower capital needs by the manufacturer. Furthermore, some manufacturers and processors actually receive direct financial assistance from wholesalers. In the food canning industry, for example, it is not uncommon for wholesalers to make advances to the canner in order that the latter may purchase raw materials and meet his payroll requirements.

Another important service is *simplification of accounting and credit problems,* owing to the fact that wholesalers carry the accounts of hundreds or thousands of retailers, with the result that manufacturers need only account for sales made to a much smaller number of wholesalers or other large buyers. Since orders from wholesalers are larger than from most retailers, the per-order cost of accounting and shipping activities is lessened. Similarly, by carrying the accounts of retailers, the wholesaler reduces the loss from these accounts for, as already shown, he is in a better position than is the manufacturer to make investigations and grant credit to small retailers. Wholesalers as a class generally enjoy a good credit rating, usually pay within the cash discount period, and sales to them do not involve a great amount of credit risk or bad debt loss.

Industrial Distributors

Industrial distributors are wholesale merchants, operating in the main like regular wholesalers engaged in the distribution of consumer goods, although differing from them in the customers served and kinds of products handled. On an aggregate basis, industrial or business users constitute the second most important class of customers of wholesalers, accounting for some 32 per cent of wholesalers' sales, as compared with 46 per cent for retailers buying for resale, and 15 per cent for other wholesale establishments purchasing for resale. As used in business parlance and in certain trade publications and associations, the term industrial distributor is narrowly restricted to the operations of wholesalers who market supplies, equipment, machinery, and parts for manufacturing establishments, mines, oil wells, public utilities, railroads, and similar customers. More broadly viewed the term may be applied correctly to any merchant wholesaler who sells primarily to business or institutional customers who purchase items for business use rather than for resale of the same item in the same form.

The terms supply and machinery distributor, machinery dealer, mill supply house, and mine and mill supply house are often used to refer to the industrial distributors selling to horizontal markets. Other terms applying to industrial distributors in various vertical markets are beauty and barber supply house, dental supply house, laundry and dry cleaning supply house, undertakers' supply house, railroad equipment dealer, ship chandler, and hotel and restaurant outfitter.

In general, the industrial distributor renders services to both seller and buyer similar to the regular wholesaler in consumer goods lines. One service is that of acting as a purchasing agent for his customers. A mill supply house may have a stock of 5,000 to 10,000 items even when it serves only one line of industry. Stocks of 50,000 to 70,000 items are not unknown in the case of large distributors who have members of several industries as customers. They watch the offerings of manufacturers and attempt to forecast the needs of their customers by carrying wanted items in stock. To do this they are forced to choose from the offerings of many manufacturers, even hundreds or several thousand within some particular product classifications. All the items assembled by the distributor are consolidated into one catalog, a notable convenience to the industrial purchasing agent.

Other services to customers include the ability of the distributor to buy in large quantities with resulting transportation economies, thus often making possible the quotation of lower selling prices than could be obtained if goods had to be purchased direct from manufacturers. Stocks are maintained close to customers' plants. This facilitates buying and often prevents heavy losses through the ability of the distributor to prevent plant shut-downs by the quick supply of vitally needed articles. Customers also gain by reducing their inventory of repair parts if a reliable distributor maintains a complete stock. By pooling the reserve for many customers, a smaller total stock is needed.

Distributors' salesmen are trained to give technical advice to customers. Some of them may be better engineers than those employed by the buyer's plant, for they have acquired special knowledge through serving many customers. They inform customers of the newest products and their relative merits, indicate when and what savings a customer will be able to make by installing new equipment, and often help in solving specific problems vexing the buyer. Since such salesmen can be more specialized as to line than the purchasing agent, their advice on probable market changes is often eagerly accepted.

Like other wholesalers, industrial distributors often finance their customers by favorable credit terms. It is far simpler for a purchaser to establish credit with a few distributors than with many manufacturers. Accounts also are correspondingly simpler. Finally, the distributor's policy of protecting his customers on goods sold to them means more than do the guaranties of some manufacturers. Industrial distributors serve their sources of supply by providing a competent sales force, one that can call on a larger number of customers more frequently than is feasible for direct selling manufacturers. One survey revealed that the typical industrial distributor employs 5 salesmen, each of whom makes about 8 sales calls a day and serves about 145 accounts. Thus, the typical distributor represents about 40 sales calls each working day, among 725 customers. An industrial goods manufacturer selling through a network of some 200 noncompetitive distributors located in different cities would make his product potentially available to about 145,000 distributor customers.

Visualize the task of the manufacturer of industrial brooms, belting, lubricating oil, or roof paint were he to call on all possible users, a number coextensive with industry itself. Another important service to the manufacturer is that of storing goods near the point of demand. Since the manufacturer, by use of distributors, greatly reduces his number of direct sales contacts, his credit and accounting problems are proportionally simplified. When one thinks of the services of the industrial distributor to both buyers and sellers, one is led to conclude that he fills an important niche in the scheme of industrial distribution and that he has a secure place so long as he continues to serve efficiently.

Classes of Regular Wholesalers

In the foregoing discussion, regular wholesalers have been treated as a homogeneous group and this is characteristic of them in terms of services to customers and suppliers. There is considerable disparity, however, in terms of the extent of the line of goods handled and size of the territory which they serve, each of which is an important competitive factor.

Line of Goods

On the basis of line of goods handled, wholesalers are classified as *general-merchandise,* general-line, and specialty wholesalers. Least numerous are the general-merchandise wholesalers who carry a variety of goods in several distinct and unrelated lines of business. Such wholesalers are of greatest importance in serving retailers in the more sparsely populated areas of the country. Because they serve general stores, many hardware outlets, automobile accessory dealers, electrical appliance shops, some furniture stores, drugstores, plumbing supply retailers, and other dealers, variety is truly wide. Owing to changes in the environment for marketing, the trend has been away from this type of organization and toward specialization in some one line of trade.

General-line wholesalers, sometimes called full-line wholesalers, carry a complete stock of some one type of merchandise, corresponding roughly to a substantial majority of the total merchandise requirements of customers in a major line of trade or industry classification. While less numerous than specialty wholesalers, general-line organizations are usually much larger and tend to be the dominant form of wholesaling volume-wise in the important jobbing lines such as drugs, hardware, and groceries, or, in industrial marketing, the general-line factory or mill supply house. The principal competitive advantage of the general-line wholesaler is ability to supply a large proportion of the total merchandise needs of his customers.

Specialty wholesalers, often called short-line distributors, stock a narrow range of products. Examples are frozen food wholesalers in the grocery trade, pharmaceutical specialists in the drug trade, notions jobbers in the dry goods trade, beer wholesalers, "fine" paper merchants who limit their wholesaling activities to paper of printing quality, appliance wholesalers who confine their activities to the distribution of one or two manufacturers' lines, and distributors of mechanical rubber goods or power transmission equipment. Such wholesalers operate principally in welldeveloped markets where there are many retail outlets in the immediate vicinity. Because of the narrow range of products sold, order size tends to be smaller than for general-line competitors, and thus operating expenses are usually higher. Specialty wholesalers compensate for this disadvantage by more expert sales knowledge, a more complete assortment of goods within the range of products handled, and the ability to render prompt order-filling and delivery service.

Radius of Operation

From the standpoint of territory normally served, regular wholesalers are classified as local, sectional or regional, and national wholesalers. Local wholesalers operate within a single recognized wholesale trading area or within the trading area that can be served more advantageously by them than by wholesalers located in competing wholesale trade centers. They are the most numerous class and account for the bulk of the business done by regular wholesalers. Reasons for such dominance include the wholesaler's familiarity with market conditions, close and frequent contacts with customers, and speed, as well as the low cost of delivery service.

Sectional wholesalers operate over a large area that includes a number of wholesale trade centers and usually covers several states. Minneapolis, Denver, St. Louis, Dallas, San Francisco, and Atlanta are representative locations of such firms. *National wholesalers,* as the name implies, cover all or a large portion of the United States. The competitive position of sectional and national wholesalers is somewhat similar, and varies in each class depending upon whether the wholesaler covers his territory from a single establishment or whether he operates a multiunit organization.

Sectional and national wholesalers operating from a single place of business are much like local wholesalers in their home markets. When selling in distant territories, however, they are at a competitive disadvantage to local wholesalers who have a lower cost experience or who have a speed of service advantage. To compensate for this, many sectional and national wholesalers have integrated vertically, by assuming some functions normally performed by manufacturers. Some have extensive lines of private branded merchandise which is produced according to the wholesaler's specifications and which is heavily promoted to the trade. When selling in distant markets, sales efforts are devoted chiefly to such private branded items for which direct price comparisons are not possible. Because sectional and national wholesalers are much larger organizations as a rule, they carry many more items than many local wholesalers and derive some patronage from an appeal based on their extensive variety and assortments.

In lines of trade where transportation costs are high or where speed or service is of paramount importance, sectional and national wholesalers are able to cover a large area only by the operation of branch houses or a chain of wholesale establishments. In this manner they are able to move heavy or bulky merchandise into local markets at a transportation cost competitive with local wholesalers and are able to supply merchandise to retailers on a competitive schedule of delivery service. Illustrative of some of the leading national chain wholesalers are Consolidated Grocers Corporation, McKesson and Robbins in the drug trade, The Graybar Electric Co., and the American News Co.

SPECIAL TYPES OF WHOLESALERS

While the great majority of wholesalers are of the regular or fullfunction type, certain other classes are of unusual interest either because of their limited-function character or because of differences in the level or plane of distribution on which wholesaling operations are carried on.

Limited-Function Wholesalers

The term limited-function wholesaler is applied to a variety of specific types that have placed emphasis upon reducing, eliminating, or modifying certain well-established functions ordinarily performed by regular wholesalers. Their development over a period of several decades has not been accidental, but in line with the other marketing changes. Chief among these are:

- The rapid growth of chain organizations during the 1920's and 1930's,
- Increased buying in urban centers and in types of stores which do not normally purchase from the wholesaler,
- Development of cooperative wholesaling,
- The growing tendency of some kinds of manufac- turers to sell directly to retailers.

These changes have forced regular wholesalers to modify certain policies and at the same time provided an opportunity for limited-function wholesalers. As will be shown below, such wholesalers as a class have certain advantages and a degree of mobility which has allowed them to adapt their services to changes in demand. The most important types are drop shippers, retailer-cooperative warehouses, cash-and-carry whole-salers, and wagon or truck distributors. Altogether, these several types. accounted for only 4 per cent of the total business of wholesalers.

They are, however, of considerable interest for several reasons. First, as is apparent in the ensuing discussion, each type tends to be concentrated in one line or in a few lines of trade, with the result that each is of substantial competitive significance to its principal rivals. Second, the analysis of maverick types tends to sharpen one's comprehension of regular or orthodox wholesaling while at the same time illustrating the opportunity for specialists to emerge to meet particular kinds of customer needs. Finally, each of the principal methods used by limited-function wholesalers is of much greater importance than the sales made by that kind of institution, since the same methods are also used as supplementary marketing methods by some regular wholesalers and by many manufacturing companies which carry on wholesaling functions through their own facilities.

Drop Shippers

The drop shipper (sometimes called desk jobber) is so known because of the trade practice of referring to a shipment made directly from the factory to a retailer or industrial user as a "drop shipment." Drop shippers usually have an office but no warehouse, since they do not take physical possession of the goods. They are true wholesalers, however, because *they take title to the goods* and assume responsibility for the shipment after it leaves the factory.

If a claim against the common carrier is necessary, it is filed by the drop shipper. If the shipment is rejected upon arrival, he must assume responsibility unless rejection was due to some fault of the supplier. He extends credit, collects the account, and incurs all the sales costs necessary to secure orders. Drop shippers are of major importance in two lines of trade: coal and coke, and lumber and construction materials. Carload shipments to retailers and industrial users are almost universal in these two industries, which makes warehousing unnecessary and gives the drop shipper an opportunity. Furthermore, the commodities are bulky and much can be saved by the elimination of handling and storing by the wholesaler. They are also of some importance in petroleum, farm products, and heavy machinery. Since some costly functions are not performed by drop shippers, their operating expenses are relatively low, being about half those of service wholesalers in the same kinds of business. Entrance into this type of operation is fairly easy because a large fixed investment is not needed. Acquaintance with the trade and the confidence of a manufacturer that orders sent to him are bona-fide and that hence the drop shipper can collect and remit to him are important factors in their success.

The principal limitations to this business are inherent in its nature. Opportunities to make sales are limited essentially to customers that purchase in the same quantity that the wholesaler buys; moreover, buyers must anticipate their needs to an extent that permits delivery from factories or mines, rather than from local warehouse stocks. Finally, manufac-turers often frown on this method of wholesale distribution.

Retailer-Cooperative Warehouses

The origin, development, and operating characteristics of retailer-cooperative establishments. They are classed as wholesalers because they are usually set up as a corporate entity distinct from the retail interests that own them; and they buy, take title, and resell merchandise on their own account, sometimes even to nonmember retailers. Their operations as limited-function wholesalers are similar to those of cash-and-carry wholesalers discussed below, although many provide regular delivery service and offer merchandising counseling assistance like that of the regular voluntary group wholesaler.

Cash-and-Carry Wholesalers

In 1958 wholesalers operated 1,860 establishments on a cash-and-carry basis. This method of operation was largely a product of the 1920's when many such businesses were established to give retailers a chance to meet chain store competition or to keep them from joining a cooperative which featured lower costs to prospective members. Since chain competition has been strongest in groceries, the cash-and-carry outlets are strongest in that line, where they commonly operate as specialty distributors.

Some cash-and-carry wholesalers operate as single establishments; but most of them are in multiunits, either branches of a full-function wholesaler or units of a chain of such establishments. Assortments are limited to staple merchandise with a relatively quick turnover. Salesmen are not used nor is much advertising employed. Many cash-and-carry wholesale establishments are operated much like supermarkets, permitting (or requiring) the customer to select his own merchandise, physically assemble his order, check-out through a central transaction processing station, and load his merchandise in his own car or truck.

Cash-and-carry wholesalers usually sell at lower prices than regular wholesalers, primarily because of cost savings which result from the curtailment of services to the trade. If a retailer is located close to a cashand-carry establishment, so that he can readily assume the transportation function, and if he can pay cash for his purchases, he can effect some savings by patronizing such a source. On the other hand, there are obvious disadvantages. Because of the streamlined stocks which are carried by most cash-and-carry operators, the retailer must patronize certain other wholesalers to maintain his store inventory. Furthermore, he does not receive the benefit of important informational and advisory services of full-function wholesalers.

From a social viewpoint, the cash-and-carry plan of operation transfers certain well-accepted wholesaling functions from wholesaler to retailer. Usually the retailer cannot perform these services as well as the wholesaler and this is the principal factor limiting the market opportunity for cash-and-carry establishments.

Wagon Distributors

The persistence of marketing terminology is well illustrated by the universal practice of referring to one type of limited-function wholesaler as a wagon distributor, whereas for many years a truck has been used rather than horse and wagon. Such wholesalers differ from the regular wholesaler principally in the combination of selling and delivery in the almost simultaneous performance of these functions, although orders may first be received by telephone and then distributed. An inventory of merchandise is carried on trucks which are operated by driver-salesmen. The retailer's requirements for merchandise are determined at the time of the sales call and orders are filled immediately from the stock carried on the truck. Wagon distributors are of importance principally in the grocery trade, and their stock is usually limited to specialty items or fast-moving perishables, which bear a good margin of gross profit but involve risk of deterioration or which require constant attention. Common examples include potato chips, oleomargarine, cheese products, frozen foods, and specialty processed meat items. Normally the wagon distributor carries a very limited range of merchandise items and sells for cash.

From the foregoing description, it might be assumed that wagon distribution would entail low costs of doing business. One trip for both sales and delivery, one man to do both, low or no credit costs, quick turnover of a limited stock, and simplified record keeping suggest a favorable operating cost situation. The facts show the reverse to be the case. Average operating expenses are considerably higher than for regular wholesalers handling comparable lines of merchandise. A principal reason for the high costs of wagon distribution is the very narrow range of merchandise items handled, which gives rise to a low order size and necessitates many calls to obtain a signigcant volume of business.

Rack Merchandisers

Somewhat akin to the wagon distributor in certain aspects of operation is a relatively new wholesaling institution, the rack merchandiser or rack jobber. Rack merchandisers are classified as full-service or regular wholesalers, however, inasmuch as they normally carry an extensive line of goods, sell on a credit or consignment basis, and provide a wide range of services both of a wholesale character and also of a retailing nature. The term rack merchandiser, or rack jobber, arises out of the common practice of the distributor of installing his own display racks which are stocked with merchandise thereon displayed for sale. Rack jobbers are of importance chiefly in supplying nonfood items to grocery retailers, such as drugs, toilet articles, housewares, and notions. They developed with the expansion of nonfood merchandising in grocery stores, especially of the supermarket type, capitalizing upon the opportunity to supply grocers with merchandise items that they were not used to procuring from normal sources of supply.

On a typical sales call, the driver-salesman inspects the retailer's stock of merchandise, determines whether any items need be replaced, brings merchandise in from his truck in quantities believed salable by the retailer before the next call, price-marks the merchandise, and places it on the shelves of the display rack. Most rack jobbers actually sell on what amounts to a consignment basis, with the salesman collecting on each visit, just for merchandise sold since the last visit, and standing ready at any time to take back or replace any unsold or unsalable items.

Assembling Wholesalers

Assembling wholesalers differ from regular wholesalers of consumer and industrial products and from most limited-function wholesalers in an important respect. Instead of buying in large quantities, breaking bulk, and selling and delivering to customers in smaller quantities, as is usual in wholesaling, assembling wholesalers buy from numerous small farms, assemble the goods into economical shipment quantities, and sell them in larger quantities than those purchased. The assembling wholesaler has no sales force in the usual sense because he always has a regional or central market outlet for his produce at a publicized competitive market price. His main task is that of observing prices in central markets and buying from local sources at a lower level of prices that provides a margin adequate to cover expenses of operation and allows a reasonable net profit.

Assembly is not the only service of these merchants, for grading is also essential. Cream station operators use tests to determine butterfat content. Buyers of apples and citrus fruit usually operate packing houses, and assemblers of grain operate elevators with equipment for both grading and storing. They are thereby able to ship commodities of a definite size and grade and thus can fill exact demands. Assemblers perform the finance function, for they pay cash and do not receive their returns until sales are made, often weeks later in the case of certain fruits. They assume risk when they buy on current quotations and sell at a future time. Because of their specialized knowledge and situation, they collect and interpret market news.

Smaller assembling wholesalers often combine some other form of business operation with that of the assembler. For example, in small communities it is common to find grain assemblers selling farm feeds and fertilizer. This provides an opportunity to utilize physical facilities and personnel more efficiently and tends to even out somewhat the seasonal character of the business. Assembling wholesalers have declined substantially in number of establishments and sales volume significance, owing to the conditions which were analyzed in connection with the discussion of the bypassing of local and terminal markets for agricultural commodities.

Split-Function Wholesalers

Some wholesalers are vertically integrated in the sense that they operate on two different levels of the channel of distribution. This may involve operation on both of wholesale and retail levels or it may consist of two distinct types of wholesaling activity.

Semijobbing by Wholesalers

Marketing both at wholesale and at retail is occasionally done by regular and by limited-function wholesalers. When a wholesaler sells at retail as well as at wholesale, he is usually known as a *split-function* wholesaler or as a *semijobber*. That retail sales are normally only incidental to the main business of conducting a wholesale firm is shown by the fact that they constitute less than 2 per cent of the sales made by all wholesalers. But in some lines of business, such as automotive supplies or farm average products, retail sales by wholesalers are much more significant than the average figure would suggest. Some wholesalers operate as semijobbers because of the opportunity to make a substantial volume of sales at retail through the same facilities that are used for the wholesale operation. Some automotive parts wholesalers, for example, make sales at retail prices to any person who visits their establishments. In other cases, wholesalers actually operate retail stores. An example is provided by a long-established Ohio wholesale grocery organization that built a number of supermarkets in order to obtain an assured market for a substantial amount of business within its trading area.

Some retail sales by wholesalers result from the initiative of persons who believe that if they buy from wholesalers, they can secure goods at lower prices. Friends of the of the wholesaler and of his employees often importune him to sell to them at the same price which he charges retailers. Many wholesalers resist; others succumb to the pressure and make such sales at prices which range from just over the price paid by retailers to just under the amount charged by retailers. Many wholesalers follow a rigid policy of never making such sales, because they do not believe that it is either fair or wise to compete with their own customers. Other wholesalers, frequently those not particularly successful, are willing to sell to anyone who can pay for the merchandise and thus, in effect, operate as "discount house" retailers.

Semijobbing by Retailers

Somewhat different is the case of the retailing organization that assumes some wholesale functions and thus engages in semijobbing. The common motivation for such integration is the desire to buy on terms more favorable than those available to the usual retailer. Sometimes a manufacturer's salesman may suggest that the retailer solicit orders from some friendly competitors and thus purchase from the manufacturer at better wholesale prices based upon the larger quantity. Other retailers merely print a letterhead and call themselves wholesalers because certain manufacturers will quote them wholesaler prices even though they do not perform a single wholesaling function. The more common practice is, however, that of pooling orders under the leadership of one retailer, or of a large and adequately financed retailer ordering more than he needs and selling the surplus to nearby retailers. Prices received are usually somewhat under those charged by the regular wholesaler, since fewer services are provided on such transactions.

Redistribution by Wholesalers

Somewhat analogous to semijobbing is the activity of certain wholesalers that market on two different levels of wholesale distribution. About one-sixth of the total sales of wholesalers is made to other wholesale establishments that buy for purposes of resale, although the relative importance of such sales varies considerably among different kinds of businesses. Sales by wholesalers to other wholesale organizations tend to be common under certain wellrecognized conditions. First, it is especially common in lines of trade where wholesalers are heavily engaged in importing merchandise, thus giving rise to the opportunity to redistribute to other wholesalers engaged in domestic marketing. This type of redistribution is especially common among coffee, tea and spice wholesalers, precious stone distributors, and gift and art goods wholesalers. Second, redistribution by wholesalers is commonplace when certain processing or packaging operations are carried on in connection with the operation of a wholesale business, as in the case of piece goods or paper converters. Third, when the final plane of wholesale distribution consists of numerous wholesalers or jobbers that operate on a small scale and are widely dispersed, redistribution through other wholesalers is common, as illustrated by fertilizer and agricultural chemical distributors, wholesalers of automotive repair parts, and wholesalers of tobacco products, all of which types make many sales to other resellers at wholesale.

Competitive and Legal Implications

A split-function establishment operating on two or more distinct levels of a distribution channel poses some unusual competitive and legal questions. For example, in the marketing of automotive repair parts, certain manufacturers of items such as oil filters, spark plugs, and fan belts sell to redistribution wholesalers, who market to smaller auto parts jobbers as well as to retailers or automotive repair shops. The redistribution wholesaler receives a functional discount to compensate him for the function of redistribution.

This gives rise to potential problems of price discrimination and unfair competitive advantages when he sells the same items directly to retailers or users, in competition with other wholesalers (often his own customers) who do not receive such a discount. Similar questions arise in connection with semijobbing establishments. In certain interpretations of the Robinson-Patman Act, it has been held that a semijobber is entitled to receive the wholesaler's functional discount when one is offered by a manufacturer only on that part of his purchases which is to be resold at wholesale and that he must pay the price ordinarily paid by other retailers on the portion to be resold by him at retail. Because of the practical difficulties of such a classification of a semijobber's purchases of any one commodity, there has been a tendency to curtail the dual functioning of an enterprise or to form separate corporations for the purpose.

4

Integrated Wholesaling

While wholesalers are indispensable in the marketing of a wide variety of products, they are by no means universally used as instrumentalities in the channel of distribution. In the case of manufactured goods, for example, it is estimated that wholesa-lers are involved in the marketing of slightly less than one-half of consumer products, about one-fifth of industrial products, and (on an f.o.b. factory value basis) about one-third of all manufacturing output. Some other institutional arrangement is used to accomplish the task of wholesaling for about two-thirds of all manufacturing output. In many cases this is done by integrating the wholesaling task with other business activities.

NATURE OF INTEGRATED WHOLESALING

The term *integrated wholesaling* means that the functions or activities of wholesale marketing are combined in ownership (and often in physical facilities as well) with agricultural production, manufacturing, or retailing. It invol-ves the incorporation within a single business organization functions that are normally or at least commonly performed by separate and distinct business entities, operating on different levels of distribution channels. Integrated wholesa-ling is, therefore, a type of forward or backward verti-cal integration, distinguished from horizontal integration which involves joint ownership and operation of functionally similar units on the same plane or level of distribution. Vertical integration is, however, often accom-panied with some degree of horizontal integration, since both tend to be mainly characteristic of large-scale organizations.

MINIMAL UTILIZATION OF WHOLESALERS

In a few lines of trade, the wholesaler has declined in significance, and in others he was never an important factor. The nature of and reasons for integrated wholesaling can be better understood by giving specific attention to certain industrial market and consumer market examples of minimal utilization of wholesalers in distribution channels.

Industrial Market Examples

Much of the industrial market is composed of expensive but technically complex machinery and installations. Because expert advice is often necessary to determine the needs of the user, and in some cases specifications for the manufacture of special products must be drawn by the salesman, wholesalers' representatives having a large line of products are not well fitted for such sales. Demonstrations call for special knowledge possessed only by men trained in the qualities of one line of machinery. Since many such products are of high unit value, direct contact is economically justified.

Semimanufactured goods and parts which enter directly into the manufacture of other more finished items are commonly marketed on the basis of very large contracts, often calling for delivery at periodic intervals. Such products are also frequently made to the specifications of the industrial purchaser thus calling for direct channel relationships.

In the case of agricultural commodities marketed as raw materials, assembling wholesalers tend to be bypassed in favor of direct farmer to processor marketing when commodities are highly perishable and when processing plants are conveniently accessible to farmers as is usually the case when an area assumes specialized production characteristics. Farmers producing cream in Wisconsin or Minnesota, leading dairy product states, are likely to sell direct to local creameries. In Kansas or Nebraska, where there is less emphasis on dairy farming, processing plants are less numerous and more widely scattered. Farmers in these states are more likely to sell to a local assembler who ships cream to processing plants located at some distance.In the early years of the poultry industry, it was common to sell live birds to local market wholesale poultry dealers who, in turn, would arrange for shipment to poultry processing firms in major central markets. A specialized commercial broiler industry has developed on a large scale since the mid-1930's, with the most significant concentrations of production in the Delaware-Maryland-Virginia peninsula and northwest Georgia. In these and other important poultry regions, it is common for processors to finance poultry raisers by supplying them with hatchery stock and feed. When the poultry is ready for the market, processors obtain the birds directly from raisers, process them, and then ship dressed birds by fast motor truck to major eastern market centers.

In the marketing of highly perishable commodities with a short processing season, growers and processors are mutually interdependent to an unusual degree. The grower wants to be assured of at least one market outlet before planting, and the processor who markets a given quality of product under an established brand name desires assurance of sources of supply for particular quantities of specific varieties of produce. This has given rise to the common practice of contract negotiations between growers and processors in advance of production, especially in the fruit and vegetable canning and beet sugar industries. Such contracts customarily provide for the farmer to supply the processor with the output of a given number of acres. Prices are sometimes stipulated, or the contract may provide for a specific formula according to which prices are to be calculated at time of delivery. In some cases where the processor has strict quality requirements, he may furnish seed or plants, arrange for periodic crop spraying and dusting, and may actually undertake to harvest the crop at maturity.

Consumer Market Examples

The grocery, drug, hardware, and dry goods trades have always been considered jobbing lines, that is, lines of trade in which the wholesaler predominates. In certain other lines of business, as in automobile accessories other than tires, tobacco products, plumbing supplies, and electrical goods, the wholesaler has been used as the principal method of moving goods from manufacturer to retailer or contractor. In practically all lines of trade the wholesaler has been utilized at least to some degree. There are some industries, however, in which sales are most commonly made by manufacturers to retailers without the use of independent wholesale merchant middlemen.

In the automobile industry the wholesaler was at one time dominant but is now of negligible significance. In the early days of this industry (prior to World War I), the industry was characterized by uncertain sales and a low volume of production, manufacturers and retailers with weak financial resources, and a highly concentrated manufacturing centre (the Detroit area) serving a broad national market. Under such conditions manufacturers sold automobiles predominantly through wholesale distributors to retailers. The distributor organization permitted manufacturers to concentrate on engineering and manufacturing problems when the industry was in the developmental stages; it filled an important financial gap because manufacturers lacked the capital resources required for wholesaling; it performed the storage function necessitated by the seasonal sale of cars; it provided a decentralized system of warehouse depots required to render prompt delivery service to dealers in distant markets; and it provided intensive selling in local markets of the kind needed to build a retail dealer organization.

During the 1920's and 1930's the automobile industry experienced rapid growth and its characteristics were modified in a manner that minimized the need for wholesalers. Manufacturing companies grew in size and were able to command needed capital in the national money markets. Manufacturing was decentralized through the construction of assembly plants in various parts of the country. Sales finance companies developed to provide special services in financing dealer inventories and sales of automobiles to consumers. Dealers grew in size and stature and concentrated their efforts on one manufacturer's line of cars; as a consequence, they had large annual purchasing requirements from a single source of supply. As a result of these environmental changes, adaptive behaviour took the form of largely supplanting the independent wholesale distributor with direct sales from manufacturer to retailer. The ready-to-wear apparel industries are examples of situations in which wholesalers have never been of great importance. The men's clothing industry expanded rapidly following the War between the States, as a result of mass production developments stemming from the manufacture of military uniforms during the war period.

From the very outset, most manufacturers sent out traveling salesmen to call upon retail clothiers. The production of men's suits is an extremely complicated undertaking requiring a long manufacturing cycle. Orders are usually obtained from retailers in advance of production. The unit value is high, dealers are not relatively numerous; and they must make a substantial investment in inventory. These factors, characteristic of the industry in its early stages as well as in modern times, gave rise to the need for direct contact between manufacturer and retailer. Manufacturers who sell direct to clothing stores and department stores account for 70 per cent or more of the total industry volume of men's suits, and manufacturers who distribute through their own retail stores account for about 20 per cent (e.g., Bond Clothing Co. and Richman Bros. Co.).

The women's ready-to-wear apparel industry is characterized by a concentration of consumer shopping in large shopping centers; by a speedy manufacturing cycle, enabling most vendors to give prompt delivery from the factory on reorders of popular styles; by a limited number of concentrated manufacturing centers which are also wholesale buying markets for retailers; by marked seasonal shifts in the character of demand; and by rapid fashion obsolescence. The major retail outlets operate on a fairly large scale, consisting chiefly of department stores, departmentized specialty stores, and chains of women's ready-to-wear establishments. More than 85 per cent of the output of women's dresses, coats, and suits is sold direct from manufacturer to retailer. In spite of the dominance of direct selling in these industries, wholesalers are used to some extent, especially in supplying smaller retailers in communities most distant from the major market centers in which manufacturers are concentrated. Wholesalers are of considerable importance in merchandising more staple items of apparel and accessories, including men's work clothing, underwear, hosiery, and millinery.

Wholesalers pla a very limited role in the distribution of some perishable products and other commodities which are manufactured or processed chiefly by local establishments. In the field of meat products, the activities of wholesalers are limited chiefly to specialists in specific kinds of meat items who are located in major cities, and who often cater primarily to special segments of the trade such as restaurants and hotels. Most meat products sold in ordinary grocery stores and meat markets come directly from meat packing plants or from wholesale branches operated by the major meat packing companies.

Bakery products, dairy products, and carbonated bottled beverages are examples of products which are manufactured in all cities of significant size and which are sold almost altogether direct to retail stores. While the foregoing examples are selective and limited in number, they serve to illustrate how marketing channels tend to be adapted to particular conditions, which vary from one industry or trade to another.

REASONS FOR BYPASSING WHOLESALERS

When manufacturers take the initiative in establishing direct marketing channels, the effort to circumvent the wholesaler is usually prompted by one or more of the following principal motives:

- Necessity of moving perishable or style goods through trade channels with the greatest possible speed;
- Desire to secure closer control over the product;
- Desire for economy;
- Dissatisfaction with the wholesaler's services;
- Pressure from retailers or industrial users who prefer to buy direct.

Other motives of lesser importance may consist of:

- A desire to sell a small portion of the output direct for purposes of experimentation in an effort to improve regular channels;
- Need for supplementing inadequate wholesaling facilities existing in some of the manufacturer's markets with his own wholesaling outlets.

Perishable Nature of Goods

Perishability is a characteristic that tends to make the direct sale of some goods desirable. Some commodities are subject to rapid physical *deterioration,* as is the case with baked goods, dairy products, and meat. It is important that few handlings be involved and as little time as possible elapse in the movement of such items from processor to retailer.

Direct contact in the sale of such items enables a manufacturer to follow up his product and prevent the resale of stale and unsuitable merchandise bearing his label, in this way safeguarding the good will of the consuming public. It also enables him to oversee the care and treatment accorded his product prior to its sale to the ultimate consumer.

Perishability may also result from rapid *obsolescence,* as is the case in much fashion merchandising. Loss occurs when ladies' ready-to-wear, shoes, or millinery are delayed in passing from manufacturers to retailers. Hence wholesalers have found small opportunity to handle such merchandise, largely restricting their efforts to articles for which fashion changes are less frequent, less drastic, or more predictable.

Desire for Closer Control Over Product

Certain manufacturers strongly desire close control over their products until they reach the ultimate user. This is true, for example, of some manufacturers of furnaces, refrigeration, or factory machinery where success in the long run is dependent to a substantial degree upon the quality of servicing work. In order to insure proper installation and service, manufacturers have in many instances taken over wholesaling functions. In the case of some specialty goods, it may be advantageous for the manufacturer to control also the entire sales programme. Some manufacturers have attempted to accomplish this, at least in part, by integrating the wholesaling and the manufacturing tasks and processes.

Economy as a Motive

A desire to reduce marketing costs by undertaking the performance of the wholesaler's functions leads many manufacturers to direct selling, either with or without branch houses. Many believe that greater volume can be secured, thus reducing manufacturing overhead, and perhaps also the cost of selling may be less than the margin allowed to the wholesaler. Many, however, have learned to their sorrow that elimination of the wholesaler does not eliminate his functions. They have also learned that frequently he can perform these functions more cheaply than can the manufacturer. Many manufacturers have come to the same conclusion; they admit that economy is not usually the basic motive for going around the wholesaler. Economy may be effected only when the manufacturer performs the wholesaling functions more efficiently than, or at least as efficiently as, does the wholesaler.

Dissatisfaction with Wholesaler's Services

An important reason for circumventing the wholesaler, even in lines in which he is generally utilized, is dissatisfaction with his services. Where this feeling exists, it is based on one or more of three grounds. Wholesalers have been charged with:

- Lack of intensive cultivation;
- Indifference or even hostility to a manufacturer's advertising or sales programme promotion;
- Pushing private brands at the expense of competing brands of manufacturers.

While such allegations are sometimes founded in fact, they often result from a misunderstanding of the nature of a wholesaler's operation. A regular, general-line wholesaler ordinarily carries a number of brands in each product classification and handles a wide range of product classes. He cannot justifiably single out one manufacturer's product line for intensive selling attention unless he has some special incentive for so doing. Manufacturers who desire to obtain extra selling or merchandising effort from wholesalers usually find it necessary to provide compensation for this by means of additional discounts or promotional allowances, or by giving a wholesaler exclusive rights for distribution within his area of operation.

Direct-Buying Pressure

Pressure for direct channel of distribution relationships often comes from retailers or from industrial customers. In the hope of obtaining lower prices or gaining certain other buying advantages, large-scale retailers and industrial or business users generally desire to buy merchandise directly from manufacturers. Patronage of wholesalers is then confined largely to fill-in orders. Many smaller stores have attempted direct buying, frequently through participation in one or more buying groups. Advertising allowances and special discounts have often been secured from the manufacturer by large direct-buying retailers, in addition to the lower prices.

In some instances, pressure by retailers for direct-buying arrangements has been accompanied by threats of discontinuing the manufacturer's brand unless such a request is granted. If the retailers in question account for any significant proportion of the manufacturer's sales volume, he may be forced to choose between losing their business or acceding to their wishes.

CONDITIONS FAVORING INTEGRATED WHOLESALING

Regardless of the strength of motives that a manufacturer may have for circumventing the wholesaler in the channel of distribution, this may be impossible or highly impractical. Unless motivation is accompanied by the presence of certain conditions favoring integrated wholesaling, circumvention of the wholesaler cannot be feasible or economical. The most important of these conditions are a large size of order, a concentrated market, management capabilities, and the feasibility of using partial substitutes for the wholesaler's services. As is shown in the following discussion, certain of these conditions may arise out of the nature of the product, the circumstances of the manufacturer, or the characteristics of the market.

Large Order Size

When it is possible for the manufacturer to make sales in large dollar amounts, then the costs of integrated wholesaling, including maintenance of a sales force, delivery to customers, accounting for sales, and handling credit and collection problems may be relatively small. Such a condition may exist if customers are large-scale organizations, if they handle a very specialized line of goods, if the product is of high unit value, or if the manufacturer sells a wide line of merchandise.

Large-Scale Buyers

Large-scale retailers and industrial or institutional customers ordinarily purchase substantial proportions of their total requirements directly from manufacturers at advantageous prices, or through representatives other than wholesalers. They buy in large quantities, obtain quantity discounts, secure economies in transportation, and can often store just as efficiently as a wholesale firm. In fact, savings frequently amount to more than that, because they need not employ wholesale salesmen or create outlets for the goods they buy. Furthermore, large retail institutions and industrial users are in a position to maintain an efficient buying staff or purchasing department and to secure favorable terms of credit. While some manufacturers refuse to sell direct to the retail trade even when goods are purchased in large quantities, because of resentment on the part of wholesale distributors, most of them offer chains and other large retailers merchandise at jobbers' discounts or even more favorable terms. Retaliatory measures by wholesalers are sometimes taken against such manufacturers. The trend, however, has been in favor of direct sale to all large retail enterprises, although a surprisingly large amount of merchandise is bought by even the largest retailers from wholesalers, sometimes as fill-ins and often because the retailers may not care to stock certain items in their warehouses.

Specialized Costomers

Because specialty stores handle only a very limited variety of merchandise, their purchases are usually concentrated with a single supplier or with a few manufacturing resources, resulting in fairly large sizes of orders even for small stores. If a store's business consists chiefly of one kind of merchandise, such as men's coats and suits, typewriters, shoes, musical instruments, or cameras, the goods are bought by retailers, and consequently sold to them by manufacturers, in large quantities. Instead of buying a quarter of a dozen suits once or twice a week, a men's clothing store usually places several major orders per year. "Fill-in" orders may be placed by mail without any personal contact between the merchant and a manufacturer's sales representative. Essentially the same situation obtains in industrial marketing. Even quite small manufacturing plants have large purchasing requirements of certain types of materials entering directly into manufacture, owing to the typical highly specialized character of output of the small factory.

Unit Value of Product

Numerous products are of such high unit value that only a few units of an item represent a sizable sale. Such commodities are often of a type that require a considerable stock investment by the merchant, service to be given in connection with sale or installation, and the maintenance of a stock of repair parts supplied by the same manufacturer. Examples of such consumer products are automobiles, typewriters, pianos, major electrical appliances, furniture, and furnaces. Some of these products require such close working arrangements between retail dealers and manufacturers that exclusive agency agreements are made. High unit value of industrial installations and major items of industrial and business equipment contributes to the prevalence of integrated wholesaling by manufacturers of such items, either on a direct-fromfactory basis or through a branch office system.

Yet even in the case of many such products the wholesaler or industrial distributor occupies a strategic position. Many brands of major appliances, for example, are sold through wholesalers, on an exclusive agency basis. Such an arrangement permits the manufacturer to concentrate his efforts on manufacturing and demand-creation activities. Manufacturing schedules can be planned well in advance, because wholesalers often agree to market a certain quota. Wholesalers also may operate a central service station, thereby aiding dealers or users in their territory with repair business.

Size of the Line Produced

If the manufacturer produces complete lines or families of products, the tendency is to lessen the importance of the wholesaler. Individual orders from retailers or business users under such circumstances may be large enough to justify direct selling by the manufacturer. This is apparently one of the major reasons for integrated wholesaling by certain manufacturers of paint and allied products, cosmetics and toilet goods, sporting goods, cookies and crackers, and office machinery and equipment. In most such instances of successful integrated wholesaling, at least some favorable conditions in addition to extent of line are also present.

Some long-line manufacturers with a history of integrated wholesaling have greatly improved their market position by changing to distribution through wholesalers. The H. J. Heinz Co., for example, distributed its famous "57 Varieties" (actually many more) of food products through its own system of wholesale branches with stocks. The company also had its own sales organization and supported its wholesale distribution system with strong national advertising. The high costs of wholesaling a limited line (in comparison with the thousands of items distributed through regular grocery wholesalers) tended to restrict personal sales effort and retail distribution to large metropolitan areas. In the late 1950's Heinz abandoned its historic direct-to-dealer system in favor of the use of wholesalers, in order to expand its distribution in small communities and rural areas which account for a sizable proportion of the national food business. The Scott Paper Company which markets a very wide line of industrial paper items through its Industrial Packaged Products Division attracted considerable trade attention in 1960 when it abandoned a programme of widespread direct-to-user selling in favor of almost complete emphasis upon distribution through wholesale paper distributors, with resulting higher levels of sales, fewer shipping points, and reduced selling, handling, and accounting costs.

Extent of product line is a factor contributing to the feasibility of integrated wholesaling only when products are somewhat homogeneous, or are sold in combination to the same classes of retail outlets or to the same type of industrial users. Many factories, however, make by-products which, though profitable, do not fit into their regular lines of merchandise. A paint manufacturer, for instance, may sell linseed oil meal—a cattle feed—which he secures as a by-product when oil is extracted for the paints he manufactures. Unless such a manufacturer is large enough to develop integrated channels for both the major products and for the by-products, wholesalers must usually be used for the marketing of at least one of them.

CONCENTRATED MARKET

When the buying market for a manufacturer's products is highly concentrated, little travel expense is involved in retailer-manufacturer relationships and transportation economies may be realized. This may be attributable to a density of outlets or to the existence of a strongly developed central market which is visited by purchasers.

Density of Outlets

In the most populous metropolitan areas, large numbers of retailers in the same kind of business are situated in a confined geographic area. Such a concentration of customers may facilitate circumvention of the wholesaler, even in the distribution of convenience goods where transportation costs are an important factor and sales to retailers are frequent. There is such a large number of retail grocers or druggists in a city like New York or Chicago that a manufacturer may justify the establishment and maintenance of local warehouses to which merchandise is shipped in carload quantities and from which prompt deliveries are made to retail stores. Because of the proximity of stores, salesmen may be able to make a large number of calls per day at reasonable cost. A manufacturer who pursues such a policy in major cities may find the wholesaler indispensable in sparsely populated districts where the costs of selling and delivery are too burdensome to justify direct distribution to retailers.

Markets for many industrial products are similarly concentrated. Manufacturers selling to a horizontal industrial market consisting of all manufacturing industries find it significant that nearly one-half of the total number, of manufacturing establishments are located within about 1 per cent of the total number of counties in the United States. Various vertical markets are much more concentrated than this. Manufacturers of machinery and equipment used in shoe manufacturing, for example, find a considerable proportion of the largest users concentrated in four areas, around Boston, St. Louis, in central and southern Ohio, and in Tennessee.

Location in Central Buying Markets

For many items of fashion merchandise, central markets are well developed and are frequently visited by retailers. Manufacturers located in such markets can make a substantial volume of sales to retail store buyers while the latter are in the market. New York City is the leading market for almost all items of women's apparel, but Chicago, St. Louis, Dallas, Los Angeles, and San Francisco are also of substantial importance. Many manufacturers of furniture and house furnishings are able to sell direct to retailers without incurring much travel or selling expense by maintaining a selling office in the Merchandise Mart in Chicago which is an important market for such products.

Qualifications and Capabilities of Management

The management of the manufacturing enterprise may be well qualified and fully capable of coping with manufacturing problems but may lack the facilities or the ability to deal with the numerous marketing problems incident to the performance of the wholesaling functions when selling directly to retailers or industrial users, especially when potential customers are numerous and widely scattered. In such cases it may be wiser by far to confine operations to manufacturing and to let regular marketing institutions undertake the marketing task, unless the size and financial strength of the enterprise permit an expansion in facilities and management for the proper integration of the two sets of functions.

Feasibility of Using Partial Substitutes for Wholesalers

If a manufacturer is well equipped to assume part of the wholesaler's functions, but not at all of them, he may be able to utilize some special form of marketing organization as a partial substitute for the wholesaler. Some manufacturers who find it desirable and feasible to maintain their own sales organization utilize public merchandise warehouses to handle the physical supply functions of wholesalers. In brief, they receive shipments from the factory, store merchandise, fill orders from stock, and handle deliveries to the manufacturer's customers. They are often operated in conjunction with a manufacturer's sales branch. When a contact is entered into with a public warehouse, there is no outlay of capital, no obligations for a lease are involved, and warehouse space may be contracted or expanded as warranted by trade conditions. Thus, warehousing offers an opportunity to manufacturers of certain goods who seek to go around the wholesaler to keep distribution within their own control.

Where there is no need for maintaining stocks of merchandise in local markets, the manufacturer may be able to utilize the selling services of one of the types of functional middlemen. Each such middleman sells, on a commission arrangement, products of several manufacturers. In the furniture, men's furnishings, and sporting goods field, it is rather common for manufacturers to sell through manu-facturers' agents. These middlemen sell more economically than the manufacturer, because they carry several different lines which they sell to the same trade. Orders are transmitted to factories and direct shipments are made to stores.

WHOLESALE ESTABLISHMENTS OF RETAILERS AND MANUFACTURERS

When wholesalers are circumvented in the channel of distribution, the essential nature of wholesaling activities is clearly revealed. Whether the initiative is taken by retailers or by manufacturers, ways and means must be provided to perform the functions that would otherwise be rendered by independent wholesalers. In some cases, the physical aspects of wholesaling activities are so fused with manufacturing or with retailing, as the case may be, that they are difficult to perceive. When integrated wholesaling is carried on extensi-vely, as in the case of a large, multi product manufacturing company, or in the case of the large, multi establishment retailing organization, separate facilities are usually provided for wholesaling activities.

Integrated Wholesaling by Retailers

The extent to which retailers have attempted to perform the wholesaling functions when buying direct is difficult to estimate. Smaller retail organizations have generally passed on the wholesaling functions to the manufacturer, but larger companies establish chain store warehouses or other places where reservoirs of goods are held until needed by the store. A chain store warehouse is essentially a wholesale place of business. In many respects its operations are quite analogous to those of a regular wholesaler. It receives goods, maintains inventories, breaks bulk, delivers and bills the merchandise to retail units, and employs supervisors to inspect stores and assist store managers much as do wholesalers' salesmen.

Reliable data on *total* costs of performing wholesaling functions in chain store warehouses are not available for any recent year from Census sources. Based on historic compari-sons and recent trends in payroll costs and related data, it is estimated that average operating expense ratios of chain store warehouses are at least one-third less than the average operating costs of regular wholesalers handling comparable types of merchandise.

The relatively lower probable cost of chain store warehouses may be explained by several factors. First, a large part of the goods included in "sales and billings" of chain store warehouses, especially perishable items, actually moves direct from manufacturer or other supplier to store rather than to chain store warehouse. If the expenses were expressed as a per cent of the total goods actually *handled* in and through the warehouse, costs would no doubt be higher. Second, the chain store warehouse serves a captive group of customers; hence there is no need for a sales force to solicit business from the retail units. Third, since the retail units are under the same ownership, it obviates any necessity for credit investigations or for collection expense. Fourth, delivery can be streamlined and made less frequently.

At the same time, a chain store warehouse undoubtedly incurs more so-called retailing expenses than does the wholesaler. Many such warehouses maintain personnel and accounting records for company retail stores, and much of the retail sales promotion and advertising work of the organization is performed by personnel employed in the warehouse office, which also often serves as administrative headquarters for the company or for a geographic division thereof. For these reasons, higher operating expenses may be expected for chain store warehouses. Inasmuch as chain store warehouses function very much like regular wholesalers in many ordinary respects and operate in the same kinds of locations with the same types of personnel and equipment, it is reasonable to conclude that whatever differences there are in total operating expenses probably issue from the distinguishing characteristics indicated above and not from a difference in the level of general operating efficiency.

Indeed, within the grocery trade, certain progressive wholesaler sponsors of voluntary chains are known to have operating expense ratios as low as those commonly achieved by corporate grocery chain warehouses, thus demonstrating that there is no *inherent* economic advantage for chain store warehouses in terms of operating efficiency.

Operating cost data for department store warehouses have never been collected and published, but it is known that many such establishments can be operated at a relatively low cost in comparison with the value of goods handled through them. As in chain store warehouses, there is no cost for selling or credit extension between the warehouse and the retail departments. A very large variety of items is handled, with the result that seasonal storage requirements of some merchandise are largely offset by different seasonal peaks in other departments. The rate of turnover and volume of business are such that fixed costs of operation are spread over a very large sales volume. In contrast with the typical chain store warehouse, merchandise items moving out of the usual department store warehouse tend to be heavy or bulky items which are delivered direct to the ultimate consumer. Thus the department store warehouse is not engaged in such an extensive range of wholesale redistribution activities as is the wholesaler or the chain store warehouse.

Integrated Wholesaling by Manufacturers

In lines of business where wholesalers are ordinarily an important link in the chain of distribution, most manufacturers have found it necessary to establish branch wholesaling systems in order to effect distribution *to nonintegrated retailers*. This usually takes the form of branches where stocks of merchandise are maintained, either in the manufacturer's owned or leased warehousing facilities or in space occupied in a public merchandise warehouse. Manufacturers' sales branches without stocks, which are only about two-thirds as important numerically as branches with stocks, and which do only about one-fifth of their business with retailers, are relatively much more significant in industrial marketing so that their total volume exceeds that of the branches with stocks. They operate in a manner that is much more comparable to the drop shipper or to the manufacturers' agent than to the regular wholesaler. Operating expenses of manufacturers' branches with stocks are generally somewhat lower than those of merchant wholesalers. In 1958 the average cost ratios for all lines of business were 10.8 per cent and 13.4 per cent of sales, respectively, for these two types of operation. Several reasons may be advanced to explain the lower cost ratios for manufacturers' branches. First, these establishments sell a much larger proportion of their goods to other wholesale organizations for resale than do merchant wholesalers. Such transactions ordinarily involve much larger quantities than sales to retailers and are accompanied by relatively low selling and handling costs.

Second, the entire range of wholesaling functions is not performed in most manufacturers' branches. In many instances, some activities ordinarily performed by merchant wholesalers are performed in manufacturers' headquarters offices with the result that the cost of the activities, even though performed by the company, is not reflected in the operating costs of the *branches.*

Illustrative are personnel management activities, sales promotion planning, often credit management and accounting, and other office work. Another factor is that manufacturers' branches are heavily concentrated in major metropolitan areas. For the most part, they do not attempt to call on retail stores in sparsely populated areas or on the smaller retail stores, wherever located, which are the most costly customers of regular wholesalers.

When the above conditions are given proper weight, it appears that sales branches would probably experience considerably higher operating costs than regular wholesalers, if strictly comparable activities were performed, similar services rendered, the same types and classes of customers served, and the same lines of merchandise involved in the same proportions.

The only Census of Business classification of manufacturers' sales branches with stocks that is reasonably comparable with merchant wholesalers is the "food and kindred products" trade. Establishments here classified sell on a wide geographic basis, reaching a large proportion of the total retail grocery outlets in all classes of cities. In 1958 their operating cost amounted to 10.3 per cent of their sales volume, as compared with only 6.4 per cent for general-line grocery wholesalers. This reveals that the typical manufacturer with a branch wholesaling system must operate much like a specialty wholesaler, spreading costs over a small range of products in comparison with the regular wholesaler.

5

Functional Middlemen

The analysis of various specific institutional arrangements for wholesaling of the performance of a group of wholesale market middlemen who do not take title to the goods in which they deal and who are known as *functional middlemen, agent middlemen,* or as they are collectively designated by the Census of Business, *agents and brokers.*

GENERAL NATURE AND IMPORTANCE

Organizations falling within this group are known as functional middlemen since they specialize in only a limited number of the various functions which are necessarily performed in the wholesaling process. The most useful test as to whether a given middleman is a merchant or functional middleman hinges upon whether or not he *acquires title* to the goods he sells or distributes in the regular course of his operations. If he does, and operates in the wholesale field, he is a merchant middleman and falls within some one of the types. Absence of title ordinarily frees a middleman from a number of costly and laborious tasks, hence the use of the term "functional" with its connotation of limited functions and functional specialization. Two main subdivisions of functional middlemen are agents and brokers, the distinction depending basically upon continuity of representation of the principal rather than upon legalistic grounds. As a class, functional middlemen once accounted for about one-fifth of the total sales of all wholesale establishments, but this ratio has declined to about one-seventh of wholesale trade, as indicated by the following data:

Year **Agents and Brokers** **as a Per Cent of Total Sales** **of All Wholesale Establishments**	**Number of** **Sales of Agents and Brokers**	
1929	18,388	20.7
1939	20,903	19.4
1948	24,377	17.3
1954	22,131	15.9
1958	26,567	15.5

The data on *number of establishments* do not indicate the *total number of agents and brokers;* and the sales volume ratios, while somewhat indicative of their competitive position, actually understate it. The reason for this is that the Censuses of Business for 1929-48 were taken on the basis of recognizable business establishments, and the Censuses for 1954 and 1958 were limited to establishments with paid employees. Many functional middlemen, especially of the type later described as manufacturers' agents and brokers, while accounting for a substantial volume of business, structurally are very small businesses, operated by individuals without paid employees and without a regular place of business in the ordinary sense. Such agents or brokers are not properly reflected in the Census of Business data on establishments.

It is sometimes assumed that functional middlemen are utilized almost altogether to bridge the gap between the manufacturer and wholesalers handling his products or as a substitute for wholesalers. Such is not the case, for only about 51 per cent of the business done by agents and brokers consists of sales to other middlemen for purposes of resale, of which nearly three-fourths is made up of sales to wholesalers and about one-fourth to retailers. Sales to industrial users are nearly as important as sales to resellers, consisting of some 44 per cent of the volume of business done by agents and brokers. Export business and occasional sales to ultimate consumers and farmers make up the remaining 5 per cent of their volume. While some of the functional middlemen operate on the buying end of the business, by far the majority of them concentrate on the sales function; for this reason their business may be regarded generally as consisting of sales. Additional light is shed on the operations of functional middlemen by the nature of products in which they deal. Approximately three-fifths of their sales consist of manufactured goods and about two-fifths involve products of agriculture or other extractive industries.

Selling agents provide the most complete range of marketing services, serving principals on a continuing basis and generally rendering all the services normally performed by a manufacturer's own sales force. Manufacturers' agents confine their activities to a particular territory, serve on a continuing basis, and perform functions similar to a manufacturer's salesman or a branch sales office. Commission merchants do not serve continuously but are engaged temporarily and intermittently for the disposal of specific lots of merchandise which are sold by them on a commission basis. Brokers are also temporary representatives, are engaged for the disposal or purchase of specific lots of merchandise, and serve by negotiating sales or purchases which are confirmed by principals before they become binding agreements. Auction companies are an additional type that afford a temporary or intermittent type of arrangement for the disposal of specific lots of merchandise. Also sometimes referred to as functional middlemen are advertising agencies, freight forwarders who render a transportation expediting service, and factors who aid in the financing function. Each of these is discussed in Part V of the book, in connection with the appropriate marketing function in which they specialize. Still additional classifications are purchasing agents, resident buyers, export agents and import agents; since the operations of the last two are, by nature, not distinctly different from those of agents primarily in domestic trade, they are not accorded separate or special treatment.

General Reasons for Use

Even though the major types of functional middlemen differ in the specific nature of the services which they render, they have certain common characteristics which indicate why they are employed in the channel of distribution. All the major types serve, at least to some extent, as a substitute for a manufacturer's own sales force. Most of them, however, serve a number of manufacturers of similar products or of products which are sold to the same types of customers. Through a process of combining several products or product lines, a functional middleman is usually able to spread the costs of operating a wholesaling establishment over a much larger sales volume than is possible for a single manufacturer. Marketing costs are therefore lower in relation to sales volume. An important general reason for the use of functional middlemen is, therefore, economy.

Because of the low cost of selling through functional middlemen, manufacturers are often able to extend the radius of their operations. They can effect sales in distant and sparsely populated market areas that could not otherwise be served by their own selling organizations.

A third reason is that functional middlemen are specialists in marketing. Numerous small manufacturing firms producing a narrow line of goods are concerned chiefly with manufacturing problems. They are often perfectly content to allow others with a broader base of experience to assume a large amount of responsibility for the performance of marketing functions. In many plants, the sales volume is large enough to support only one executive, often the actual owner of the business, and he is usually a factory specialist not well qualified by education, training, experience, or interest to cope with the complexities and dynamics of market situations.

Fourth, all major types of functional middlemen are ordinarily compensated in the form of a commission or brokerage fee, which is in direct relation to the amount of sales volume produced on the manufacturer's line. Thus, to the extent that the manufacturer shifts marketing functions to such middlemen, he also shifts the costs of performing them. Marketing costs then assume for him a predetermined percentage relationship to sales. While this may involve large dollar sums expended for the services of functional middlemen in years when sales volume is particularly high, many manufacturers welcome such an escape from the continuing expense of attempting to hold a selling organization intact in years when conditions are adverse. Essentially the same reasons account for the use of functional middlemen in the marketing of agricultural commodities.

SELLING AGENTS

Selling agents, as was previously indicated, perform the greatest variety of services of any of the functional middlemen and assume the highest degree of responsibility for marketing operations. Their importance is not always fully recognized, because in some lines of trade they are more frequently known as commission houses, selling houses, or by other similar terms. The variety of terms arises not so much from differences in functions as from historical usage in different trades.

Nature of Operations

A selling agent serves his principals on a continuing contractual basis, receives a commission for his services, does not take title to the goods, assumes responsibility for selling the entire output of his principal, gives advice on styles and patterns, furnishes financial aid, and assists in carrying or actually carries credits for the client.

Historically, selling agents have been most important in the textile trade, but their wide use in the sale of coal has created a second great field of activity. In both of these trades, selling agents have tended to decline in importance, owing to changing conditions. Many small textile firms have been absorbed through a process of merger with or acquisition by competitors, suppliers, or customers, thus resulting in a smaller number of larger and often vertically integrated firms that do not require the use of functional middlemen. In the coal industry, selling agents have suffered by a tendency among large users (e.g., steel companies and certain public utilities) to integrate vertically, thereby controlling their source of supply through the ownership of so-called "captive mines." Nevertheless, textiles and coal are still two of the major areas of activity for selling agents.

They also operate in a number of other lines, principal among which are metals and metalwork, clothing and furnishings, grocery and food specialties, and construction materials, especially lumber. Selling agents usually represent several mills or manufacturers producing allied and supplementary lines of goods of a noncompeting nature, although some confine their activities to the marketing of the output of a single mill. When several clients are represented by a single agent the goods of the different producers need not be essentially different or noncompeting, but such is generally the case. Some selling agents are corporations that own, or are owned by, textile mill companies; in either case they often also sell related products made by companies with which they have no ownership affiliation.

Functions of Selling Agents

Services rendered by selling agents to any one client vary considerably, depending upon the arrangement governing the particular relationship. Consequently, rates of commission vary greatly, depending upon the functions an agent performs, nature of the goods, sales resistance that must be overcome, style risk involved, and the bargaining position of agent and principal. Commissions for selling alone generally range from 2 to 5 per cent, with extra charges for additional services.

Selling

The principal function of all selling agents is to provide their clients with a selling organization for the disposal of their output. They frequently take orders several months in advance which serve as a basis for the mill's production schedule. Selling is conducted partly from salesrooms maintained at different market centers, and partly through salesmen who cover the trade. Larger selling agents operate their business on a departmental basis, sometimes employing specialty, local, and traveling salesmen within a single department.

Product Planning

A second important function, particularly in textile and related trades, is product planning advice. Mills producing goods of seasonal design find it essential to secure as much up-to-date style information as possible. This is a costly process when undertaken by a single manufacturer. Selling agents, by distributing their costs over several mills, are enabled to maintain representatives in important style centers and obtain authentic information on the latest styles, patterns, and designs, or to subscribe for such services.

These representatives attend theaters, fashion shows and exhibitions, and fashionable society resorts and functions, for the purpose of observing what style leaders wear or how they react toward exhibitions by leading designers or couturiers. On the basis of such data, styles, designs, and patterns are submitted to clients, sometimes for adoption and sometimes only as suggestions subject to the exercise of the mill's prerogative. If the recommended designs are adopted, the mill makes up samples and submits its estimate of the cost of the goods. Designs for the seasons are then chosen and salesmen are sent out with the samples to secure orders.

Selling agents also furnish reliable market and price information for the guidance of the purchasing activities of the mills. Some go even further and supervise mill production and receive daily reports concerning production progress on the various orders, on the theory that such information is essential to a proper correlation between manufacturing and selling. It not only makes possible intelligent direction of the sales force, but enables the agency to safeguard the observance of promises regarding delivery dates. When financial aid is extended, such data further help in checking up on the effective utilization of the loans.

Financing

A third function of selling agents is to render financial assistance to manufacturers they represent. It is a very important service when the clients are weak financially and far removed from financial centers.

Credit and Collection Service

Finally, selling agents, particularly when they make direct loans to their clients or "cash their sales," often perform a complete credit and collection service. Under such circumstances they must approve all orders, maintain a credit department, and collect all accounts, thereby freeing the manufacturer from such work. Many selling agents guarantee all credit extended by them, render bills for the goods, receive payment and collect overdue accounts, and in turn remit to the mill after charges have been deducted, or remit the full amount collected and then bill the client for commissions and other charges.

When Employed

From the foregoing consideration of functions, it is apparent that the selling agent can be used most advantageously when the manufacturer operates on a small scale, needs financial assistance, produces a limited variety of products which require wide distribution, and needs continuous representation in the market. Small-scale operation and a limited line may make the cost of sending one's own sales force over a wide territory at all times prohibitive. Brokers are best used when there is no need for continuous represen-tation, and manufacturers' agents are best suited when sales assistance is needed for only a part of one's sales area and financial aid or product planning assistance are not required. Hence the selling agent fits into a place not well occupied by the manufacturer's own sales force, the broker, or the manufacturers' agent. The principal disadvantages in using selling agents are, first, that the manufacturer is altogether dependent upon one outside organization for sales and, second, that it is sometimes difficult to coordinate manufacturing schedules with such an outside organization that sells for several different firms.

MANUFACTURERS' AGENTS

Of the various other types of functional middlemen, the manufacturers' agent (or manufacturers' representative as he is popularly designated in some trades, but not to be confused with a manufacturer's sales employee) comes closest to approximating the variety of services rendered by the selling agent. In spite of some degree of similarity, there are nevertheless marked contrasts in the nature of the operations of these two types of agents and the conditions under which they are used.

Character of Operations

Manufacturers' agents sell a part of the output of two or more client manufacturers. They differ from selling agents in the following major respects:

- The territory of a manufacturers' agent is limited, while that of a selling agent is unlimited. Territorial size varies considerably, ranging from a single city in some instances to a combination of several states in others.
- Manufacturers' agents have little, if any, control over prices, discounts, credit terms, or other conditions of sale, whereas it is common (although not universal) for selling agents to determine such matters. Manufacturers distributing through manufacturers' agents commonly carry on their own advertising and sales promotional activities, or determine the character of the advertising and selling work to be done by the agent.
- While the selling agent undertakes to sell the entire output of his clients, the manufacturers' agent sells only a part of it, within the territory assigned to him, and according to some broader marketing plan usually pursued by the manufacturer in distributing through other agents assigned to noncompeting territories or through his own sales force in part.

Commissions received by manufacturers' agents vary considerably with the different lines of trade. For all such agents, average commission rates are about 6 per cent of sales. The range is from less than 2 per cent for commodities which are sold in very large volume and when sales are made with relative ease to more than 20 per cent for items which are usually sold in small amounts and when sales are accom-plished with difficulty. Although nearly five times as nume-rous as selling agents, manufacturers' agents account for only 40 per cent more in volume of sales. The typical establishment is small, often consisting of a single individual, and only occasionally comprising more than several employees. A few agents operate on a considerable scale, however, and employ a large number of salesmen, each of whom is assigned to a group of specific accounts or to a specific sales area within the agent's territory. Larger agents sometimes represent as many as twenty-five different manufacturers and smaller ones as few as two or three. Their form of selling representation permeates almost all lines of manufacturing; but they are of greatest importance in the distribution of machinery and equipment, specialty groceries and foods, dry goods, electrical goods, metals, clothing, apparel accessories, hosiery, furniture, and automotive accessories.

Functions of Manufacturers' Agents

Most manufacturers' agents are concerned almost exclusively with the selling function, providing continuous sales representation for the manufacturer in the assigned territory. In addition, they are commonly a source of marketing information, feeding back to the manufacturer information on competitive conditions, product preferences, and suggestions for product changes.

About 25 per cent of the manufacturers' agents provide some warehousing facilities and make deliveries from stock carried on consignment from manufacturers. This is more common for agents operating in the industrial goods field than in consumer goods. Even then, stocks are usually limited to items which must often be supplied on an emergency basis or to repair parts. In the majority of cases, drop shipments are sent by the factory directly to the purchasers, unless pooled cars are used, in which case the agent may take charge of the distribution of the goods after the carlot has been broken.

When Employed

There are several circumstances which favor the employment of manufacturers' agents. First is the financial consideration. Numerous manufacturing firms do not have adequate financial resources to establish their own sales organization, particularly when an extremely wide market must be covered. This situation obtains in the textile trades where some mills have grown in size and in financial strength sufficiently to free themselves from the selling agent but still lack the capital and experience necessary to assume complete control of all selling operations. Manufacturers' agents thus afford a desirable stage of transition.

Second, like other types of functional middlemen, manufacturers' agents are used by companies that produce a single product or a narrow line of goods with a unit value too low to justify the expense of maintaining a sales force.

A third favorable condition is when distribution is desired in sparsely populated territories or in markets located at a great distance from the factory. A manufacturing company may employ its own sales force for the disposal of its products in dense markets but may prefer to be represented by manufacturers' agents in sparse market areas where the potential business is small and traveling expenses are high. Distant markets present similar handicaps. This accounts for the fact that so many eastern and middle-western manufacturers, regardless of size, employ manufacturers' agents in the Rocky Mountain and Pacific Coast states. A manufacturer located in the Far West is in a similar position with regard to representation on the Atlantic Coast, particularly when few commodities are produced.

Fourth, manufacturers' agents are used to advantage for introductory purposes. A manufacturers' agent may sometimes be employed as a means of securing entrance to a certain group of prospective buyers. He serves as a passport, a *billet d'entrée*. Finally, manufacturers' agents are useful where continuous representation in the market is needed and hence brokers and commission merchants cannot be employed to advantage, but where sales possibilities do not justify a full-time salesman.

While distribution through manufacturers' agents is commonly carried out under the above conditions, it neverthe-less often presents some problems for the manufacturer. One of the most important is that of selecting agents who can provide the desired type of sales representation and who do not already represent competing manufacturers. A second problem is that of territorial assignments. The territory assigned to a specific agent must be integrated with the territory normally covered by him for other clients. It is quite a complex undertaking to make a selection of agents which provides complete selling coverage of the manufacturer's total market, without overlapping of territories. Third, since agents are independent businessmen, it is difficult to coordinate their activities and to have a group of them sell according to a manufacturer's planned marketing strategy.

COMMISSION MERCHANTS

By way of contrast with selling and manufacturers' agents, commission merchants, brokers, and auction companies are not ordinarily engaged on a continuing contractual basis, but rather for the disposal of a specific lot of goods or for a single transaction. While similar in this respect, commission merchants differ from brokers and auction companies in other ways, particularly with respect to the method of consummating a transaction and with reference to the actual handling of commodities.

Nature of Operations

Commission men often have physical possession of the goods they sell, warehousing them or at least displaying samples of lots offered for sale, contacting potential buyers with a view to obtaining the best possible prices, and generally performing the sales function. They operate with considerably more freedom than brokers in that they have the power to accept an offer from a buyer without obtaining confirmation from the principal, although the principal often stipulates a minimum price in order to protect his own interests against possible abuse. In fact, the principal need not even be identified to the purchaser, for the commission merchant makes the sale as if the goods were his own, extends credit at his own risk, renders a bill to the purchaser, collects the account, and submits to his principal an accounting of the transaction, together with remission of the proceeds less the commission charged for his services. As the term commission merchant is used in this discussion, it refers only to firms that operate primarily in this manner, that is, sell on a consignment basis goods to which they do not acquire title. Many commission houses actually blend this activity with merchant wholesaling by taking title to goods, a practice often criticized because of the opportunity it gives for abuse. As an agent of a principal, it is the function of the commission merchant to effect a sale at the highest possible price, whereas in purchasing on his own account such an operator is naturally interested in buying at the lowest possible price.

Thus there is a definite conflict in interests when goods which are submitted by principals for commission sale are purchased by the commission man for his own account. When they buy on their own account with full knowledge of the fact by everyone concerned, there is not the same opportunity for abuse because the seller knows that he is dealing with a merchant whose interests conflict with his own and he must, accordingly, assume responsibility himself for making the best possible arrangement.

Since the present discussion is confined to commission operations that constitute the bulk of the operations of particular wholesale establishments, the commission method of sale is more important. Many wholesalers who take title to most of the goods in which they deal operate on a commission basis to some extent.

Measured by sales volume importance, commission merchants constitute the second most important group of functional middleman. Only a small proportion of the total sales of commission merchants consists of manufactured products. The great bulk of their activities is in the field of agricultural marketing, both consumer farm produce and raw materials, and the nature of operations varies somewhat with the class of commodity involved.

Fresh Farm Produce

A commission firm dealing in consumer fresh farm produce receives the product from growers or shippers; handles, conditions, and otherwise prepares it for market; sells in its own name, without divulging the name of its principal, for the best price available; collects and remits the proceeds to the shipper after deducting its commission, transportation charges, and any expenses incurred for cartage, storage, and repacking. In making remittance, the firm renders an *account sale,* consisting of a statement showing what disposition has been made of the consignment, even before collections have been made from the buyers. An account sale is often rendered within 24 hours after consummation of the sale. Except when restricted by specific instructions from the owner, the commission merchant has full control of the selling and can exercise his best judgment and ability.

He either sells in car lots on the railroad track or else breaks bulk, carts the goods to his place of business, and makes sales and deliveries in small lots. He is entrusted with the management, control, and disposition of the goods he handles and has a special property in them, including a lien for his interest and his commission.Commission dealing in consumer farm produce was widely practiced in a former era when marketing methods were crude, goods unstandardized, transportation facilities inadequate, slow, and uncertain, and knowledge of market conditions was insufficient. Under such circumstances, few merchants were willing to assume risks involved in outright purchase of agricultural products at point of origin. Prices offered were therefore too low to induce producers and local middlemen to sell outright. So long as these conditions prevailed, the commission business flourished. Two major long-range developments have resulted in a gradual decline in commission dealing in favor of an increasing outright sale by local shippers to regional or central market purchasers. First, the use of commonly accepted standards and grading systems, coupled with improvements in speed and special handling facilities in transportation, have made it possible for merchant buyers to be more confident of the quality and condition of goods when received at regional or central markets. Second, improvements in communication and the dissemination of market information have reduced risks by making it possible for shippers and wholesalers to avoid market gluts with their disastrous consequences.

In certain cases, the commission method also became unpopular with shippers. Some firms abused their trusted status by buying consigned produce *for their own account* at lower than market prices, thus reaping a benefit at the shipper's expense. Opportunities for such abuses were most prevalent when a considerable distance separated commission merchant and shipper and when marketing information was limited and disseminated slowly. Thus, long-run developments have contributed to the shipper's desire to make outright sales, as well as to the commission merchant's willingness to buy for his own account.

Whereas formerly commission men seldom bought any produce outright, many such houses now handle on a consignment basis no more than a small part of the goods they sell, the greater portion being bought on their own account, except in large cities where commission dealing is more prominent. In such cases the middleman has truly become a merchant, so that the designation *merchant* is more descriptive of his function than the older term commission *man* or commission *house*. Even the newer term presents a distorted picture of the actual situation. Here is a case where methods of doing business have changed without a corresponding change in the name of the firms, either because of the desire to emphasize their readiness to serve clients in the sale of consignments or because of good will that may be attached to the old name, or on account of mere neglect to effect a change that is not regarded as vital.

Livestock and Grain

Commission dealing is extremely important in the marketing of livestock and grain at major terminal markets. Terminal markets for livestock are at some considerable distance from the typical farmer and not conveniently accessible to him. Thus, he finds it expedient to sell livestock through an intermediary, usually a livestock commission firm, which may be an independently owned business or owned by a livestock cooperative marketing association. A livestock shipment is consigned to a commission firm which takes custody of the animals upon arrival at the facilities of a stockyards company. The stockyards firm does not engage in buying or selling, but merely provides physical facilities for the care and handling of animals for a rental fee. Salesmen for commission firms and terminal buyers are expert judges of quality and are well informed about supply and demand conditions generally and for specific grades of individual species. Sales are effected after buyers' inspection of individual offerings and are consummated through a process of bargaining and haggling. The commission firm receives a fee for its services and renders a prompt accounting of the transaction to its principals. Commission dealing in grain differs in several respects. Most grain that moves to terminal markets is assembled in local growers' markets. Thus the central market commission firm usually represents a local assembling elevator rather than a farmer. Grain shipped from country points is consigned to a commission firm which takes custody of rail car shipments upon arrival at the terminal market. It makes immediate arrangements for grading according to government standards. Samples are taken from arriving cars and the grain is sold on the basis of such samples on the floor of an organized commodity exchange.

The continuing significance of commission dealing in livestock and grain is explained by several factors. First, there is little opportunity for the abuses that have been associated with this method historically in the marketing of fresh farm produce. This is explained by the public character of transactions in terminal markets and by widely and rapidly disseminated price quotations for specific grades of livestock and grain. Second, there is always a ready market for these commodities at the prevailing market price for a given grade. The shipper, therefore, has little fear that the commodities will not be sold upon arrival. Third, most commission firms are members of an organized exchange or other group and sell according to rules and standards of ethical conduct which prevent, among other things, abuses and unfair dealings with shipper principals. While the commission firm's relationship with its principal is confined to responsibility for the sale of a particular consignment, most shippers make frequent or periodic use of some one commission firm that has rendered satisfactory service in the past.

Factors Governing Use of Commission Merchants

Commission merchants are used by sellers who need an immediately available outlet for goods, which can be consigned without complicated advance or continuing arrangements and where shippers can be assured of immediate efforts to sell. Thus, with little effort and at no cost except on sales actually made, the manufacturer or agricultural producer can draw upon the resources of an experienced marketing organization in a market area of his choice.

The use of commission merchants by manufacturing organizations tends to be restricted to those that make a highly standardized product, undifferentiated by brand name, and for which no special demand has been created by promotional effort. In such instances, the procedure used by manufacturers in their dealings with commission merchants varies from that ordinarily employed by shippers of agricultural commodities, in that they may not give the house physical possession of a shipment. Instead, samples, results of a chemical analysis, or grade specifications may be submitted, together with a description of quantities offered for sale and any limitations imposed upon the freedom of the commission operator with respect to minimum prices or delivery dates. Thus, commission outlets are well adapted to the sale of highly standardized products, since goods of that type can be more easily sold when not in physical possession of the seller.

BROKERS

From the standpoint of sales volume, brokers are the third most important type of functional middlemen. They operate, however, with the most limited freedom in consummating transactions and perform fewer costly functions than the other types.

Services

The principal service of the broker is that of bringing buyer and seller together. He is a "go-between," assuming no title risks, and not being looked upon as a permanent representative of either buyer or seller. A broker does not take title to the goods in which he deals nor does he usually have physical possession of them. He does not handle the goods nor does he finance his clients. His is purely a negotiatory service or function. He finds buyers for merchandise under one set of conditions; under another he seeks out suppliers. In the first instance he represents and is paid a brokerage fee by the seller; in the second case he represents a buyer and is paid a fee by him. When demand is normal, the broker is more likely to represent sellers. But when supply is limited, or certain grades are hard to obtain, he more often represents buyers. Some brokers specialize in representing buyers, but most of them specialize in representing sellers.

When Brokers Are Used

Like other marketing institutions, the use of brokers is governed by certain well-established conditions which may be expressed in the form of principles. First, when production is seasonal the broker is an efficient aid. Were he not used, the producer would be compelled to organize a sales force for work during a short selling season, discharge it when the task is finished, and rehire it the following year; else pay his men for an entire year but use them for but a part of the time. Either alternative would involve prohibitive expense. Brokers can be called upon when the product is ready for sale, used during that period, and be again ready the following year. They are immediately available and bring their knowledge of the market to the aid of the manufacturer for the time he needs it.

Second, brokers are useful when producers are small and the market is scattered. Since they are paid only when they serve their clients, and since they can be secured in all markets, a food processor may, by the use of brokers, touch all markets without establishing a sales force of his own. Similar conditions explain the use of brokers in the cotton piece goods trade. Here, many producers are small and not well financed, the market is very broad, and the broker is the ideal agent for reaching it. A third principle is that when goods are highly standardized and available from many sources, buying brokers are effective. Since they know all possible sources in detail, they render a special type of service by aiding the buyer to contact the best source of supply, without divulging the name of his principal until after the transaction has been consummated.

Brokers often act as agents for agricultural producers and country shippers of farm commodities, also as agents of central market wholesale middlemen or processors who wish to buy carload lots of agricultural commodities from shippers at assembly points Since brokers do not have physical custody of shipments their operations are confined to commodities that can be exchanged on the basis of description. Sale through brokers is especially important when a shipper wishes to "try the market" by getting offers from one or more buyers prior to consigning goods to a particular destination. This may be illustrated with reference to northwestern apples. When a carload is available for shipment, the seller, who may be a large grower, a cooperative association, or a local middleman, writes or telegraphs a description of the offering to one or more brokers The broker then canvasses the trade diligently and gets in touch with dealers who are likely to buy the goods and sends the vendor the best bid obtainable.

When buyer and seller have agreed on a price the broker notifies the shipper to forward the car f.o.b. usual terms, and to send a draft attached to the bill of lading on the broker's bank. Permission is usually given to inspect the merchandise prior to acceptance, unless official inspection services are available at the shipping point, and the goods are sold f.o.b. cash track, in which case payment is due immediately and all risks thereafter are assumed by the buyer. On accepting the car, the buyer orders his bank to pay the draft and proceeds are remitted to the shipper. If the car is not accepted and complications develop, the broker may be given authority to settle the dispute and make proper allowances.

When a broker represents a buyer, he gets in touch with sources of supply and secures offers which are then transmitted to his principal or client for acceptance or rejection. If contract terms and conditions are satisfactory, the broker notifies the vendor and his part is completed. Brokers are widely used by smaller manufacturers of consumer goods, particularly items of the convenience goods types and especially many items that are purchased in large quantities by wholesale grocers and chain store warehouses in the food trades. The economy that a manufacturer of such products achieves by using brokers to sell to such customers is suggested by the following typical brokerage fees: nationally advertised canned fruits and vegetables, 2 to 2 ½ per cent; less well-known brands of canned fruits and vegetables, 3 per cent; canned milk, 5 cents per case; woodenware items (e.g., toothpicks and clothespins), 5 per cent to 7 ½ per cent; frozen food products, 3 per cent to 4 per cent; sundries, such as insecticides, 6 per cent to 7 per cent.

Brokers are used in the distribution of all but a small per cent of the refined sugar sold in the United States. Specialized brokers who operate on a large scale in major metropolitan markets receive a commission of 5 cents per 100 lb. bag, but sales in many smaller areas are negotiated with the cooperation of two brokers, in which case a total brokerage fee of 8.75 cents is divided between them. In spite of the fact that the channel of distribution is unusually long, often involving two brokers between the sugar refiner and wholesale distributing organization, distribution costs are among the lowest for all food commodity groups. Total brokerage fees have been estimated to amount to less than 0.75 per cent of the final selling price of sugar.

Limitations

Brokers are not always an ideal agency. Their principal advantage, that of being a widespread, quickly available and economical marketing institution, is in part offset by their somewhat impersonal interest in the transaction. To be sure, their fee depends on negotiating a deal successfully, but they are not laboring under quite the same incentive as is a manufacturer's own sales force. They are not subject to the same control nor the same stimulation. Some have their favourite clients and do not always give equal representation to all. It is hard for a distant shipper to know whether failure to sell in a certain market is due to the weakness of the broker or to his failure to quote the right price. But thousands of small canners and other small manufacturers find it impossible to operate their own force and must depend on the broker; or if the goods must be handled or continuous representation is required, one of the other types of functional middlemen must be called into service.

The Food Broker

The foregoing discussion has served to indicate the operations of most organizations known as brokers. The dynamics of marketing is illustrated by the fact that many firms, originally established and operated in this manner, and still known to the trade as brokers, have nevertheless altered their activities over, the years in response to changing market situations. This is particularly true of food brokers who are members of the National Food Brokers Association, a group said to include more than 40 per cent of the brokers dealing in food products. Members of this association have agreed upon a code of ethics and general operating procedures which distinguish them to some extent from other brokers operating in the food and other fields.

It is asserted that such brokers are actually manufacturers' agents or sellers' representatives. It is their policy to act only for sellers and to receive compensation only from them in any transaction. The position of such brokers as agents of sellers is explained in part by the fact that this has been customary practice in the food field, also undoubtedly by the influence of the brokerage fee provision of the Robinson-Patman Act, which prohibits receipt of brokerage fees except for services rendered, which means that no fee can be received from a seller when a broker operates as a representative of the buyer, and vice versa. The question as to whether a food broker should be classed as a genuine broker or as a manufacturers' agent is a matter to be resolved in each individual case, depending upon the presence or absence of continuing contractual relationships pertaining to operation in a limited, exclusive territory. Actually, the operations of many *food* brokers bear a closer resemblance to those of manufacturers' agents than to what may be designated as *bona fide* brokers.

Such a food broker, in addition to representing only sellers, confines his activities to a definite territory which usually consists of the wholesale grocery trading area of the key city in which the office is maintained. Within this territory the broker is ordinarily the sole sales agency of the principals who engage his services, and he serves them by negotiating sales with grocery wholesalers, chain store buyers, and institutions. He receives commissions on all sales made by the principals within the broker's specified territory regardless of how the sales are actually effected—an arrangement justified by the merchandising service rendered by such brokers and which, in some instances, is highly developed.

Many food brokers have a missionary sales staff that calls upon independent retail stores and units of chain store organi- zations. While the broker ordinarily transacts business with wholesalers and chain store buying offices, his missionary salesmen solicit orders from new retail accounts; the orders are then turned over to regular wholesalers who maintain stocks, provide delivery service, and render other wholesaling services. The merchandising service also includes the activities of explaining the manufacturers' advertising programs to retailers, soliciting dealer cooperation in local advertising, getting the dealer to use point-of-sale advertising material, and arranging for store and window displays of the principals' merchandise. Because the broker's missionary sales staff works with the products of several manufacturers, this can be done at lower cost than experienced by most manufacturers who attempt to organize comparable merchandising services for themselves.

AUCTION COMPANIES

Auction companies comprise a third type of functional middleman that provides sellers with a temporary or intermittent opportunity to market specific lots of commodities. The auction method of sale is encountered only occasionally in the marketing of manufactured goods but is of great importance in the marketing of certain agricultural commodities.

NATURE OF AUCTION OPERATIONS

Auction companies provide the facilities and mechanism *for public exchange*. Facilities are usually available to all sellers who wish to offer commodities and to all commercial buyers (except in tobacco auctions where buyers must be licensed for tax-collecting reasons) who wish to bid on them. Sales are usually well publicized in advance or are held at specific times well known in the trade. Exchange is effected in accordance with definite rules, with sales made to the highest bidder. For its services, the auction company receives a fee which is usually charged as a small per cent of the value of the commodities sold. Auctions are of chief significance in the marketing of certain fruits and vegetables in terminal markets and in marketing tobacco and livestock in producing regions. They are also used for selling furs in terminal markets, and live poultry and certain fruits and vegetables in growing regions. The nature of auction operations varies somewhat according to the marketing requirements of the major types of commodities commonly sold by this method.

Terminal Fruit Auctions

Fruit auctions located in certain large cities are a significant institution in the marketing of fresh deciduous and citrus fruits and various specialty edible produce items. In the mid-1930's thirteen such auctions handled some 36 per cent of the total sales of fresh citrus fruits and 13 per cent of fresh deciduous fruit sales. By the late 1950's these proportions had declined, respectively, to 16 and 6 per cent, and the number of terminal market auctions declined from thirteen to nine. The diminishing importance of terminal fruit auctions is an aspect of a general trend to bypass terminal markets for agricultural commodities. Specifically, it is attributed to the growing tendency of arge chain grocery organizations and large wholesalers to make direct purchases in growing regions. Terminal markets still, however, serve as a significant source of supply to institutional buyers, independent grocers and specialty fruit and vegetable stores, small corporate and voluntary chain groups that do not operate their own produce warehouses, dispersion market produce jobbers, and large chains when purchasing fill-in requirements and smallvolume specialty produce items (e.g., apricots, plums, grapes, tangerines, nectarines). Cooperative shipping associations supply about two-thirds of the volume of commodities sold through such auctions and the remainder is accounted for by assembling wholesalers and certain large individual producers. Upon the arrival of cars at the auction, goods are unloaded and placed in storage, usually adjacent to the auction room. Next is the separation of goods into lines or lots consisting of packages of the same brand, size, and grade from a single car. Samples are then selected at random by representatives of the auction company and made available for inspection by prospective buyers. Sales are made on a strictly "as is" basis, but on the assumption that samples have been fairly taken. A catalog showing all lots to be offered and essentials of grade and size is prepared and used by the auctioneer and the buyers. Clerks record the transactions as they occur, and the buyers arrange for removing their purchases. Usually credit is granted for 10 or 15 days, although some sales are for cash only.

Tobacco

The auction method of sale has been found well suited to the sale of tobacco largely because of difficulties in grading. Small differences in quality are often responsible for rather substantial differences in value. Buyers and sellers therefore prefer a system of exchange based on visual inspection of lots offered for sale and competitive bidding. More than 90 per cent of the tobacco crop is sold through *loose-leaf auctions* which are conducted in large tobacco warehouses located in many cities throughout the southern tobacco-growing states. Before offering tobacco for sale, the farmer sorts it into different lots according to colour and other factors relating to quality. Each lot is placed in a separate basket, weighed, and graded by a federal inspector. Bidders at the auction are representatives of tobacco manufacturing companies and smaller speculative buyers. Sales are made with great rapidity, usually at the rate of 350 to 400 baskets per hour. Farmers receive payment within a few minutes after close of the auction.

Livestock

Marketing of livestock through local or *shipping point auctions* has increased considerably since the 1930's. It provides the farmer who does not wish to ship to terminal markets with the opportunity to sell locally on the basis of competitive bids. Auctions constitute the principal method of selling hogs from the farm but are also used for other important forms of livestock. Throughout the United States there are more than 2,000 livestock auctions, located principally in rural marketing centers and concentrated heavily in southern and southeastern states which are most remote from terminal market facilities. Sales are made to meat packing companies, other farmers who buy animals for feeding or breeding purposes, and, to a limited extent, to speculative buyers. Auction company personnel receives livestock consigned for sale and cares for animals after sale until shipment is made. Animals are sold in a sales ring to the highest bidder. In small markets, it is common to restrict the operation of the auction to one day per week in order to concentrate supply and demand factors.

Advantages of Auctions

A significant advantage claimed for the auction method of sale is the free play of supply and demand thus made possible. It brings the buying power of the market together and stimulates active and unrestricted bidding. Consequently, it exerts a stabilizing influence on the market to the benefit of both buyer and seller, the latter presumably securing as high a price as market conditions warrant. Auctions also afford a market for goods which must be sold quickly because they are perishable or which enjoy no established market, although best results are not secured on ungraded or defective merchandise. It is further claimed that auctions are an inexpensive method of selling, especially for livestock.

Auction company charges and commissions amount to about $2.25 per head to sell cattle, $0.63 per head for hogs, and $0.42 for sheep or lambs. Publicity incident to auction sales renders the vendor some assurance of fair dealing. Prices are made public immediately after sale by means of trade publications, newspapers, and through price-realized catalogs. This publicity affords another advantage in that auction-established prices on certain products serve for guidance in later private transactions.

Disadvantages of Auctions

Because full play is given to the forces of supply and demand, wide price fluctuations are common at auctions. If supply is small and demand brisk, prices soar, but drop precipitously when the reverse is true. Such variations may be greater than justified by the entire market situation. A second disadvantage is that it is time consuming. At private sales, buyers can visit several wholesale suppliers, compare prices and quality, and make decisions in a short time. If they buy on the auction they may be forced to wait some time—often some hours—until the merchandise in which they are interested is offered.

Objection has also been raised to certain practices which tend to distort actual supply and demand conditions. Sales may be influenced by "puffers," "by-bidders," or "cappers." These are fictitious bidders who have no idea of making actual purchases but are employed by sellers to boost the price. This practice is forbidden by all auction companies and is believed to be practically absent on the terminal fruit auctions. Similar in effect and also against the rules is the practice of some receivers to bid on their own goods in order to raise the price. This is not normally necessary as the seller has a right to set a minimum before the sale starts and, usually, to withdraw his offerings before they are actually sold. A final objection is that the auction method is unfair to some vendors. Those whose goods are sold early in the day sometimes receive more than do consignors whose offerings are sold some hours later.

6

The Buying Function

In every transaction someone engages in buying. Goods or services may be purchased for industrial or commercial use, for resale, or for ultimate consumption. The buyer may be one who specializes in performing this function, one who does buying along with many other business activities, or an ultimate consumer satisfying a personal want. In any event, there is no better indication of the importance and pervasive nature of the buying function than the fact that someone buys every time a sale is made. Buying is significant not only as a differentiated specific function but also as an economic activity, the understanding of which is basic to modern concepts of customer-oriented marketing management.

BUYING—AN ACTIVE MARKETING FUNCTION

While buying is a basic marketing function, it is often improperly relegated to an unimportant position. It is sometimes erroneously assumed that it is of a *passive character*—merely the opposite of selling. Quite to the contrary, buying does not take care of itself, but is indeed an *active* function.

The skill used in buying has an important influence in determining the relative value of what is purchased by the consumer. The constant increase in the variety of products offered to him, the growing tendency to procure more goods and services in the market rather than to produce them in the home, the multiplicity of brands, the frequency of relatively small quality differentials, and the widely differing services offered by stores, all combine to add to the difficulty of the consumer's choice and to stress the importance of his being able to buy with intelligence. The active character of buying is especially conspicuous in the case of the consumer. Traditionally, he has taken the initiative in the exchange process. When wants are recognized and the consumer is ready to act upon them, it is customary for him to seek out a seller or sellers. When a salesperson comes into contact with the consumer-buyer, the process of exchange is often nearly completed. This is dramatically emphasized by the small proportion of retail business which is accounted for by house-to-house canvassers or other sellers who take the initiative in seeking out prospective consumer-buyers, and, by way of contrast, by the predominant proportion which is accounted for by regular retail establishments that are visited by a purchasing-minded public. Developments in simplified selling or self-service merchandising accentuate the importance of consumer buying activity.

The more the retail selling and service functions are curtailed, the greater becomes the task and responsibility of the consumer as a buyer. While there is a substantial amount of pre-buying stimulation in the form of aggressive retailer and manufacturer advertising and sales promotion activity, the number of items competing for consumer attention is so vast and diverse that the ordinary person must play an extremely active role in making the purchases that satisfy his wants. It may be observed, however, that buying is often as active when examined from the standpoint of the firm as it is in the case of the ultimate consumer.

Unless buying of raw materials, semimanufactures, and the many items of equipment and supplies needed for the production process is effectively accomplished, manufacturers handicap themselves in their ability to compete with those who may be more skillful in the performance of this function. Ability to select from many offerings just what will sell best and to determine the most economic quantities to be bought at a given time is one of the prime tests of the efficiency of both wholesaler and retailer. Moreover, buying is closely related to other marketing functions. Its practices and policies are often determined, in part at least, by the financial position of the purchaser, the availability of adequate and economical transportation and storage facilities, and the degree to which standardization has been accomplished. Risk is often reduced by the adoption of proper buying policies. Skillful buyers make use of reliable and pertinent market information from a variety of sources. Goods purchased for resale must be selected primarily with reference to what the market will absorb. In short, this marketing function is closely related to the functioning of almost every part of our marketing system.

SPECIALIZATION IN BUYING

That buying is a very active and quantitatively significant function cannot be questioned when it is considered that manufacturing companies and middlemen ordinarily employ specialists to perform this activ-ity. In manufacturing establishments a key employee, generally known as the purchasing agent, sometimes bearing the title of Vice President in Charge of Procurement, is responsible for the function. All wholesale merchants have buyers who generally occupy the position of executives, the number depending upon the size of the business and the number of different merchandise departments involved. Larger retail stores employ buyers who are also usually the managers of merchandise departments. Quite a number of large department stores have more than 100 buyers each. In the chain store field the buying function is either centralized or divided between the central office and the individual retail store unit. Among smaller independent stores, the buying function is usually the responsibility of the proprietor or one of the partners, but it is almost invariably one of the most important of their activities.

WHAT BUYING INVOLVES

Like the other marketing functions, buying may be subdivided into a number of important elements or responsi-bilities. The most important of these are:

- The selection of kinds of goods,
- The determination of quality or suitability,
- The determination of quantities,
- The selection of sources of supply.

Selection of Kinds of Goods

Freedom in determining the kinds of goods to be purchased varies from one type of business to another. In many lines of manufacturing the materials to be bought are fixed automatically by the nature of the product manufactured. The manufacturer of cotton textiles must buy cotton yarn or raw cotton, and the butter manufacturer must have cream. Installations and industrial equipment are determined largely by the nature of the manufacturing process, with the result that there is sometimes rather limited freedom in their purchase. For most merchants, on the other hand, the determination of kinds of goods to be purchased is a real problem, since the firm may not constantly handle exactly the same merchandise.

While within certain limits most wholesalers and retailers find their choice of merchandise circumscribed by their clientele and competition, nevertheless it is a rare mercantile business which does not have some latitude. This problem has been aggravated considerably by a pronounced tendency for many types of stores to expand or diversify their merchandise lines. Self-service grocery stores, for example, have sought to handle any type of merchandise that is suitable for sale by self-service methods. In seeking new items to purchase, they have been attracted by the higher margins obtainable on numerous items normally handled by drug-, de-partment, or hardware stores. As a result, numerous advertised brands of proprietary remedies, toilet preparations, cosmetics, housewares, magazines, and alcoholic beverages have been successfully added to the lines carried by many supermarkets.

Drugstores, hardware stores, and other kinds of business, feeling the pressure of this competition, have also sought to expand their offerings by invading fields hitherto foreign to them. Similarly, most variety chains have abandoned their limited-price position, and some have become in essence junior department stores. Department stores, in turn, have expanded their sales volume by the addition of departments for sporting goods, cameras and photographic equipment, and other kinds of merchandise that have been sold traditionally in specialized types of establishments. Many marketing establishments have made costly mistakes in experimental attempts to diversify their merchandise offerings. For most small establishments, experience has indicated that new items cannot ordinarily be added successfully *unless*

- they are in keeping with the general character of the business as reflected by firm name, atmosphere, location, and advertising and promotion policies;
- They can be sold according to the present method of sale and by present employees;
- Sufficient space and capital investment can be devoted to the new merchandise to offer customers a reasonable range of choice within the classification to which it belongs. Obviously, these rules have not been important limiting factors for very large wholesale or retail firms where it is more feasible to add specialized personnel or facilities to handle the merchandising of items not closely related to those previously sold.

Determination of Quality

A second major buying responsibility relates to the determination of the suitability of goods for business use or for resale. This is a matter of quality, which involves consideration of materials, workmanship, grades, sizes, designs, colors, and patterns.

To a large degree manufacturers determine the quality of goods purchased by the characteristics of the products they make. For example, furniture sold in the highest price ranges demands materials far different from those used in making furniture to sell on a price basis. Although the final product depends greatly upon the skill of craftsmen assigned to its manufacture, minimum qualities of materials must be established. In many lines of manufacturing, however, there is an opportunity to exercise choice in selecting qualities for purchase. Sometimes additional labour may be applied to cheaper materials with resulting equal end results and a net cost reduction. While the specifications for materials are usually dictated by the requirements of the product being manufactured, final product design is often determined, at least in part, by the prices at which materials of varying qualities can be purchased.

Determination of quality is of especial interest in the purchase of business supplies. Good purchasing practice involves obtaining the *right quality for a particular purpose*—not the highest obtainable quality. This may be illustrated with respect to paper which is available over a wide range of quality. To purchase such a product which is either not good enough or better than necessary involves potential waste. Take the case of a large insurance company that has substantial paper requirements. For inter-office communications that are promptly read and quickly discarded, only minimum quality standards need be observed. For documents which will be kept a long time and handled often, however, much attention must be given to various quality factors which are relevant to preservation.

Retailers and wholesalers have a somewhat similar problem. Their market must be analyzed to determine the quality of merchandise which will appeal to prospective buyers. Often such a study reveals that a considerable part of the community desires either higher or lower qualities than are being supplied by stores. Not only must quality be determined, but merchants must give careful consideration to the salability of various sizes, materials, patterns, colors, and designs before entering the buying market.

Consumer demand is not, however, the sole consideration in determining just what qualities to buy. This may be illustrated with respect to the marketing of fresh peaches. Generally speaking, the consumer wants peaches which are ready to eat when purchased and prefers those that are picked from trees in a near ripe state. In the very early part of the season, however, peaches are usually quite expensive and sell rather slowly on both wholesale and retail levels of distribution. At this time, produce jobbers and retailers wish to buy peaches which are picked green because they will keep longer and can be handled with less risk of damage or spoilage. Thus, quality considerations are dictated by cost and handling factors rather than by consumer preference. Later, as supplies become more abundant, prices decline, and the volume of sales increases markedly. Both wholesalers and retailers are then more willing to handle peaches which have been picked in a more mature state and which are more satisfactory to the ultimate consumer.

A somewhat similar situation exists in ready-to-wear apparel establishments and other stores selling style merchandise. Consumer demand may dictate quality decisions for the most part, but in some instances there are other reasons for purchasing a given quality. Some retailers will buy a few items of more expensive quality than can be readily sold to their clientele. Their reason may be that the highest priced items make the next higher priced items in the line appear less expensive by comparison. Another motive may be to use the higher quality items chiefly for prestige purposes—that is, for display to give the store more of an atmosphere of elegance and fashion leadership than it would have if it confined its offerings solely to qualities that it can merchandise profitably. All of this suggests the wisdom of not confining motivation research to consumerbuyers or to industrial users, but of extending it to buyers of consumer goods on both the retail and wholesale levels of distribution.

Measuring Quality

While it is important to determine the desirable quality before buying, it is equally important to ascertain just what quality has actually been supplied by a seller. When quality factors are related to consideration such as flavour, visual appeal, or fashion, tests of quality are confined substantially to the judgment of the purchaser. Many aspects of quality are, however, precisely measurable. The process of analysis is used to determine the composition of an alloy or the purity of a chemical substance. Physical tests are employed to obtain the tensile strength of metal or the bursting strength of paper cartons. Precision measurements are used to find out whether the thread count of woven fibers or the thickness of sheet steel are within stated tolerances. Tests of performance are appropriate to determine how well paint will wear on a surface or how well automobile tires will last in use.

Many manufacturers utilize their own testing facilities for this purpose; others employ commercial testing laboratories. In some cases the test is made to determine the effective price, which may depend on the quality actually delivered. More often the test is made to prevent acceptance of products the quality of which is lower than was ordered. Many large retailers have installed testing laboratories for similar reasons, realizing that they must know the quality of merchandise which they sell if they are to serve their customers well. Certain trade associations perform a similar service for their members.

Determination of Quantities

A third important buying responsibility is ascertaining the proper quantities to be purchased. In wholesaling and retailing concerns this is based upon planned sales, and in manufacturing enterprises it is based upon manufacturing schedules which are ultimately dependent upon the sales volume anticipated. In some factories scheduling is altogether or largely based on orders already received and little or no manufacturing for stock takes place. In such instances, the manufacturer may defer the purchase of materials until he has orders for his product. Most manufacturers, however, cannot defer the purchase of all materials until they have orders in hand, since to do so would mean undue delays in delivery. All merchants are forced to carry some stock, and most merchants must carry substantial inventories. For them quantitative considerations in purchasing must rest upon estimates of future sales.

The sales estimate may be made directly in terms of numbers of units of merchandise to be sold, i.e., dozens, hundreds, pounds, barrels, tons, etc., or first in terms of dollars and cents. Expressing planned sales in money is a convenient common denominator for indicating total potential sales of a diverse and varied line of merchandise. The sales estimate or plan in terms of dollars becomes a valuable "yardstick" for measuring actual sales against planned sales. Obviously, where the manufacturer or merchant begins with a sales estimate in terms of value he must convert the dollar-and-cents figures into merchandise units.

In retail stores that handle fashion merchandise, careful sales plans are made twice a year, once for the spring and summer season and again for the fall and winter season. Planned purchases are derived from such estimates. For example, a shoe retailer may anticipate sales of $150,000 for the fall and winter season. If the merchant expects to realise a gross margin of 30 per cent of sales, then 70 per cent of sales or $105,000 may be spent to purchase shoes for this season. It would ordinarily be very bad judgment to spend the entire $105,000 before the season of retail sales arrived, since that would greatly increase the expense of operating the business through higher costs in obsolescence, deterioration, interest, rent, and taxes.

It is necessary, therefore, to decide just how the $105,000 in purchases is to be distributed over the period. That is, the buyer must decide how much merchandise shall be purchased or delivered before autumn and how much shall be spent for merchandise to be received during each of the autumn and winter months. If actual sales fall below the planned total, it will be necessary to curtail purchases. If actual sales exceed planned sales, then additions must be made to the sum allotted for the season's purchases.

Most retail and wholesale establishments that deal in staple commodities do not find it necessary to formulate such sales plans in order to buy intelligently. The typical grocery, hardware, or drugstore is supplied by wholesale firms in the vicinity and can obtain immediate replenishment for most items. Similarly, tobacco wholesalers reorder from manufac-turers of cigarettes who maintain inventories in most major cities. Such merchants need anticipate their requirements only a short time ahead to determine quantities to be bought.

Quantity Versus Small-lot Buying

While the total quantity to be purchased *over a period of time* is derived from anticipated sales volume, most manufacturers and merchants have considerable latitude in determining the quantity of specific products to be ordered *at a given time*. Such decisions are often a matter of policy, determined after consideration of the advantages of placing large orders and the disadvantages of such a practice.

Among the various *advantages of quantity buying*, the ability to obtain merchandise at lower cost is a foremost consideration. Many sellers quote special prices on large orders because the costs of selling and shipping are relatively less than on small orders. Price concessions may take the form of lower list price quotations, extra discounts from list prices, or "free deals" involving, for example, an offer of one dozen units of free merchandise if a merchant orders a full gross at one time rather than a mere one or two dozen. Substantial transportation economies are often associated with large orders. This is especially true if a full carload or truckload is purchased instead of an ordinary freight shipment, or if a freight shipment of 100 pounds or more is purchased instead of a considerably smaller amount. When large quantities are purchased, fewer orders are placed, which means that less time and effort may be required to perform the buying function, fewer incoming shipments need be received and checked, and a small number of invoices is to be accounted for and paid. Quantity buying is often stimulated by speculative desires. This is especially true when market prices are rising, and buyers wish to profit thereby, or when conditions of scarcity are anticipated, as in a national emergency.

While it offers many inducements, a number of *disadvantages also result from quantity buying*. The practice may lead to a decreased stockturn rate through a larger average stock on hand without a corresponding increase in sales volume. This, in turn, tends to accelerate depreciation both from physical deterioration and from style obsolescence. As against the possible speculative gains of quantity buying there must be offset the possible losses due to declining prices. Buying in smaller quantities gives more flexibility to the merchandising programme, since the smaller inventories make it possible for the merchant to change his stock to bring it into conformity with changes in demand. Buying in larger quantities sometimes results in an inability to take advantage of late season bargains and other special opportunities. Furthermore, the larger stocks of goods which result from quantity buying practices spell higher costs of owning or carrying a merchandise inventory. Illustrative are greater interest costs on capital invested in inventory, larger requirements for storage space, greater insurance needs, and higher taxes on inventories, as well as greater depreciation or obsolescence losses.

Selection of Sources of Supply

A fourth major buying responsibility is determining the firms from which purchases are to be made. If it be assumed that decisions regarding kinds, qualities, and quantities of goods have been made, and if buying decisions were altogether objective and impersonal, it would appear that suppliers would be chosen on the sole consideration of price. The lowest price, it might be argued, would point inevitably to one particular vendor as the most logical source of supply, except where the same price is quoted by several suppliers which may be the case under conditions of either oligopoly or extremely keen competition. This sometimes holds true when an inflexible purchasing system is prescribed, as in the case of many government agencies where the purchasing agent must accept the lowest of a number of competitive bids. In business practice generally, many factors enter into the picture, often with the result of making this facet of buying very complex.

Factors Governing the Choice of Suppliers

Price is obviously a very important consideration, for different vendors often quote different prices on goods of varying quality. The vendor's price quotation must be considered in relation to transportation costs, if these are to be paid by the buyer, especially if suppliers are located at a considerable distance or if the goods are heavy or economically bulky. The ability of a supplier to make *prompt delivery* is often most important. In some cases, this may be a prime consideration, as when repair parts are needed to keep from shutting down a factory. Retailers of fashion merchandise are willing to pay premiums for immediate delivery when the demand for a specific fashion is great and stocks are depleted. *Terms of sale* sometimes vary among vendors and are considered in the selection of suppliers. Cash discounts, which are offered to encourage the payment of bills before the expiration of a regular credit period, are often an important inducement, especially to firms that are in a healthy financial condition. The length of the credit period is important to many buyers, particularly those in weak financial condition.

The vendor's general reputation for *reliability* is often a patronagedetermining factor. This may relate to integrity in observing the terms of contracts, making deliveries on schedule, or supplying goods that conform with samples or contract grades.

Buyers are often influenced by the *distribution policies* of vendors. If a manufacturer sells direct to some retailers, some wholesalers may refuse to consider him as a source of supply. If a manufacturer operates some retail stores of his own, this may cause ill will among retailers, especially in shopping areas where the manufacturer's stores are located. Some manufac-turers select only a few outlets for their products in each community, and many have only one exclusive representative. When a retailer or wholesaler is so selected, he is likely to be more favorably inclined toward the seller than in a case where a seller distributes his product widely through a large number of competing establishments.

Sales promotion policies of vendors also influence their selection as sources of supply. A maker of women's dresses may purchase the fabric of a particular cloth manufacturer because the latter's consumer advertising will help in the sale of the dresses made from it. Some manufacturers win the favor of retailers because of assistance provided in local cooperative advertising, point-of-sale display materials, demonstrations, direct mail advertising, or sales training programs for the buyers' employees. The ability of a vendor to provide *continuity of supply* is often very important. Retailers do not like to patronize wholesalers who are often out-of-stock on important items and have to "back-order" them. In industrial purchasing, this factor is especially significant in connection with raw materials and supplies which are used regularly.

The selection of vendors is sometimes resolved on the basis of *reciprocity*. This is especially true in the industrial marketing field where large quantities are usually involved in a single transaction. Although this is not a scientific way of selecting suppliers, it is often rationalized by the attitude of "buying from those who buy from us, and thus we help each other." Just because a possible supplier is a customer does not mean that he is a good supplier on the basis of more rational considerations explained above. Some companies carry a policy of reciprocity to the extreme. A manufacturing company, for example, analyzes its sales to oil companies and distributes its purchases of supplies such as lubricating oil to each company in relation to the approximate volume of each oil company's purchases from it.

When a number of different potential suppliers are all satisfactory on the basis of the factors herein considered, the actual selection of sources is likely to hinge on the human equation. The personality, character, and technical proficiency of the *vendor's salesman* is frequently the factor that swings the balance of decision from some alternatives to others.

Concentration of Purchases

The practice of buying from one source or a small number of suppliers is known as concentration of purchases. Although often a phase of quantity buying, a policy which limits the number of suppliers is practiced because of certain special advantages. Price concessions other than regular quantity discounts, better terms of credit, special help from the whole-saler or manufacturer in solving merchandising problems, and an opportunity for prior selection of desirable merchandise are often of enough importance to justify a policy of concen-tration. Moreover, such a policy tends to minimize the chance of overstocking, largely through a reduction in the number of brands, styles, patterns, designs, or price lines. Some retailers and wholesalers concentrate their purchases in order to secure an exclusive agency or in order to become affiliated with a voluntary chain organization.

Rigid limitations on the number of resources is not, however, always a wise policy. Some wholesalers and retailers find it necessary to buy from many sources to secure the best assortment of style goods. Good buying strategy calls for alertness for special offers which often preclude concentration, because such offerings may come from suppliers not normally patronized or from newly established sources. Many industrial purchasing agents make it a policy to develop a number of supply sources for important materials to insure continuity of procurement under circumstances that might jeopardize normal operations.

Scientific Developments in Buying

The performance of the various sub functions or elements of buying has been considerably modified by the growing use of sophisticated techniques or practices, including value analysis, vendor rating programs, determination of optimum order quantities, and automatic reordering. Such techniques are highly technical in application; hence, it is essential to limit the present discussion to an indication of their nature and significance to marketing.

Value Analysis

Value analysis as consisting of formal analytical procedures used to relate design and function of purchased products to cost, with a view to reducing cost substantially through modification of design, change in specifications, different method of manufacture, change in source of supply, possible elimination of an item, or incorporation of a new item. Value analysis differs from former buying methods in two ways—first, in the wide scope of its activities which involve participation by all departments of a business concerned with the use of resale of products being purchased and, second, in the carefully planned, methodical approach to the problem of getting the most *ultimate value* from money spent.

It tends to take the emphasis away from the net cost of the item being purchased and focuses attention on eventual total costs. For example, one manufacturer had been satisfied for years with a lacquer the cost of which was substantially lower than competitive makes. One gallon covered 250 square feet. Through value analysis techniques, the purchasing department identified a much superior but higher-priced lacquer which covered nearly twice the area per gallon. While the invoice price of this lacquer was substantially greater, the ultimate cost of using it, per unit of finished product, was reduced by 30 per cent.

Vendor Rating

Closely akin to and often considered as a part of, or a supplement to, a value analysis programme are formal procedures for evaluating vendors. Traditionally, vendors have been evaluated on the basis of relatively few factors, with high priority often attached to the criteria of lowest purchase price and convenience and reliability of supply. Many business firms have developed elaborate check lists, often comprising 30 to 50 specific rating criteria, which are used periodically to evaluate alternative suppliers, with a view to identifying those who best serve the total needs of the purchaser on an over-all basis. While value analysis is concerned largely with functional attributes of a physical product, vendor analysis goes beyond, to consider the other values available from suppliers and which, therefore, are an important aspect of productive purchasing.

Optimum Order Quantities

From the preceding discussion of quantity versus small-lot buying, it is evident that the optimum quantity to purchase of a given item depends upon a wide range of complex variable factors including the following: risk of losses from deterio-ration and obsolescence; costs of storing or warehousing inventories; financial costs of carrying inventory, such as interest on investment, insurance, and taxes; risk of lost sales or interrupted manufacturing operations owing to a lack of availability; transportation costs which may vary on a per unit basis with quantity purchased; discounts or price concessions related to quantity bought; and acquisition costs such as those of processing purchase orders and handling accounts payable transactions.

The number of such variables is so large, their applicability varies so much from one product class to another, and the number of items to be purchased by most businesses is so great that traditionally the determination of purchase quantities has necessarily been largely a matter of subjective judgment, often taking into account only the most obvious of such variables, such as quantity discounts and transportation economies. However, under modern conditions of automatic data processing by means of high-capacity electronic computers, it is relatively easy to use mathematical formulas which relate all of the variable factors listed above, for the purpose of determining the optimum quantity to purchase for each one of thousands of items which are *regularly* bought in substantial amounts. It is, moreover, feasible to do this as frequently as changes occur in any of the variable factors included in the formulas.

Automatic Reordering

In many large organizations, electronic computers are used to reduce the amount of human judgment involved in routine reordering of staple items continually maintained in stock. This necessitates the prior determination of minimum stock levels for individual items, based on factors such as historical rates of sale, optimum reorder quantities (as discussed in the preceding section), normal stockrepleni- shment time, and safety factors (stock "cushion") to allow for random or unpredictable needs (e.g., delays in transit or occasional sales in unusually large quantities). Once a minimum stock quantity for an item is determined, computers can be used to reduce reordering to a semiautomatic or completely automatic basis. All information about changes in stock levels is fed into the computer. New purchases or receipts are added to previous balances, and all sales or use information is deducted, with the result that data are constantly available within the computer to reveal the current inventory figure for each item.

A computer can be programmed so that it prepares daily a list of all items for which the amount of stock on hand, plus the stock on order, is less than the previously determined minimum. The computer can also indicate the number of units that should be ordered to bring the inventory (plus commitments) up to desired levels. This results in semia-utomatic reordering, since the buyer need give attention only to computer determined replenishment requirements of those items listed on such special reports.

In some cases reordering is completely automatic in the sense that the computer is programmed to prepare an actual purchase order for a predetermined optimum purchase quantity whenever the stock on hand and on order falls below specified minimums. The buyer then needs only to signify approval of the computer-prepared purchase order by signing it.

Marketing Significance

While the various scientific or analytical procedures discussed above have been growing in importance, their application has been confined mainly to large-scale buyers and even then principally in connection with goods which are purchased regularly. Extensive use of such procedures involves two prerequisites—specialization of a fairly high order in the buying organization and volume of sales sufficient to warrant the use of expensive data processing equipment. Such procedures are of rather limited value for new items for which there is no historical information on use or resale, for items the sale of which is relatively unpredictable owing to changing consumer tastes or fashion, and for items needed only occasionally. Nevertheless, their application has been widespread in industrial purchasing, particularly for materials used in manufacture and for supply items with a high consumption rate. It has also been extensive in wholesale distribution warehouses (whether operated by manufacturers, chain store companies, or regular wholesalers), particularly those dealing in numerous items continuously maintained in stock as, for example, groceries, hardware, drugs, and automotive supplies.

The impact of such procedures has been to place buying on a more scientific plane, with the result that the buying function is controlled more rigidly by predetermined criteria. As a consequence many sellers have been forced to adapt their marketing operations more closely to the requirements of customers who have committed themselves to any or all of the buying procedures here discussed. This has made it much more difficult for the seller, in appropriate cases, to count upon his own selling effort to bring about changes in buying practices. Such procedures have also had an important bearing upon more scientific approaches to the physical distribution of goods.

BUYING PRACTICES

Various practices are followed in contacting resources, appraising their selections, and making purchases. Buying may be accomplished through central market visits, by negotiating with salesmen who visit the purchaser's premises, by means of trade registers and directories, in cooperation with other buyers who have similar needs, or by delegating the authority for purchases to a central agency.

Visiting the Market

In a number of lines of business, leading central markets have developed, and these are regularly visited by merchants or store buyers who wish to make purchases. New York City, for example, is both an important manufacturing and buying centre for women's clothing. Other cities such as Chicago, Miami, St. Louis, Dallas, San Francisco, and Los Angeles are of importance as centers of supply for the same merchandise and are visited annually by merchants.

The major market for furniture and home furnishings is in Chicago. Hundreds of exhibitors have offices and show-rooms in this city in, or in the vicinity of, the Merchandise Mart, which is a famous market centre with 93 acres of floor space. Other major furniture markets include New York, Dallas, Atlanta, Los Angeles, and High Point, North Carolina. A general trend in both apparel and home furnishings markets has been for the number of centers to increase with more emphasis upon regionalism. This has made it possible for larger numbers of buyers from all parts of the country to visit at least one market centre, but it has also created problems for many manufacturers who now find it necessary to display merchandise in a greater variety of market centers. A number of considerations affect the frequency of market visits. Buyers from stores located in communities remote from central or regional markets, even though interested in style merchandise, may go to market but once or twice a year or not at all, while those near at hand make frequent visits. Buyers from large firms usually visit markets more often than do representatives of the smaller houses. Retail stores which feature special sales at short intervals make frequent market trips to procure merchandise for these sales.

Trade Shows

A great deal of buying activity takes place at special trade shows which are held periodically, usually annually or semiannually, in many lines of business—for example, toys, house wares, hardware, office equipment, scientific instruments, packaging materials, and materials-handling equipment. Such shows are usually held in a major city with hundreds or thousands of exhibitors displaying their wares in temporary booths established for the duration of the show in hotels or exhibition halls. Some of the well-known shows of this type are held in connection with national, regional, or state trade association conventions so that buyers can combine buying trips with attendance at business meetings of their association. Trade shows are of such outstanding interest in lines in which they are common that considerable attention is devoted to them in trade magazines.

Buying on the Purchaser's Premises

All kinds of business firms do a large part of their buying on their own premises, either by mail orders or through suppliers' salesmen. Mail orders sent to suppliers are the least important for most organizations. They are usually based on catalogs furnished by vendors or information contained in trade registers and directories. Many retail stores and wholesalers use the mails for fill-in orders which are placed in the interval between salesmen's calls or visits to market centers. This method is also commonly used in industrial purchasing, especially for routine or occasional buying of supplies, tools, and stocks of repair parts.

Buying from salesmen is the second form of purchasing on the buyer's premises and is doubtless the most important single form of buying. Most independent dealers in convenience goods buy a large part of their stock from wholesalers' salesmen who visit the store. Much style merchandise, even that sold in the very largest department stores, is purchased from manufacturers' salesmen who visit the store with samples of ready-to-wear items supplied by New York garment houses and other similar resources. Buyers for wholesale establishments, factories, and governmental units also spend a considerable amount of time with suppliers' salesmen who call at their offices, and a large proportion of their requirements is bought in this manner.

Group Buying

The practice of *cooperative combination of orders from a number of buyers* so that relatively large purchases can be made at attractive prices is known as group buying. This practice is used occasionally by some wholesale and retail merchants in a wide variety of trades but is especially important among groups of department, dry goods, and apparel stores that have combined orders of many articles to the mutual advantage of participants. Arrangements for group buying are often made by resident buying offices. These arrangements include plans for group participants to visit the central market at the same time. Samples of the type of merchandise under consideration are collected and examined by the attending buyers who express their preferences by voting upon various offerings. Quantities desired by the participants are then pooled into a combined order and a price is negotiated with the resource.

The principal advantages of group buying lie in the lower prices usually secured from vendors, the fact that the merchandise may be produced to specifications of the group and packaged or labeled with the group's brand name, and the use of the combined judgment of a group of qualified experts in selecting merchandise. Group buying has, however, met with only limited success. For this there are several reasons. First, some lines of goods must be selected with the particular needs of each store's clientele in mind.

The pooled judgment of a group of buyers from different stores does not always result in the selection of just the type or style of goods which a given store needs. Second, many buyers have failed to cooperate fully in such purchases because of the tendency of the plan, if successful, to minimize the value of their individual buying skill. Third, some manufacturers refuse to make offerings to cooperative groups because sales can be effected only at such low prices as to make the business economically unattractive or impossible to justify under the price discrimination provisions of the Robinson-Patman Act.

Central Buying

An important buying practice, limited substantially to large multi-unit organizations, is that of central buying. Its distinguishing feature is that *authority and responsibility for purchasing are vested in a central office rather than in the individual operating units* involved. This practice is widely used by almost all types of large retailing chains, to a limited degree by independent retailers of fashion merchandise through arrangement with resident buying offices, to a considerable extent by multi-unit wholesaling and manufacturing companies, also by various governmental units that have a central purchasing organization for different divisions or departments. In some shoe or apparel chain stores, for example, there are no buyers in the individual stores. Local store managers are chiefly responsible for sales and have responsibility for buying only to the extent of providing the central office with daily or other frequent stock control information that indicates the sales of various items and changes in the inventory situation. The central office buyer makes all market contacts, handles negotiations with suppliers, and makes actual purchases. On the basis of individual store stock and sales reports, merchandise shipments are made to them as directed by central office personnel, either direct from factories or from a central warehouse operated by the chain. In the grocery, variety, and drug fields the practice varies from this pattern. Store managers or other key employees check the stock periodically and requisition or order merchandise as needed, but from warehouse stocks or catalog listings that have been made available through central office negotiations.

Similar practices are sometimes followed in industrial or governmental purchasing. A large manufacturer of automotive equipment may operate a number of different factories, widely scattered geographically. If each of them requires similar equipment, materials, or supplies, the individual requirements are sometimes consolidated and purchased centrally.

Specific procedures used in central buying vary from one type of industry to another and often among different firms within a particular industry or trade. Regardless of variations in detail, central buying is generally adopted to obtain specific advantages which include the following: greater skill and specialization in the buying function than would be possible if each unit did its own purchasing; lower merchandise costs through the negotiating power which comes from consolidating the requirements of the various units; ability to take advantage of favorable market opportunities through continual contacts with suppliers; and economies in purchasing and accounting obtained by combining what would otherwise be a large number of individual transactions, each entailing the same unit costs for office procedures.

Specification Buying by Contract

When a firm exercises rigid control over the quantitative and qualitative characteristics of an item being purchased, the practice is known as specification buying. This type of buying is quite frequently accompanied by a contractual arrangement in which the buyer agrees to purchase stipulated quantities of goods for delivery at periodic intervals or as requisitioned, and at prices which either are set forth in the contract or are to be established in terms of some formula which is incorporated in the agreement. Contracts sometimes involve commitments for a substantial proportion of the seller's total output and may cover all or a major part of the purchaser's requirements for a period of many months or even a year or more.

Because of the rather substantial character of many such contracts, they are often negotiated through high-level executives of both parties. This buying practice is encountered in various segments of business, including retail chain and mail order companies which sell products under their own brand names, wholesaling companies that feature private brands, manufacturing companies that require materials of certain specifications for further processing or for incorporation in their end product, and governmental purchasing units, especially the military organizations.

Various considerations underlie such contractual arrangements. In the case of manufacturers, the assurance of a continuing supply of raw materials at a predetermined price is often the dominant motive. On the part of some purchasers, contracts for periodic delivery of instalments may be dictated by a desire to secure quantity prices without assuming the burdens incident to carrying heavy average inventories.

Many merchants have also attempted to secure the advantages of quantity buying without assuming the disadvantages through placing contracts for the periodic future delivery of large orders. Some large retailing concerns, for example, enter into contracts calling for the delivery of a certain number of pairs of hosiery each month for a period of months. Such contracts involve careful manufacturing specifications. Colors and shades are usually not determined at the time when the original contract is made but are furnished by the buyer from time to time during the life of the contract.

The manufacturer finds such an agreement advantageous in that it enables him to plan a production programme and to buy raw materials more intelligently. At the same time the purchaser profits by securing a quantity price and an assured supply without increasing his average inventory and, by supplying currently a schedule of colors and shades, he is enabled to adjust his stock to shifting consumer preferences in colour and shade.

Buying Committees

Owing to the proliferation of new product offerings in the post-World War II era, many merchandising organizations have removed ultimate responsibility for adding or eliminating new products from an individual departmental buyer and have assigned authority for final judgment and decision on such matters to a buying committee. While such committees are used in many kinds of retailing and wholesaling establishments, they are most common in the supermarket industry where about 90 per cent of the larger organizations report their use. Under the buying committee arrangement, a departmental buyer handles all purchasing responsibilities for items regularly stocked. He also sees salesmen for new products and collects all relevant information about new items which are presented. He may reject a new item, but if it meets with his approval he still does not have the authority to buy it. Instead, it must be presented to the buying committee which considers not only matters of departmental significance, but also reviews proposed new items in terms of corporate objectives. Each new item presents certain problems relating to limited shelf space, capital investment in inventory, promotional requirements, ware-house storage and handling, and competitive significance. It is largely due to these over-all problems that buying responsibility for new items is often assigned to buying or merchandising committees.

Specialized Buying Agencies

The dynamics of marketing is vividly illustrated by a number of agencies which have emerged as specialized buying institutions. Their economic justification rests upon ability to render a unique service at a low cost to a group of firms with common buying problems.

Resident Buying Offices

A well-established segment of our buying structure is the resident buying office. Principally serving department, general merchandise, and apparel stores, these offices have largely supplanted private central market offices which were formerly maintained by some larger independent stores. Resident buying offices developed for the purpose of supplying central market representation for merchants and of relieving them from the necessity of making frequent trips to central markets. Such offices represent many retailers in the same line of business, and because of this fact they are able to render many services at a relatively small cost.

By means of a staff of experts constantly in touch with market developments, the resident buying office is able to keep its client stores in touch with the best sources of supply. The office becomes the headquarters of visiting buyers who are guided in their purchases by office buyers of comparable lines. Style bulletins and other market information are sent to member stores at regular intervals and, in general, the office acts as their representative in the market. Some group buying and central buying is sponsored by resident buying offices, and many fill-ins are selected by its buyers for member stores.

Payment for the resident buyer's services by a fixed yearly fee is a common practice in this field, the amount being fixed by the estimated sales of the store during the period of the contract. Smaller stores are often served by resident buyers who may receive payment in the form of commissions on sales made for certain manufacturers. Resident buyers are an increasingly important factor in the distribution of ready-to-wear and certain dry goods lines. Distance from the market and the importance of style merchandise to the individual merchant are the principal factors determining the extent to which they are used.

Several hundred resident buying organizations are located in New York City in the so-called "garment district" in midtown Manhattan. Many of the larger organizations have branches in other principal markets for fashion merchandise, including Chicago, Los Angeles, San Francisco, and certain foreign countries.

Independent Purchasing Agents

Several independent business firms, known as purchasing agents or purchasing companies, provide a buying and market information service for wholesalers of consumer goods and for industrial distributors. Typical is an organization in the wholesale hardware and mill supply trade which serves many wholesalers by locating sources of new, superior, imported, or scarce merchandise and in other cases by securing attractive price quotations for them. Descriptions of thousands of items are supplied to the wholesalers in the form of a loose-leaf price book. Whenever the client believes that he can do so advantageously, he places orders with the purchasing agent, who in turn transmits them to the proper supplier for shipment. Each client pays a monthly membership fee for the services thus rendered. Similar organizations serve hundreds of wholesale grocers.

Purchasing agents of this type render an important service and constitute an important element in the distribution of certain lines of goods. Their freedom to develop and operate was somewhat curtailed by the Robinson-Patman Act, for this law forbade collection of brokerage fees from sellers except for services rendered to such sellers rather than to buyers. It had been the practice of the purchasing agent to collect brokerage fees from sellers and to remit at least part to their clients, a fact which gave the clients a price advantage as compared with their competitors who bought directly from the same supplier or through the regular broker who kept his entire brokerage fee.

Prevention of this and other types of price discrimination was one of the primary objects of the law. The result has therefore been that membership fees must be large enough to cover the cost of the purchasing agent's service, a fact which has somewhat reduced his importance as an agent for placing orders but which has in no way lessened the value of the market information provided. In many trades brokers are sometimes employed by buyers to locate advantageous sources of supply, particularly for seasonal commodities or for items in short supply. When so utilized, the broker performs some of the functions of the independent purchasing agent.

Commissioners

In purchasing goods in foreign markets buyers are frequently under the disadvantage of a lack of knowledge of good sources of supply and are further handicapped by a lack of knowledge of the language. To assist such buyers, individuals known as commissioners or commissionaires are found in foreign markets. It is the function of the commissioner to bring the buyer into contact with proper vendors and to function as an interpreter. When the American buyer is not abroad, the commissioner keeps in communication with him, furnishing him with samples and information about goods. The commissioner represents the buyer and receives his compensation from him.

Buying and the Law

Owing to its significance as one of the two exchange functions of marketing, buying comes within the purview of certain public policy regulations. Since the whole subject of government and marketing is dealt with at a later point, it is sufficient here merely to note some of the more important legal implications.

Under the Sherman Antitrust Act, a buyer is prohibited from conspiring with other buyers whereby as a group they agree not to make purchases from certain sources of supply, when the agreement would be in restraint of trade, thus foreclosing a market or channel of distribution to one or several potential suppliers whose policies do not meet with the favor of the buyers who are in collusive agreement. Such an agreement is in violation of the law *per se,* regardless of actual effect. A buyer may also be guilty of unfair methods of competition in trade or commerce, under the Federal Trade Commission Act, if he joins with others in formulating lists or directories of buyers, where the purpose or intent of such lists is to cause suppliers to sell only to those whose names appear thereon. Under the Robinson-Patman Act it is unlawful for a buyer operating as a wholesaler (or retailer) also to presume to act as a broker and thus receive a brokerage fee on merchandise purchased for resale as a merchant.

The Act limits the payment of brokerage fees to parties that are acting on behalf of, or are controlled by, the party making the payment. Also under the Robinson-Patman Act it is unlawful for a buyer knowingly to induce or to receive a discrimination in price which is prohibited by the law. As this matter has been viewed by the courts, it pertains primarily to cases in which a buyer, knowing full well that there was little likelihood of a cost saving or other legal defence by the seller for a price discrimination, nevertheless received or proceeded to exert pressure for lower prices than could be legally justified by the seller. These few illustrations are sufficient to indicate that regulations exist which, to some extent, limit the buyer as well as the seller in situations involving monopolistic, trade restraining, or unfair competitive practices.

7

The Selling Function: Advertising

A major function for most business firms today is that of establishing and maintaining a market for their products. In the case of such simple business enterprises as roadside markets, ordinary display and the more elementary forms of personal selling are the only expression of this function. On the other hand, many manufacturers, middlemen, and producers of business or personal services conduct elaborate campaigns to arouse or stimulate demand for their products, or to divert such demand from competitors. In each case the business organization is engaged in one of the most essential marketing functions, that of demand creation or selling.

MEANING OF DEMAND CREATION

Throughout this book the term demand creation is used in the rather loose, broad, and very general way that has become customary in all discussions of advertising and personal selling. For example, the word demand must not be interpreted to mean a stubborn insistence upon the product advertised, for seldom is it meant to be other than a mere recognition, a favorable impression, or a preference with respect to it. More important, the word "creation" must not be interpreted to mean as bringing into existence something which has not existed before, for usually it refers to the bringing into consciousness and action motivations that have been dormant or otherwise ineffective. Actually, then, instead of "creating demand" in the literal sense, what selling effort (including advertising) does is to arouse, stimulate, or direct a prospective buyer's conscious or dormant desire for want satisfaction that results in action with reference to a given product, service, or seller.

METHODS OF SELLING

Two principal methods are involved in the selling function: *advertising* and *personal selling*. Advertising is any *paid* form of *nonpersonal* presentation of goods, services, or ideas to a group by an identified sponsor. Personal selling, on the other hand, is the process of personally assisting and persuading a prospect to buy a commodity or service or to act upon an idea. The presentation may be formal, in the nature of a carefully rehearsed sales talk, which is presented in substantially the same manner to all prospects, or it may be and usually is informal.

Certain other terms commonly used in the sales field, such as publicity and sales promotion, should be understood in this connection. *Publicity* is *any* form of commercially significant news items or editorial comment about products or institutions published in space or broadcast time that is *not paid* for by the sponsor, although the term is sometimes used in a broader sense to include advertising. *Sales promotion* includes those selling activities that supplement both advertising and personal selling, coordinate them, and render them more effective. It includes sampling, displays, demonstrations, and various kinds of non recurrent selling effort.

RELATION OF ADVERTISING TO PERSONAL SELLING

Advertising and personal selling are not as a rule in competition but rather supplement each other. A marked characteristic of personal selling is that the message is usually delivered to a definite prospect. Advertising, except for direct mail, on the other hand, must appeal to the mass mind, or at least to the average individual within some market segment to which the appeal is directed. Moreover, personal salesmanship is adaptable. The message can be adjusted to the individual prospect and appeals can be selected which are of most importance to him. The speed of delivery and the language of the sales argument can be adjusted to the prospect's training or general intelligence. Objections can be met as they arise, and thus effective demand can be created.

Advertising is used, as a rule, to assist the salesman. It aims to give preliminary information and to break down resistance which might operate to prevent the later, effective delivery of a sales message. Advertisements in trade magazines can be used, for example, to tell the story of a certain type of business machine and to suggest that many companies have used such machines with success. Purchasing agents and mechanical engineers are much more apt to give a careful hearing to the salesman for a machine of this kind when he calls than would be the case if they knew nothing about the machine in advance of the call. Thousands of people may receive favorable impressions about a certain kind of automobile because of the manufacturer's advertising, but as a rule it is not until after further selling effort by the dealer's salesman that a purchase is actually made. Although commonly supplementary to each other, either of the two methods of selling may be used exclusively. Many unbranded and unadvertised raw materials and some manufactured commodities are sold without advertising. Many articles are sold by mail through advertising and without any personal salesmanship. The proportion of total goods sold by advertising alone is, however, exceedingly small. Furthermore, modern distribution is normally based on the use of both methods, neither one entirely supplanting the other.

RATIONALE FOR THE SELLING FUNCTION

Selling effort (including advertising, personal selling, and sales promotion) is largely a phenomenon of the twentieth century. It did not exist in the conspicuous and important way that we know it today prior to the attainment of a high level of industrial production in our private enterprise economy. Moreover, selling effort as we know it in the United States is not now to be found in parts of the world characterized by low levels of industrial production; neither does it exist in areas where the buying behaviour of consumers is regulated in a planned economy, ruled by a dictatorial government. Of all the marketing functions, selling is the least understood and the most maligned, even though numerous theoretical economists, marketing authorities, and business leaders have attempted to provide some rational explanation for selling costs and selling effort. Some understanding of the various theories aimed at explaining the basis for selling effort should prove helpful in evaluating the selling function from a social point of view, from the viewpoint of marketing management, and from the standpoint of the individual acting in the capacity of a consumer-buyer.

Material Opulence.

Substantial emphasis upon the selling function is ascribed by some to material opulence as reflected in the relatively high level of income and purchasing power characterizing our economy. It is claimed that "The need and the opportunity to persuade people arise only as people have the income to satisfy relatively unimportant wants, of the urgency of which they are not automatically aware." Hence, "Our proliferation of selling activity is the counterpart of comparative opulence." According to this view, two attributes of selling are emphasized. One is its capacity to initiate the spending cycle, and the other is its contribution to the aggregate level of income which attends its widespread use. While both of these factors are important, they do not account for the most essential characteristic of selling effort. To be sure, for example, the potential response to selling effort is determined in large measure by the level of purchasing power and to that extent this view provides a partial explanation for the emphasis placed on the selling function in our economy. But all that is thus explained is the *level* of selling expenditures in the aggregate and not the basic reason why such expenditures are made at all even in a less opulent state of economic well-being.

Firm Differentiation

An explanation of selling effort in terms of firm differentiation is commonplace, particularly in many theore-tical economic treatises. This thesis holds that selling costs arise out of the attempts of competing business units to build a protective barrier against their rivals. Selling effort, it is claimed, provides a more secure position in terms of the level of the company's sales, its degree of product acceptance, enterprise image, or some other aspect of its market standing. This conception leads to an investment approach in the management of selling costs, particularly for advertising programs intended to promote a brand or the company name. While there is substantial justification for this theory, it fails to distinguish the selling function from other aspects of business activity designed to achieve firm differentiation, such as patents, product research, and location. Moreover, it fails to account for selling effort that is not primarily of a competitive nature.

Demand Manipulation

Selling effort has frequently been defined in terms of demand manipulation, a somewhat objectionable term because of its connotation. By implication, the buyer (commonly viewed as the ultimate or individual consumer and ignoring the status of business purchasers as targets of a large amount of selling effort) is overwhelmed by selling pressure. To use an analogy, he is swayed by the seller much like clay is shaped by the potter. This is the attitude of critics who object to the kinds of things people buy and sometimes to the idea. Such a concept of selling suggests a desire of the critic to impose his value standards upon the general consuming public. Obviously, a more realistic view is that sellers, by using various advertising appeals and selling techniques, can persuade buyers to respond favorably to offers of goods and services. Consequently, demand manipulation in itself, especially when used in a derogatory manner, is incomplete as an explanation because it attributes a response to selling effort but does not explain why the response occurs.

Information

Perhaps the more widely held thesis on the rationale for the selling function is that its task is to provide information. As initially stated, the theory suggests that because buyers act rationally and should be sovereign in their decision making, the sole task of the selling process is to provide information about the product or about the seller. Any effort beyond that is unnecessary and, therefore, unproductive of an essential economic service.

Basically, this was the view of the early economic classicists who accepted demand as given (and hence not subject to change in nature, size, or direction), supply rather scarce, and man quite rational. Under such circumstances, all that a seller needs to do is to provide the necessary information concerning his product, its price, and availability, and that would comprise the totality of the selling function. It is interesting to note, however, that not all economists accepted this view of selling effort. Alfred Marshall, the developer of neoclassical economics, recognized the importance of persuasion as part of selling effort when he indicated that when a manufacturer makes a commodity, the demand for which could be increased with resulting internal economies, it may be "worth his while to sacrifice a great deal in order to push its sales in a new market." Indeed, the expenditure for this purpose may even exceed that "which he devotes directly to the manufacture.

Contemporary writers on the subject apparently overlook the views of Marshall and his followers in economic thought when they adhere to the theory that the only function of selling effort is one of providing information. In doing so, they shun the persuasion ingredient of the selling function in order to avoid buyer irrationality and ethical overtones about the seller suggested by it. This position is obviously weak theoretically and completely unrealistic. Much advertising and personal selling effort may not even impart any information but may be aimed at securing attention, reminding, or creating favorable impressions through colour and symbolism. Moreover, even so-called informative advertising and selling are designed to influence buyers and thus effect sales. Hence, an explanation of selling effort in terms of communicating information, while possessing some merit with respect to a substantial proportion of all selling activity and an essential ingredient of it, fails to capture the fundamental characteristic of most selling which is persuasion.

Creation of Possession Utility

While all of the foregoing viewpoints cast some light on certain aspects or facets of the selling function, at least in a partial way, the clearest rationale lies in its creation of possession utility. A product consists of the satisfactions or benefits derived from its use or consumption, and production is the creation of all economic values or utilities, including those of form, time, place, and possession, as well as activities or functions that facilitate in the creation of these values.

Accordingly, the selling function is part of the productive process since it creates possession utility by affecting or effecting the exchange process. In advertising, owing to the usual remoteness from the act of title transfer, it is more a matter of affecting the process. Through personal selling, on the other hand, actual transfers of title and hence changes in legal possession are commonly effected in a direct way. Both aspects of the selling function, however, are parts of the process of exchange and consumption of goods and services.

Satisfaction in ultimate consumption or business use of goods and services issues from the selling function in a number of ways. Buyers are aided in establishing exchange contacts when sellers take the initiative, thus providing great savings in time or convenience, as compared with any possible hypothetical situation in which it would be necessary for buyers to take the initiative in all exchange activity. Under modern concepts of customer-oriented marketing management, the selling function aids in interpreting available goods and services in terms of the needs and wants of buyers. From the point of view of the individual buyer, selling activity satisfies an apparent desire for variety. This partially accounts for the wide range of selling techniques which are designed to arouse interest and provide differentiation. From an aggregate point of view, the selling function has an influence upon a variety of matters of social concern. It is generally conceded, even by its critics, that it contributes to a level of consumption and hence of total production that is much larger than would exist in the absence of selling effort. It also has an important relationship to the distribution of consumer and business expenditures by product classes. Thus it makes a contribution to the allocation of economic resources and employment in different industries and in various lines of commercial trade.

ADVERTISING AS A BUSINESS ACTIVITY

Ultimate consumers and business purchasers are continually exposed to advertising in one form or another. Whatever the form, the advertiser's message generally appears as a simple presentation. Obscured behind the scenes, however, are a score of important business decisions that have a bearing upon the impact made on the buyer. In many companies, decisions relating to the nature of the role of advertising in the total marketing effort are a crucial aspect of marketing strategy. Various types of advertising must be considered for different specific purposes; ideas are conceived and advertisements are prepared as a result of careful plans made well in advance of publication; media are selected to convey the prepared message to the prospective recipients; and, for some or all of these decisions, a special institution known as the advertising agency is often employed.

Types of Advertising

The many types of advertising may be classified in a number of ways. Furthermore, the various classes commonly recognized are not mutually exclusive but are often different ways of looking at the same thing. For example, advertising may be classified as *institutional* or *product,* depending upon whether it is aimed primarily at establishing a favorable attitude toward the advertiser or at the development of demand for a given product. It may be classified, on the basis of the advertiser's status, into *manufacturers', wholesalers', retailers', or cooperative* advertising. Again, advertising may be classified as *consumer, trade, professional,* or *industrial,* in terms of the audience to which it is directed. It may also be classified on the basis of the principal appeal, that is; whether the purpose of such an appeal is to arouse and direct demand toward a specific product or to a given general class of products.

Advertising in the Marketing Mix

When a business firm has identified the market or market segment to which it wishes to make its strongest appeal, it must decide how much of its total promotional effort shall be allocated to various different elements of marketing strategy that may induce prospective customers to buy. The term *marketing mix* is commonly used to denote the amount of *relative emphasis* placed upon different components of a firm's marketing programme. Possible components of such a programme for many companies would include advertising, personal selling, pricing, relationships with other institutions in distribution channels, physical availability of product, after sale service, special sales promotional activities, financing of customers, and so on. Obviously, a firm with limited resources cannot allocate an unusually large *share* of its total marketing effort (funds) to some one component of a marketing mix without making some sacrifice or compromise about the magnitude of the expected contribution of other actual or possible components of the mix. A firm's ability or willingness to devote a substantial share of its marketing mix to advertising is influenced by two sets of factors—one relating to the characteristics of the goods or services being marketed and the other to the characteristics of advertising as they pertain to the particular firm.

Factors Relating to Product

Product attributes generally accepted as favorable to heavy emphasis upon advertising in the marketing mix may be listed as follows:

- *Favorable primary demand situation*: Advertising is likely to be effective when there is a substantial opportunity to expand the total market for a product, as illustrated by household air conditioning, motor boats, and hearing-aid devices.
- *Significant product differentiation*: When a product offers benefits not readily available from close substitutes, advertising is likely to be especially productive. Differentiation may exist in the physical attributes of a product (e.g., special formula or materials) or in its application or use (e.g., shoe polish packaged for ease of application without getting one's hands or clothes soiled), or in ease of branding (e.g., Sunkist citrus products) or may take other tangible or intangible forms.
- *Hidden values*: Advertising appeals based upon user satisfaction are often effective to a high degree when the product has some values not readily apparent to a prospective user, as in the case of many mechanical devices and certain types of drugs and medicines.
- *Emotional basis for buying*: When the purchaser's motives for buying have a strong emotional basis, as illustrated by many health and personal appearance products, advertising can be a strong influence in shifting consumer preferences or in getting new potential users to try a product.
- *Factors Relating to Advertising*. Certain characteristics of advertising as one form of promotional effort either encourage or discourage heavy emphasis on it, depending upon the situation of the marketing organization. These are as follows:
- *Nature of advertising expenditures*: Large-scale advertising requires substantial outlays for current expense. Unlike investments made

in plant or store equipment, advertising costs cannot ordinarily be financed through outside sources and amortized over a period of time. Thus, large-scale advertising tends to be limited to big firms with favorable working capital positions.

- *Low selectivity*: The more limited a firm's distribution or the thinner its market in terms of number of potential customers, the more difficult it is to utilize media in the mass communication field. Many firms encounter serious difficulty in the selection of media which reach an audience that corresponds well with the intended market, either geographically or in terms of customer characteristics.
- *Inflexibility through time*: Major advertising campaigns involve planning that must take place long in advance of the execution of the advertising programme. This is especially true of network television, magazines, and national campaigns in newspapers. Thus, the firm that must stand ready to adjust quickly to changing market conditions finds that the potential contribution of advertising to its total marketing effort is limited.

Advertising Media

The vehicle or carrier through which an advertising message is conveyed to its intended audience is known as an advertising medium. The major classes of media and the relative importance of each are indicated. The prominence of newspapers is explained by the fact that the bulk of local retail store advertising is carried in this medium. Each of the major classes or types of media may be further subdivided; magazines, for example, can be divided into weeklies and monthlies, or into men's, women's, children's, home or "shelter," general, and so on.

From the standpoint of the advertiser, the different types of media may be complementary or competitive. Each type has its value, is favored under given conditions, and is subject to certain limitations. Several types are often used simultaneously in well-rounded advertising campaigns, each supplementing the others.

Media selection is one of the most perplexing problems of advertising management, both with regard to classes of media (e.g., radio versus outdoor advertising) and specific media within classes. Choices of classes of media are influe-nced substantially by cost factors and by the requirements of a particular advertising programme (e.g., voice, colour, motion, graphic illustration, length of message, durability or perishability of message), as these are related to the technical characteristics of each class of media.

Choices of specific media within classes are also influenced by cost factors, particularly per 1,000 readers, listeners, or viewers, by the quantitative and qualitative characteristics of media, and by the manner in which such characteristics correspond with the market the advertiser intends to reach. Quantitative factors include such items as the number of subscribers (readers, viewers, listeners), their location, income status, and spending patterns, as revealed in many cases by elaborate market research studies provided to advertisers by media. Among the significant qualitative factors are the editorial policy of the medium, nature of contents or programs, status or personality of the medium, and qualitative characteristics of the audience, as these may be revealed by research or presumed from the qualitative characteristics of the medium.

The major classes of media have adjusted dynamically to changing times and each one, through innovation, has become somewhat more readily substitutable for the other. This is illustrated by the increasing availability of high-quality colour illustrations in newspapers; ability of advertisers to buy pages in split-run, regional issues of certain leading magazines; magazine concept of network broadcast media, whereby the high cost of sponsoring programs is shared by a variety of advertisers; and the growth of colour broadcasting in television.

Product Advertising by Manufacturers

While the details of manufacturers' advertising programs vary with the kind of product and character of the company, a common function is that of *building acceptance or preference for the advertised product,* and a common pattern of managerial decisions is followed. First, the advertiser must be certain that the product to be promoted actually satisfies some basic need; otherwise, no amount of advertising can win acceptance for the product. Second, it is necessary to discover the uses or applications of the product, and confine the advertised uses to reasonable ones that satisfy important common needs. Third is the determination of distinctive characteristics of the product to be used as selling appeals. For advertising to be successful over a period of time, these should be real and recognizable distinctions as viewed from the customer's and not the seller's standpoint. Most manufacturers' advertising is characterized by an attempt to give the product a personality or identity which will make it stand out competitively. This requires close coordination between the planning of advertising and package or label design.

Other major management problems relate to the determination of the market for the product, whether general or highly restricted to a segment of the total market; the selection of media which will reach the consumers of the product and possibly also the trade; and the determination of an advertising appropriation that will be adequate to accomplish the objective of the programme. The appropriation is likely to be large per unit of product if an item is in the introductory stage of development and, hence, is not well known to consumers or distributors; it is likely to be large in total amount, but small per unit of product, if the item is in the competitive stage and similar products are being mass-produced and mass-distributed by a number of companies.

Merchandise Advertising by Retailers

Retailers' merchandise advertising differs from that of manufacturers' in objective. Whereas the manufacturer usually seeks to build acceptance or preference for his brand of product, the retailer is concerned primarily with *building good will or patronage for his particular store.* Except where exclusive agencies are common, as in the automobile field, retailers' advertisements are characterized more by variety and assortments of merchandise rather than by individual items. Stress is placed upon patronage motives such as price, selection, location of stores, or services.

In retail advertising there is also more of an attempt *to provoke immediate buying reaction* than is the case with manufacturers' advertising where a long programme may be planned to build or sustain consumer acceptance or preference. This accounts for very marked concentrations of retail advertising at times when consumer buying urges are most active, as evidenced by heavy grocery advertising on Wednesdays or Thursdays in anticipation of week-end shopping, or unusual quantities of department store advertising at Christmas, Easter, school-opening time, and on other occasions when consumers are most likely to respond to specific advertising appeals.

Cooperative Advertising

Much advertising involves the cooperative participation of a number of individual firms. Such advertising is designated as *horizontal cooperative* when the participants are functionally similar and operate on the same level of distribution. This type is particularly common where the objective is to increase primary demand for a type of product or to influence favorably public attitudes toward an industry. Illustrative are advertisements by agricultural marketing cooperatives, the cost of which is supported by charges on products marketed by members and by some trade associations.

When the participants are organizations on different levels of a distribution channel, the activity is known as *vertical cooperative* advertising. It exists in a variety of forms including advertisements by manufacturers in which distributors or dealers are listed by name, and retailer advertisements featuring a manufacturer's product, for which an allowance is granted by the manufacturer to reimburse the dealer for some part or perhaps all of the cost of advertising or promoting the manufacturer's product.

The practice of granting advertising allowances to distributors or dealers is especially common among manufac-turers utilizing a selective distribution policy, particularly in certain lines of appliances, household equipment, tires, paint, shoes, and men's and women's clothing. It is also prevalent in certain convenience goods lines, notably grocery products, cosmetics and toilet goods. In the grocery trade, for example, some 75 to 95 per cent of corporate chains, wholesaler sponsored voluntary chains, and retailer cooperative groups report the frequent use of advertising allowances for products in the following groups: canned foods, cooking and salad oils, crackers and cookies, frozen foods, lard and shortening, macaroni products, paper products, soaps and detergents, starches and bleaches, and tea.

Many manufacturers grant allowances to finance advertis-ing of their products by dealers in order to guide consumers to local sources of supply, to provide a point-of-purchase tie-in with national advertising, to stimulate the cooperation of dealers, to help gain additional dealers, and to obtain a sort of automatic control over advertising expenditures, inasmuch as advertising allowances are commonly granted to dealers in direct relation to their volume of purchases during specified time periods. On the other hand, numerous manufacturers abhor cooperative advertising allowances, believing that such allowances provide a drain on their national advertising budget, reduce the quality of copy and layout when advertisements are prepared by dealers, present many nuisance problems relating to bookkee-ping and control and in checking of dealer performance in relation to an advertising agreement, and cause many legal complications since under the Robinson-Patman Act, it is required that advertising allowances or special promotional services, when granted to some dealers, must be made available to all on proportionally equal terms.

Regardless of an individual manufacturer's viewpoint, it is difficult for him to avoid the granting of advertising allowances when this is a common competitive practice. From a broader point of view, the practice of granting advertising allowances has a somewhat deleterious effect upon retail advertising, inasmuch as the content of the advertising of many retail stores is determined more by the availability of advertising allowances than by careful judgments about what would constitute timely and interesting buying information for the consumer.

The Advertising Agency

The growth of advertising has been associated with the development of a specialized type of institution known as the advertising agency. The first advertising agents, about the middle of the nineteenth century, were space brokers for media. At that time newspaper editors were anxious to obtain advertising revenue but had no contacts with out-of-town advertisers. The first agents recognized this situation as an opportunity for rendering an economic service. They purchased or contracted for "white space" from media and contacted advertisers in distant areas, selling the space in units suited to the requirements of advertisers. Gradually the agents began to give advice and assistance to advertisers who were seeking specialized counsel in the preparation of their copy. In time the agents developed new methods and techniques and offered new services. Eventually the advertisers rather than the media became the clients of the agents.

Today the advertising agency is a service organization composed of advertising specialists, and it shares the responsibility for advertising activities with the advertising departments of clients. It is believed that advertising agencies now assist in the creation and direction of more than 90 per cent of all national advertising, more than one-half of sectional advertising, and a considerable amount of local advertising. Between 1948 and 1958 the number of advertising agency establishments increased from 3,279 to 7,720. A large per cent of total agency business, however, is accounted for by a limited number of large agencies, most of which are located in New York City.

Services of Agencies

The principal services of modern advertising agencies consist of planning, preparation, and placement of advertising. Planning requires a thorough knowledge of markets, products, distribution channels, and marketing policies. This often involves marketing research, which is carried on by or for the agency. Preparation includes developing a central idea or theme, production of advertisements, production or purchase of art work and printing, hiring radio and television talent and supervising or producing entertainment programs, and preparing broadcast media commercials.

Placement involves selection of media; preparation of advertising schedules; purchase of broadcast time or publication space; shipment of plates, copy, and instructions to media; preparation and mailing of direct advertising; and checking publications or stations to insure that advertisements were run or broadcast properly. Some of the larger agencies also provide a marketing counseling service and go so far as to advise a client on broad management policies for his business. They may assist in product development and package design; secure patents and copyrights; prepare point-of-sale promotional aids for the client's sales force; carry on public relations and publicity work; arrange and plan demonstrations and contests; and prepare training material for dealers' and jobbers' salesmen. In fact, there is almost no type of promotional service which is not provided at least by some agencies.

Why Agencies Are Used

Even the largest advertisers who maintain elaborate advertising departments find that there are several good reasons for using advertising agencies. First, the agency is independent of the advertiser and has an outside objective viewpoint which it can bring to bear on important decisions. Second, the agency has broad experience which results from its work with a number of clients having different products, selling in various markets, using various channels of distribution, and employing numerous types of media. Third, it must do a satisfactory job in order to hold the account. It is constantly alert to opportunities because it realizes that the advertiser can change agencies easily. If an advertiser developed an advertising department capable of performing all agency services, such a department would be part of the organization and could not be disposed of easily.

Fourth, the agency may spread the cost of certain technical services over a number of accounts. The payroll costs of advertising production specialists and marketing research experts is less than it would be if each advertiser had a staff comparable in skills to that of the agency. A fifth important reason is that all or a large part of the agency's service may not cost the advertiser anything. This is true because agencies obtain a substantial part of their revenue from media commissions which are not available to advertisers who buy space or time direct from media.

Agency Compensation

Advertising agency compensation is largely a carryover from the early days when the principal function of an agency was selling space for media. Most agencies still obtain the greater part of their remuneration from the media, based upon the amount of space or time purchased for clients. The agency purchases publication space or broadcast time direct from the media. With only minor exceptions, it receives a discount usually amounting to 15 per cent of the list price of the space or time purchased. For example, if the cost of a full page of space in a magazine is listed at $10,000, the recognized agency is billed for $10,000 less a 15 per cent discount, or $8,500. The agency bills its clients for a space cost of $10,000 and retains the $1,500 to defray the expense of preparing the copy, placing, and checking the advertisement. If the advertiser did not use the agency, under existing media price and discount policies, it would probably pay the magazine the full price of $10,000 and would, furthermore, have to incur the expenses of preparing and placing the advertisement.

Agency commissions from media are often supplemented by service fees paid by clients. The commission is intended to cover the service cost of preparing and placing advertising. It does not provide payment for extensive marketing research work, elaborate art work or engravings prepared outside the agency, talent for radio or television entertainment, preparation of special signs or dealer-helps, or other special services rendered or procured by the agency for the client. For such services it is customary for the agency to levy special charges based on the cost of the services plus some percentage fee agreed upon at the time the relationship is established. The agency method of commission compensation has often been criticized as illogical, inasmuch as the services of advertising agents are rendered primarily to advertisers rather than to media which pay the commissions.

It has also been criticized because the traditional pattern of commission payments became rigidly institutionalized. Various trade associations of advertising agencies and of advertising media have established criteria to be met by business firms in order for them to be recognized as accredited agencies entitled to receive such commissions. Also, it has been considered an unethical trade practice for agencies to split media commissions or to rebate any part of them to advertiser clients. The whole agency compensation pattern was called into question in the 1950's when the Department of Justice brought proceedings against various such associations under the Sherman Antitrust

Act. Early in 1956 a leading association of advertising agencies and several media associations entered into consent decrees which, among other things, prohibited practices or agreements "fixing, establishing or stabilizing agency commissions or attempting to do so" or "requiring, urging or advising any advertising agency to refrain from rebating or splitting agency commissions. These consent decrees forced a re-examination of the whole pattern of agency compensation and brought forth some experimental attempts between agencies and clients for new approaches to compensation. On the whole, however, the commission basis for agency compensation continues to be the dominant arrangement.

Agency commissions from media have not been an important factor in local or retail advertising. Newspapers and radio and television stations usually have direct contact with local advertisers. Partly because of the news value of local advertisements and partly because the large portion of revenue is obtained locally, newspapers and other local media usually have lower space or time rates for local than for nonlocal advertisers. Agency discounts do not apply to these lower local rates. This has restricted the use of advertising agencies in local advertising, because they must make a specific charge for the total value of the service rendered to local clients.

ECONOMIC AND SOCIAL ASPECTS OF ADVERTISING

In the preceding pages advertising has been discussed as an important activity, assumed to be essential to the preponderant majority of business concerns. The broader economic and social aspects of advertising are, however, a subject of considerable controversy. The negative aspects of advertising, or those facets of it which are most readily criticized or scorned, are readily apparent and widely publicized. On the other hand, the contributions and services of advertising are not well understood, even by many marketing and advertising executives. An appraisal of the economic, social, and public policy implications of advertising is essential for purposes of a functional analysis of marketing, both from a broad or over-all viewpoint as well as from the standpoint of marketing management, inasmuch as those who plan and carry out advertising programs can do so more effectively by understanding advertising as a part of the social scene.

Contributions and Services of Advertising

The place of advertising in our life is better understood if certain facts relating to the service of advertising to society as a whole are examined objectively. It was suggested that advertising did not become important until large-scale production made certain demand-creation activities necessary. Successful advertising campaigns have in turn *accelerated the movement toward large-scale production* by many manufacturers. As a rule, increase in the scale of form utility production is accompanied by decreasing costs per unit of output. There are hundreds of examples of reduction in the total cost of production and distribution through successful advertising. It is equally true that advertising and a liberal use of personal selling efforts have been made necessary in order to find a large market in which to sell the increased output resulting from quantity-production methods. *Thus advertising is both a cause and effect of large-scale activity,* with emphasis probably on the latter. In either case, the result is the same. Decreased cost of manufacturing in many cases offsets wholly or in part the cost of demand-creation activities.

Another important service of advertising lies in its *beneficial effect on the standard of living.* One measure of a nation's material progress is a cross-section of the wants of the common people. In other words, advancing civilization is accompanied by increases in the quantity and variety of wants and the means of satisfying them. Advertising has done much to encourage better homes, architecturally, mechanically, and functionally. Dozens of articles are in use in the average home of today as the result of demand stimulation by advertising. Vacuum sweepers, electric refrigerators, mechanical dishwashers, and modern floor and wall coverings are illustrations. Many advertised articles help to make the modern diet more nutritious, interesting, and enjoyable than formerly.

Since advertising facilitates the profitable exploration and development of markets for new or improved products and uses, *it has tended greatly to encourage innovation and technology.* There is no doubt but that much of the technological progress in the electronic, chemical, and automotive fields recorded in modern times can be attributed to the development of potential demands for the products and uses thus made possible.

The *educational effect of advertising* is likewise important, both directly and indirectly. It is probable that advertisements of dental creams have done more to preserve the teeth of the nation than has the personal advice of thousands of dentists. Correspondence courses which have been of great aid to many people are made possible largely because of advertising. Advertising, insofar as it is truthful, educates by providing information about hundreds of articles which might be otherwise unknown or unaccepted by the average buyer. The *indirect effect of advertising upon education* is undoubtedly even more potent. Most newspapers or magazines could not be sold at prices that would make them accessible to the masses of our people in the absence of advertising which largely subsidizes them. About two-thirds to three-fourths of the average income of newspapers and magazines comes from advertising. Most radio and television programs would be virtually impossible without sponsorship by advertisers.

Constructive advertising *lessens to a great degree the necessity for buying ability.* In the days of the more simple life it was possible for buyers to be judges of the quality of the articles they purchased, since these were comparatively few in number. It is now almost impossible for the average buyer to judge with any certainty the quality of the hundreds of articles he buys. But fortunately the use of brands, which is an essential for most advertising, makes it possible to rely on the standard quality of such merchandise, and identification enables one to avoid repurchase of unsatisfactory brands.

Criticisms of Advertising

Certain considerations tend in part, at least, to offset the social value of the services of advertising. Many criticisms have been made, and some of these are partially sound. Most of the criticisms are, however, at least partly the result of misunderstanding as shown by the following appraisal of some of the most commonly voiced and perhaps also the most important of these criticisms.

"Too Costly."

A common criticism is that the cost of advertising is too high and that such high cost adds to the price of the advertised product. This criticism grows out of an inherent characteristic of advertising as an instrument of mass communication, necessitating expenditures of large amounts of money. It is rather common knowledge, for example, that certain large advertisers spend millions of dollars annually for advertising, that advertising pages in popular magazines are priced in tens of thousands of dollars, and that the cost of producing and broadcasting certain individual television programs may run into hundreds of thousands of dollars. Such amounts appear staggering to the person of ordinary means who forgets that expenditures for advertising are significant only when expressed in relation to some meaningful standard of comparison. One way of judging the magnitude of advertising expenditures is in relation to total personal consumption expenditures. Advertising expenditures in 1960 amounted to $11.6 billion, but this was only 3.5 per cent of all consumer expenditures for goods and services.

Over a long period of years, advertising costs of about 3 per cent to 4 per cent of consumption expenditures have been typical. This basis of comparison, however, overstates the relative importance of advertising costs. Much advertising is devoted to industrial goods and services and some to goods sold primarily to government. It is, therefore, more meaningful to compare the costs of advertising to the gross national product. Over a period of years, this basis reveals that advertising costs of about 2 per cent are the common situation. Again, advertising cost, when related to the total volume of business transacted, is less than 1 per cent.

Another important approach to understanding advertising costs is in terms of units of product. In the case of cigarettes, where all important brands are highly advertised, the great amounts expended for advertising shrink into insignificance when compared to the tremendous number of units of product sold, resulting in costs of only a fraction of a cent per package. Experience varies from one industry to another. Advertising costs for certain nationally promoted brands of soap, cosmetics, and drugs amount to a significant component of final retail value. These are exceptional examples, however, and the cost of advertising for most companies is quite low when measured per unit of product sold or in relation to total sales volume involved.

The costs of advertising can also be compared with costs incurred for personal selling effort. Advertising expenses of most retail stores are only about 1 or 2 per cent of sales volume, the most notable exceptions being department stores, departmentized specialty stores, and furniture stores where advertising costs often amount to as much as 3 to 5 per cent of sales. In practically all cases this is substantially less than the expense of personal selling incurred by the same stores. Among manufacturers, advertising costs of about 1 to 3 per cent of sales volume are common experience. While there are some exceptions to such low advertising costs, as explained in the preceding paragraph, the cost of advertising is usually low in comparison to the expense of maintaining a personal selling organization in the field. If less were spent for advertising, it would be necessary for companies to exert additional personal selling effort in order to maintain their position, and *total selling costs* would undoubtedly be considerably higher. The experience of the business community has been that advertising, when properly performed, is a *relatively* inexpensive form of selling effort and that it makes personal selling more efficient, since it paves the way for the salesman.

Many critics of advertising have blissfully assumed as a criterion of pure or perfect competition the existence of a state of complete and accurate knoweldge, shared equally by all buyers and sellers in the market. At the same time, such critics often fail to state or appreciate that the task of providing such an ideal state of knowledge would involve social costs perhaps hundreds or thousands of times total annual expenditures for advertising if, indeed, it could ever be achieved at all.

Emphasizes Minor Differences

Another criticism is that advertising has tended to develop and emphasize minor differences in the construction or formulae of advertised goods in order to have "something to advertise." It is much easier to call forth additional effective demand for a product if it is new or appears to be so than when it is just another brand of the same general type as dozens already on the market. For example, it is probably true that there are many brands of advertised toothpaste which are not essentially different and which perform the same functions as previously established brands. It has, therefore, been necessary to emphasize minor chemical differences or new features in packages which are not always worth while. The effect of this is, in part, to reduce the scale of operations of the factories already producing toothpaste with the possibility of increased production costs. To the extent that this is true, the featuring of new brands, not essentially better than those already on the market, may be economically and consequently socially unjustifiable. But advertising of new brands does not necessarily divert demand from older manufacturers. In many cases additional advertising has the effect of increasing the total consumption of the article under consideration.

This additional consumption may or may not occur at the expense of other articles formerly purchased. When a new make of air-conditioning equipment is placed on the market, its advertising may increase somewhat the total sale of such equipment. In part it will divert to the new manufacturer sales which might otherwise have gone to existing suppliers. The effect may be to divert funds to the purchase of air-conditioning equipment which might have gone for clothing, alcoholic beverages, entertainment, insurance, or to savings accounts. In such a case, the social service of advertising must be judged by the relative social values of the alternative purchases.

Planned Obsolescence

A somewhat related criticism is that advertising makes possible and encourages planned obsolescence. To evaluate this criticism, it is necessary to distinguish what is generally meant by planned obsolescence from other types of product obsolescence. There is, on the one hand, *obsolescence of function,* which has to do with the outmoding of a product by the introduction of another that performs the same function in a better way, as illustrated by automatic home laundry equipment to replace old-fashioned wringer-type washers. Nearly everyone welcomes and praises the obsolescence of this type and regards it as progress. On the other hand, there is *obsolescence of quality,* or deliberate under engineering of a product, so that it will wear out quickly or be used up rapidly thus, in a sense, creating and enlarging, its own replacement demand. No sensible person can condone this type of obsolescence if the manufacturer can for the same money or for very little more provide a product that would yield more lasting benefit.

Neither the obsolescence of function nor the obsolescence of under engineering of products are usually the issue when planned obsolescence is the question at debate. Such discussions usually have to do with what has been termed the *obsolescence of desirability,* for it is this type which, to the greatest degree, is made possible and greatly facilitated by advertising. In one appraisal of the subject by a well-known advertising trade publication, this type of obsolescence was defined as "yearly or other regular superficial changes in products, styling or prestige selling appeals to persuade the public to purchase new items before the old are worn out." This criticism is most frequently directed at the durable goods industries, notably automobiles and household appliances, where annual model changes are the general practice, but it also is commonly aimed at the fashion apparel industry as well.

Proponents of planned obsolescence and its antagonists to some extent are engaged in a moral debate. Planned obsolescence would be morally indefensible if advertising of regular superficial changes in products brought about increased public emphasis upon material or conspicuous consumption at the expense of the attainment of higher social goals. It is certainly not clear that this is the case. The lesson of history is that the attainment of a high level of material well-being precedes rather than replaces the achievement of higher ranked social goals (e.g., better schools, medical care, or public recreation facilities).

Moreover, public response to the marketing strategy of planned obsolescence indicates that advertising of new models is a basic appeal to a rather pervasive desire for "newness" throughout our culture. In other words, advertising reflects rather than creates the social significance widely attached to innovation and change. This viewpoint is fortified by the fact that certain products are marketed on a basis where the main appeal is the absence of annual model changes, with the claim of little or no obsolescence, owing to changes in product which are confined to functional improvement (e.g., Rambler automobiles, Maytag home laundry equipment).

While nearly everyone abhors to some extent at least some aspects of planned obsolescence, even its critics see certain benefits which partially compensate for alleged wastes or abuses. Critics often seem to imply that consumers actually discard functioning products simply because they want to own a newer (but not necessarily an improved) product. Actually, second-hand automobiles, appliances, and even useful articles of clothing enter another market themselves, thus becoming worth while product acquisitions of consumers who cannot afford or who do not wish to make the monetary outlay for new items. Moreover, there is some merit to the argument that planned obsolescence is partially a matter of planned product improvement handled on a regularly scheduled basis. Certainly it is quite frequently the case that one model of a given make of automobile is not greatly different from the preceding model. If the annual models of any make of car are compared over a long period of years, however, a much different conclusion is reached. Such a comparison brings into evidence a continuous parade of product improvement. The automobile of the early 1920's differs from the car of today by the sum of hundreds of relatively minor year-to-year advertised differences.

Solely Competitive

Another criticism is that advertising is solely competitive and that the net result is to divert demand from one good product to another which is equally good but not superior. There can be little question as to the truth of this assertion insofar as much advertising is concerned. The potential market demand determines to a considerable degree whether or not advertising has the criticized effect.

In the foregoing illustration concerning air conditioning, it was assumed that the potential demand for air-conditioning equipment is great and that a part of the effect of the advertising was to develop additional primary demand. Had the illustration referred to bread, the effect would have been vastly different. Advertising of brands of bread has relatively little effect in increasing the demand for bread as a whole, since the primary demand for bread is well developed and is considered to be relatively stable. But who is to say that the market for bread is limited solely to the level of purchases of present users or whether it may be expansible in the sense of being only part of a larger market for starchy foods.

If one describes the market for this product in terms of its present and potential uses or satisfactions rather than in terms of its generic characteristics, the possibility of increasing primary demand appears to be more reasonable. Much advertising, nevertheless, is largely of a competitive nature wherein the selective buying or patronage appeals for a specific good or service have the effect of increasing or enhancing the market position of the advertiser rather than of increasing primary demand, even though the latter may be, to some extent, a by-product. This is, however, one of the characteristics of a competitive society. Most students of the problem recognize that much competitive effort could be eliminated were it desirable to establish a more paternalistic or dictatorial form of government. Under such circumstances it might be possible to control and even to eliminate advertising that is solely competitive. But such control would be at the expense of free competition, and freedom of competition is generally believed to be so desirable as to justify some of its inherent wastes as a necessary price for its maintenance.

Inefficiency

Another alleged weakness of advertising as conducted at present in this country is its inefficiency. To be sure, some advertising is inefficient, and doubtless all advertising is less efficient than it could be. Even among large users of advertising, jokes are sometimes made about the efficiency of advertising. Sometime about 1910 George Washington Hill, famous president of the American Tobacco Company and an outstanding innovator in advertising methods and approaches, is reputed to have said, "I am convinced that 50 per cent of our advertising is sheer waste, but I can never find out which half." To this date, this statement is a popular quotation in advertising industry meetings and often appears in press comments about the subject.

It must be understood that advertising is a relatively new art. It is not yet a science, although scientific methods of procedure are being rapidly developed. Many valuable methods and principles have been and are being evolved as the result of the contributions of psychologists and sociologists. Such study has led to improved typography, more appealing copy, and improved layout. The more widespread practice of testing trial advertisements has eliminated considerable waste resulting from poorly conceived advertising programs. Media are now selected with more skill as a result of extensive research regarding characteristics of the circulation or audience of specific and general classes of media.

Motivation research has yielded a better knowledge of consumer buying behaviour and has enabled advertisers to harmonize selling appeals with buying motives, with the effect of minimizing waste or inefficiency in the use of advertising appropriations. Other improvements in technique are constantly being developed which will no doubt lessen some of the crudities of the past. Progress in the application of more scientific procedures has indeed reached a point where many critics are more concerned about the efficiency rather than the inefficiency of advertising. This would certainly seem to be the view of some writers who regard advertising as an objectionable, manipulative art which causes people to do things they would not otherwise do, or which they should not do, if judged by the personal value standards of the critic.

Misleading and False.

An often-heard criticism of advertising is that many advertisements are misleading or definitely false. There is no doubt that this is true. Numerous advertisers have cleverly created a misleading impression even though every statement in their message, when separately considered, is literally truthful; others have quoted carefully selected findings of authoritative research studies out of context and in such a way that the quotations are construed as a product indorsement. Still others have artfully contrived to divert the reader's attention from the true nature of the terms of an offer by emphasizing headlines which give a false impression; additional advertisers have devised sensational tests which make a convincing sales argument but which have no relationship to the consumer's satisfaction from the use of the article. It is nevertheless significant that the Federal Trade Commission in its examination of hundreds of thousands of magazine, newspaper, and broadcast advertisements finds that only a very small percentage contains statements that appear to be misleading or false to a degree which justifies possible action by the Commission. No responsible citizen can condone misleading or false advertising, but to condemn all of advertising because of the objectionable practices of a deceptive minority is ridiculous. The answer, rather, is to focus attention on the control of abuses.

Control of Advertising

Popular credence in the printed word endows advertising with great potential power. At the same time, advertising is more or less centralized and is, therefore, susceptible to control. These factors no doubt explain in part the widespread control of advertising on the one hand and the complete absence, with but rare exceptions, of control over the broader area of personal selling on the other. Control of advertising has been directed principally to the elimination of falsehood, fraud, and deceptive practices and the prevention of advertising of harmful products. More recently, partly in response to consumer pressure, attempts have been made to eliminate or minimize "bad taste" in advertising and to make advertising more informative and therefore more useful in making choices. Efforts at these various controls have been shared by many types of agencies and organizations.

Federal Trade Commission and Advertising

Foremost in the control of advertising is the Federal Trade Commission which was created in 1914 by the Federal Trade Commission Act and was charged, among other things, with the responsibility of determining and preventing unfair methods of competition. One form of unfair competition is misleading advertising intended to deceive the public to the detriment or injury of competitors. The power of the Commission was greatly expanded by the passage of the Wheeler-Lea Act in 1938. This law amended the original Federal Trade Commission Act in three important respects. First, it broadened the Commission's jurisdiction to include practices that injure the public but which may not involve or injure a competitor. Prior to this amendment, action could be brought only upon complaint of a competitor who was presumably injured by an allegedly unfair practice. Now, the Commission may take action of its own accord if public injury can be shown.

The second major change pertained to the enforcement of orders issued by the Commission. The process of enforcement was regularized and shortened by making cease and desist orders of the Commission effective after 60 days unless appeals are made to the federal district courts. Furthermore, it was provided that the Commission may bring action in the federal district courts in the case of violations of such orders, and substantial penalties of $5,000 were provided for each proved violation. It has been claimed that this penalty is not sufficiently severe because a violation may involve a considerable period of time. Some unethical advertisers doing a large volume of business found that such an amount is a small price to pay for the privilege of violation. For this reason, it has been advocated that the penalty be increased or made more severe so that a fine of $5,000 or more may be imposed for *each day* of violation.

The most important of the three principal changes made by the Wheeler-Lea Act is that which pertains to the *advertising other than labeling of foods and drugs.* It definitely prohibits false advertising of food, drugs, cosmetics, and therapeutic devices. Certain infractions involving these items are rendered criminal when injurious to health or when involving intent to deceive or defraud, and are punishable by both fine and imprisonment. Temporary injunctions are provided to stop these practices pending issuance of a complaint and determination of the charges. The law also permits factory inspections and forces submittal of these commodities, when required, for testing purposes; if found harmful, their sale may be prohibited. One of the effects of this law has been greater confidence in advertising by virtue of the protection afforded. Another result is greater emphasis on specific and more informative statements in advertisements. A third result has been a re-examination of products for characteristics that could be advertised under the law. This has led to research and product improvement. In addition to its broad powers under the Wheeler-Lea Act, the Federal Trade Commission also has authority with respect to the sale, advertising, labeling or branding of certain individual commodities for which specific legislation has been enacted (e.g., Wool Products Labeling Act, Fur Products Labeling Act). Moreover, the Commission enforces the Robinson-Patman Act, which prohibits advertising or other promotional and service allowances unless they are made available on proportionally equal terms to all customers.

Still another activity of the Commission is releasing from time to time special publications in the interest of education of the business man and the consumer and to obtain voluntary, simultaneous and prompt cooperation by those whose practices are subject to the Commission's jurisdiction.

Control by Other Federal Agencies

A number of other federal agencies have some control over advertising. One of great importance is the Pure Food and Drug Administration which operates under the authority of the Food, Drug and Cosmetic Act of 1938, which was an amendment to the Pure Food and Drug Act of 1906. Under the newer law, cosmetics and therapeutic devices were brought under control in addition to food and drugs; misbranding and misleading advertising of the specified products are banned; seizure of adulterated or contaminated foods is permitted; labels must warn of habit-forming drugs; factory inspections are permitted; and no drug can be placed on the market until after it has been tested to determine whether it is harmful.

The various prohibitions may be enforced by injunction. Labeling must include the address of the manufacturer, packer, or distributor as well as facts concerning the quantity of the contents, major ingredients, and warnings against misuse of drugs. The Pure Food and Drug Administration works closely with the Federal Trade Commission. With respect to the selling function, the former agency is concerned primarily with packaging and branding. Although it watches for deceptive advertising, it usually hands over questionable cases of advertising to the Federal Trade Commission for action.

The Alcohol and Tax Division of the Treasury Department exercises powerful control over the advertising of alcoholic products. Under federal licensing regulations, this agency may require approval of all advertising and labeling of intoxicating beverages. It is very strict in the regulation of misleading advertising and has definite requirements as to the use of names for beverages and specification of exact age, type, and alcoholic content. The Post Office Department also exerts some control. Federal laws forbid the use of the mails for fraudulent purposes. While cases are relatively rare, there have been instances where the use of the mails has been forbidden to organizations that cooperated in fraudulent advertising.

State and Local Control of Advertising

A considerable degree of control is exercised over advertising in intrastate commerce. This has become effective through the widespread enactment of the so-called Printers' Ink Model Statute which was drawn up by the advertising trade publication of that name in 1911. The purpose of this legislation was to extend the "Truth in Advertising" movement to trade not susceptible to control by federal legislation. It aims, in general, at preventing in an advertisement "any assertion, representation or statement of fact which is untrue, deceptive, or misleading," by declaring such a statement a misdemeanor. This law has been enacted in 27 states and the District of Columbia, and 17 additional states have enacted adaptations of it. Only six states have no law of this kind. In addition, many cities have ordinances relating to the use of deceptive or fraudulent local advertising.

Control by the Business Community

Also of great influence is voluntary control of advertising by the business community itself. Better Business Bureaus were established primarily for the purpose of promoting more truthful local advertising, especially in the retail field and in financial advertising. Operating in the principal cities, their influence in controlling local unfair advertising practices has been salutary. Newspapers and magazines often refuse to accept certain types of advertisements, exclude certain products from their pages, and otherwise censor all advertising submitted for insertion. Following along similar lines, though much less extensively and perhaps less effectively, broadcasting companies have attempted similar controls.

The efforts of certain trade and professional associations, particularly those designed to set standards for or to censor advertisements before they are printed or stated over the airways, have also been exceedingly helpful. Finally, there are several important associations of advertising agencies, advertisers, and advertising media which have played a leading part in efforts to make advertising more useful, to place it on a higher plane, and to eliminate or minimize bad taste in advertising. This is accomplished through codes or standards of advertising practice to which the members of such associations have pledged themselves. The work of such associations is largely educational and persuasive, since they have no direct power of enforcement. Control of flagrant and intentional abuses rests necessarily with public authorities.

8

Personal Selling and Sales Promotion

RELATIVE IMPORTANCE OF PERSONAL SELLING

If age is a criterion of relative importance, then personal selling must be given prime position. In every exchange there must be two parties buyer and seller. As this bipartite condition has existed from the time that men began to exchange products, personal selling is as old as trade. It goes back many centuries before invention of the printing press which made possible the first mass advertising.

If extent of use as an exclusive selling device determines relative importance, again personal selling takes first place. To be sure, there are concerns, like mail order houses at the wholesale and retail levels, that sell entirely by means of advertising. The volume of business thus transacted is relatively small, however. On the other hand, many thousands of manufacturers and many more thousands of retailers do not advertise at all, unless window and counter displays by the latter are so considered, but make sales exclusively through personal selling effort.

Commonly, the two methods of selling are used by the same vendor to complement or supplement each other, which makes measurement of relative importance extremely difficult. If it is assumed, however, that businessmen will make the greatest expenditures in manpower and other resources where, by experience, they tend in the long run to obtain the best results, then personal selling must be judged by far the more important method of selling. The relative importance of the three main components of the selling function in the economy is indicated by the costs that can readily be identified with each. Personal selling, as measured by the compensation received by employees designated as sales workers, is more than half again as large as advertising and is some six times greater than sales promotion.

While data on compensation of sales workers comprise the best available measure of the importance of personal selling, such figures understate the true magnitude and cost of personal selling and, hence, also understate the cost of the total selling function. Not taken into account is the personal selling work of individuals not classified as sales workers, as, for example, owner-managers of small businesses and people who work at selling jobs on a part time basis. Nor do these figures make any allowance for the cost of selecting, training, supervising, and providing travel for salesmen. If all relevant personal selling activities could actually be cumulated, it is likely that their cost would comprise at least two-thirds of the total outlay for the entire selling function.

ECONOMIC BASIS FOR PERSONAL SELLING

Many people in, our present-day society believe that the work of a salesman is unproductive and hence economically unjustifiable. They entertain the idea that, at best, selling may be a necessary evil and that it adds no value to goods but increases their costs instead. The basis for this misconception, is that the mere creation of form utility is often popularly confused with production which, in its broader and more meaningful sense, includes not only form utility but also the creation of time, place, and possession utilities as well. In the vast majority of business transactions, the final value of goods cannot be accounted for without attention to the productive work of the salesman.

The rationale for personal selling activity is essentially the same as for the selling function as a whole, even though it has some aspects which distinguish it from the other types of selling effort. In the exchange process, either the buyer or seller may initiate contacts. Consumers are usually very active in this respect, especially when their wants are pressing and they have some familiarity with the kinds of goods that will satisfy their wants. Buyers for business firms are also often active in initiating exchange, particularly when they are seeking to fulfill a requirement that is of their own determination.

All kinds of buyers are, however, often reluctant or unable to make the most logical purchase when the goods providing maximum satisfaction are new or improved items, or when many alternatives are available and the knowledge of the buyer is naturally quite limited. Under such circumstances, contacts initiated by the seller and involving a human relationship with the buyer are most essential and productive. Even when buyers are most active in contactual relationships, some degree of dependence upon assistance from a salesman is the usual circumstance.

Personal selling is a natural and inevitable characteristic of a private enterprise economy in which buyers may purchase from alternative sources without compulsion. In a democratic system with a large number of complementary and competitive productive agencies, the work of the salesman is essential in consummating the exchange of products between retailers or service organizations and ultimate consumers, wholesalers and retailers, manufacturers, farmers, and wholesale organizations. It is inconceivable that we could enjoy the benefits of large-scale mass production without the work of the salesman who is the informative link between the various parties engaged in exchange.

SELLING AND SALESMANSHIP

Regardless of type of vendor or product involved, personal selling invariably comprises certain distinct steps or phases. In addition to adequate knowledge of his product, his company, and its policies, a salesman must acquire information about actual and potential customers. He must approach such customers with a view to arousing interest, establish favorable reaction, meet or answer their objections, and properly close the sale. The manner in which each of these steps is performed largely determines success and may frequently have to vary with the type of selling situation.

Service Selling and Creative Salesmanship

Two principal types of personal selling activity may be distinguished — service selling and creative salesmanship. The first type, often referred to as *low-level selling,* involves consummating a sale to a customer who has already made up his mind to buy and who knows, at least approximately, what he wants. Its purpose is to supply the prospective customer with information that will enable him to arrive at a decision to purchase the product offered by the salesman.

It involves the processes of making goods available, offering several items from which a choice can be made, explaining the differences between items, making clear the terms of sale, writing up the order, wrapping packages or arranging for the delivery of merchandise, and other types of service that aid in completing transactions. In this type of selling, the salesman is usually sought out by the buyer or at least is expected by the buyer because of some established pattern of contactual relationship.

Creative salesmanship, which is often called *high-level selling,* involves the process of arousing demand for new products or new brands or models of products, or influencing changes in patronage from one source of supply to another. To do this type of selling requires skill or art in presenting goods or services in such a manner that neutral or negative attitudes are converted into positive wants or demand. In creative selling, people are persuaded to do what they had not intended to do or had not specially wanted to do, despite basically existing wants warranting contrary reactions. This is accomplished by arousing desires that can be satisfied only by the possession of the products or services offered by the salesman. Relationships between buyers and sellers that involve service selling are often preceded by creative selling effort. Creative selling initially establishes these relationships and opens the way for repeat business, while service selling maintains and cultivates these relationships.

Spectrum of Creative Selling.

While the foregoing two types of low-level or maintenance selling and high-level or creative selling may be distinguished, each selling job usually involves some elements of both. The extent to which creative, persuasive skill is essential ranges over a wide spectrum, from some types of positions which are almost totally maintenance selling to others which are nearly altogether creative, with all sorts of variations in between. This is well illustrated by the following listing, based largely upon the type of product involved, and arranged in order of increasing relative requirements for creativity:

- Positions where the salesman's job is predominantly to deliver the product, for example, milk, bread, fuel oil.
- Positions where the salesman is predominantly an inside order taker, for example, the haberdashery salesman standing behind the counter.
- Positions where the salesman is also predominantly an order taker but works in the field, as the packing house, soap, or spice salesman does.
- Positions where the salesman is not expected or permitted to take an order but is called on only to build good will or to educate the actual or potential user, for example, detail men employed by pharmaceutical firms to make calls on the medical profession.
- Positions where the major emphasis is placed on technical knowledge, for example, the engineering salesman who is primarily a consultant to the client companies.
- Positions which demand the creative sale of tangible products like vacuum cleaners, refrigerators, and encyclopedias.
- Positions requiring the creative sale of intangibles, such as insurance, advertising services, or education.

Even within a given company marketing an established line of products, the need for creativity varies from one specific selling situation to another. In calling on regular customers, the task is mainly that of maintaining or increasing sales by providing customer service, and it is generally characterized by constancy of relationships. In calling on potential new accounts, the challenge is that of the creative development of new relationships which will induce a prospective buyer to embark upon a different pattern of behaviour. The satisfactory performance of each of these two jobs involves different problems and techniques, and the personnel requirements for each are also in marked contrast. This has led some companies to develop a sales organization consisting of two types of salesmen: one with the task of maintaining sales relationships with regular customers and the other with the job of developing new business with new customers.

Types of Personal Selling Situations

While it is not possible in a book of this scope to explore in detail all types of personal selling situations, the following paragraphs serve to indicate some of the common variations which are conditioned by the nature of the product, the channel of distribution, or the type of buyer.

Selling to Industrial Users

A salesman of highly standardized materials such as sheet steel, cement, or chemicals finds that his principal task is showing just why an order should be given to his firm rather than to a competitor who can supply materials of the same specifications. The coal or fuel oil salesman faces the same problem; although his products are not so highly standardized, they are purchased on the basis of chemical analysis of heat units. In such cases price considerations are important as are delivery dates and the general reputation of the supplier. Many orders for such goods are placed, nevertheless, because of the personality of the salesman or as the result of past relations with suppliers. Some sales of standardized goods require a great deal of technical knowledge and a high degree of salesmanship, calling for appeals to motives other than those relating to patronage. This is true, for example, in the case of the fuel oil salesman who calls upon an industrial plant that has relied upon coal as a source of heat and power. The sales presentation under such circumstances must appeal to primary motives, and it necessarily involves very detailed considera-tions such as the cost of converting burners, storage facilities needed, possible cost savings resulting from the use of the new method, and an analysis of any operating methods and procedures that may be affected by the change.

Salesmen who sell major items of equipment and installations must have a thorough understanding of the problems of the industry of which their prospects are members. A salesman of rubber belting must be able to analyse the problems of transmitting power in a particular factory and to furnish detailed specifications when he submits a price proposal. Air conditioning equipment, vertical transportation installations, and lighting fixtures are ordinarily purchased by retail establishments only after careful consideration of competing types produced by various companies. In the sale of such products graduate engineers are often employed as salesmen, because of the technical knowledge required for a careful analysis of the customer's needs. Such salesmen are appropriately called sales engineers. More than mere technical knowledge is needed by sales engineers, however, for they must be able to analyse cost savings and other advantages resulting from new installations, and cooperate with customers who have a value analysis programme. Furthermore, they must be able to arouse latent demand or in many cases create it in the sense of calling forth a hitherto unrecognized need.

Selling to Wholesalers

Salesmen who sell to wholesalers and to buyers in the purchasing organizations of large-scale retailing companies have a distinct problem. Within any specific classification of consumer goods, the number of different products which might be purchased is almost legion. On the other hand, the warehousing and capital resources of the buyer are always limited. Since the buyer can ordinarily purchase only a portion of the available offerings, he is primarily interested in the re-salability of different offerings. The principal task of the salesman is often that of convincing the buyer that there is a demand for the products in question and that retail stores will be able to make profitable re-sales. This may be achieved by an explanation of plans for advertising, by showing window or store display materials, or by proving that demand already exists by obtaining orders from retailers to be filled by the wholesaler. This latter method is a part of what is known as missionary selling. *Missionary salesmen* employed by a manufacturer work with retailers and make store demonstrations, prepare window displays, or arrange for other sales promotional activity. Orders are then accumulated from retailers and turned over to the wholesaler. Such missionary work is an important part of the demand creation activities of many manufacturers of specialty drug and food lines.

In addition to showing that there is or will be a demand for their products, salesmen who call on wholesalers must be able to discuss the general distributive organization of the company intelligently, to converse with some expertness on profit margins, and in general, to conduct themselves in a manner that inspires confidence in customers and prospects. A somewhat higher type of salesman, measured by both experience and general ability, is needed for this purpose than for selling to retailers exclusively, except in the case of sales to large retailers such as department stores, chain stores, and mail order houses where skill of just as high an order is required.

Selling to Retailers

Salesmen who represent manufacturers or wholesalers in their sales to retailers have a task somewhat similar to the one which faces salesmen who sell to wholesalers. All retailers, of course, have limited space and capital resources and are greatly concerned with the re-salability of items under consideration. Salesmen dealing with typical retailers do, however, also have a somewhat different problem. They must show the retailer that the source they represent is one from which purchases should be made. Patronage motives are of great importance. Credit policy, freight rates, speed of delivery, and personal relationship are a few of the factors entering into the situation. Usually there are a number of competitors, any one of whom could supply the desired articles.

Salesmen of this type render service to retailers by giving them advice on buying, on credit problems, on advertising policies, on window displays, and in general help their customers to become better merchants. Such requirements have tended to increase the general ability required and to eliminate persons who can merely take orders but do little or no constructive selling. In fact, many wholesaling organi- zations have made considerable progress in reorganizing their selling effort by devoting more attention to high-level selling and less to low-level selling of the order taking variety. In the food and drug fields, many wholesalers' salesmen spend most of their time in assistance work with retailers. Routine phases of ordering are sometimes shifted to retailers who determine their own purchasing requirements from preprinted order forms or catalogs and forward routine orders by telephone. This situation is most commonly encountered in cases where the wholesaler's salesman obtains agreements from retailers to concentrate their purchases with the wholesaler, so that the wholesaler is not continually pressed with the need for winning patronage. By the same token, the wholesaler's representative has more time to contact new accounts and to provide genuine merchandising assistance for regular customers.

Selling to Ultimate Consumers

All but a relatively small proportion of sales to ultimate consumers is made in retail stores or in personal service establishments. The principal differentiating characteristic of retail selling is that the consumer usually seeks out the salesman and usually has a specific want and at least an approximate idea about the means of satisfying it. It is in retail stores that *service* selling assumes the highest degree of significance. Practically all of the retail salesclerk's time is ordinarily spent in showing requested merchandise, writing sales slips, making change, wrapping packages, and maintaining the stock and the general selling area in a condition suitable for customer contacts with the merchandise. There are, nevertheless, numerous opportunities within the store for *creative* selling.

These arise out of the possibility of selling the consumer additional quantities of a desired item, selling other items related to the one that the customer enters the store to buy, and uncovering additional unrecognized needs and persuading the customer to purchase the products to meet such needs. Almost anyone who is capable of performing the service activities associated with retail selling can qualify for some kind of a position as a retail salesperson. Such selling is generally characterized by less knowledge and skill than the types of selling previously discussed. To this statement there are exceptions such as are encountered particularly in some establishments or departments selling goods of high unit value and infrequent purchase such as floor coverings, fashion apparel, and home furnishings.

The trend to self-service merchandising has shifted a considerable amount of exchange effort to the consumer and, increased his responsibilities as a buyer. There remains, nevertheless, the need for a certain amount of service selling in consummating transactions before the consumer leaves a self-service establishment. In some kinds of stores, a transition to self-service merchandising has actually opened up greater opportunities for high-level or creative salesmanship. For example, many hardware stores are arranged with open display of merchandise and cheek-out counters. Consumers who know exactly what they want and where to find it can obtain faster service by selecting their own items and paying for them at check-out stations. At the same time, salesmen do not have to spend valuable selling time on such transactions. Instead, they are free to assist other customers who can obtain greater benefits from personal selling effort because their needs are not yet made definite or they need buying counsel which involves technical product knowledge. Illustrative are purchases of power lawn mowers, paint, appliances, or plumbing fittings. A small but nevertheless significant proportion of retail sales is made at the homes of consumers by specialty salesmen. Some such salesmen are outside employees of regular retail establishments selling items like automobiles and major electrical appliances.

Others are employed by manufacturers or service companies engaged in the direct sale of products to ultimate consumers. As a rule, emphasis is placed upon ability to stimulate, direct, or divert demand rather than upon technical knowledge. Some organizations selling in the homes of consumers require their salesmen to canvass all homes in specified areas. When this policy is followed, skill in creative salesmanship is required. Other concerns selling to homes employ direct or publication advertising in order to obtain leads for their specialty salesmen. This eliminates a considerable amount of wasted effort that might ordinarily be expended in calls on prospects who do not have even a remote interest in the product. It also has the result of placing more emphasis on the service aspects of selling.

Management of the Field Sales Organization

In most large companies, particularly those marketing on a wholesale level, management of the field sales organization is one of the most important, if not the dominant, aspect of total marketing management. Some person fills the role of sales manager in all companies with more than a handful of salesmen and this task indeed becomes complex in very large wholesaling, manufacturing, and insurance companies where the number of salesmen runs into the hundreds or, in some cases, even thousands.

Part of the complexities of sales management arises out of the nature of the work of the outside salesman, which is in sharp contrast with that of manufacturing, warehousing, or clerical employees. For one thing, the salesman is in the field, on his own, working in the absence of close personal supervision. He works irregular hours, often away from his own place of residence. Much of his time is necessarily unproductive, for example, travel time, waiting to see custo-mers, broken interviews, and unkept appointments. He is constantly dealing with the public, ultimate consumers or business purchasers, external to the organization of his employer. His work situation tends to be highly variable, in that each customer's situation is a somewhat different one. Within a given company, each salesman's situation differs from that of the other salesmen, owing to variances in territory potential and characteristics; hence, less emphasis can be placed upon data which are indicative of normative performance.

The nature of the sale management task varies somewhat from industry to industry and to some extent among firms with similar product offerings.

In practically all large multi product companies, however, the same kind of problems must be faced. One of the crucial questions is how the sales force shall be organized, or how the total selling job should be specialized—by geographic area, by type of product, by kind of customer (industrial or consumer), by channel of distribution (middle-men versus direct buyers), or by nature of the selling task (development of new business versus maintenance selling). The large sales organization, particularly among expanding companies, faces a big job in selecting new salesmen. This may involve programs of recruiting, interviewing, administering psychological tests to determine aptitude for the particular type of selling, and reference checking. Training is a large part of the sales management function. It may be divided into initial training, lasting from a few days (in the case of some consumer goods items) to periods of more than a year (common for technical industrial goods), and continuing training, usually administered through sales meetings, personal conferences, and various other means of intra company communication.

The work of the sales force is commonly directed by a variety of means—through the activity of sales supervisors, by the assignment of salesmen to specific territories, by the development of schedules of call frequencies for classes of customers or specific accounts, by the use of quotas, by the use of specially devised compensation plans, and by the occasional use of sales contests. Salesmen's activities are appraised qualitatively and quantitatively also through personal supervision and by a variety of means of communication or reports indicating sales performance in relation to established quotas, number of calls made, number of sales in relation to number of calls, average size of orders obtained, travel and entertainment expense incurred, and other matters deemed of special significance in the particular case.

Owing to the peculiar nature of the outside salesman's job, as indicated above, unusual emphasis is placed upon compensation programs both as incentive and control devices. Incentive is provided, customarily, by some form of commission arrangement, either exclusively or as a salary supplement, and based on sales volume, gross margin of profit, or perhaps, sales volume in excess of quota.

Control is often built into a sales compensation programme by establishing different rates of commission for different segments of the potential market, thus emphasizing to the salesman the relative desirability of stressing sales of certain (usually the more profitable) products or kinds or sizes of orders, or obtaining business from preferred classes of accounts.

Owing to the great importance of the function, both in terms of crucial significance as a part of marketing and because of the large number of business executives so employed, the field of sales management has become the subject of an extensive field of specialized literature related to theory and practice, as evidenced by many books, periodicals, university courses, and business seminars.

SALES PROMOTION

Sales promotion was defined as consisting of those selling activities that supplement both advertising and personal selling, coordinate them, and render them more effective. It is a term that is used in the business community with a wide variety of interpretations, there being no general agreement as to the exact number or type of specific activities included within its scope.

Purpose of Sales Promotion

Sales promotion is most highly developed among large manufacturing companies that market highly advertised consumer goods. While this aspect of marketing is not restricted to such companies, its meaning and purpose are clarified by a consideration of the responsibility for the selling function in a large concern. The advertising department is ordinarily concerned with mass appeal advertising. Its major responsibility is the preparation of advertisements and their proper placement in suitable media. Personal contact with customers is usually outside the scope of its activities.

The personal salesman, on the other hand, has as his responsibility the meeting of prospective customers, delivering a sales presentation, and obtaining orders for the product or product line. He is likely to be irritated by any other activities that reduce the amount of time he is able to spend in obtaining orders. If the work of the marketing organization is confined to mass advertising and personal selling activities, the two parts of the organization responsible for these activities are likely to be working at cross-purposes and there are likely to be important gaps in the sales programme.

To supplement the advertising and personal selling departments, many companies have a sales promotion department as a third part of the marketing organization concerned directly with the selling function. This department supplements the other two by coordinating their efforts and rounds out the sales programme by maintaining liaison with dealers and consumers.

Among the most important of the numerous duties commonly assigned to a sales promotion department are the following: point-of-purchase advertising and display, dealer merchandising aids, premiums, contests, coupons, samples, and demonstrations. In small companies whose operations cannot support a specialized sales promotion department, many of these activities are nevertheless carried on by the advertising department, the personal selling department, or by the two of them working in close cooperation.

Point-of-Purchase Advertising and Display

A manufacturer of consumer goods is particularly interested in advertising and display in establishments where his product is sold to ultimate consumers, for two reasons. First, between the time that an impression is made upon a consumer by mass advertising and the time of a visit to an establishment where the merchandise is sold there may be many obstacles to purchasing. The impact of publication or broadcast advertising may have been slight; the consumer is often exposed to competing advertising which makes an equal or stronger impact; or the consumer may find competing products more prominently displayed in stores. Second, since practically all consumers visit retail stores, widespread point-of-purchase advertising is likely to be seen by nearly everyone, even by those who have not seen a magazine or newspaper advertisement or heard a radio commercial pertaining to the product. Where self-service and self-selection merchandising methods are used, the point-of-purchase display acts as a substitute for the retail salesclerk, providing information which contributes to the buying decision.

Point-of-purchase promotion effort takes two principal forms, window and interior display. A wide range of materials is used for display purposes including the product itself, dummy packages, giant package facsimiles, lithographed display cards, photographs, streamers, metal signs, floor stands, merchandise display fixtures, decalcomanias for windows and store entrances, and wall signs. A large proportion of such material is distributed free to retail stores and is newer used for the intended purpose in the retail establishment. To overcome such waste, some manufacturers have discontinued the distribution of point-of-purchase advertising material by mail but instead distribute it only through personal salesmen who have been trained in educating the dealer to the value of display and in securing cooperation for its effective use. When large window or interior display space is desired by a manufacturer, it is often necessary to compensate the dealer for its use in some manner. This is occasionally done by a cash payment but more frequently by a special deal involving an additional discount on all merchandise purchased for the display or by an offer of free goods.

Dealer Aids

A considerable amount of sales promotion effort is devoted to merchandising assistance given to dealers. Such efforts are largely confined to companies whose line of merchandise is of considerable importance to the dealer. This is the situation when a manufacturer has a wide line of merchandise or when he restricts his distribution to a very limited number of outlets that are expected to give considerable promotional effort to his line. On this basis, a wholesaler with a wide variety and assortment of merchandise is in an excellent position to use dealer aids.

Undoubtedly the most common type of assistance is in advertising. A second very important form of dealer assistance consists of training programs or educational material furnished for retail store employees selling a manufacturer's product. Some manufacturers and wholesale distributors provide very comprehensive forms of merchandising assistance that are store-wide in scope. In addition to advertising assistance and personal selling training, this may involve furnishing and installing accounting systems, stock control systems, and assistance in problems of store modernization and layout.

Incentive Travel

A form of sales promotional activity that increased greatly in use during the 1950's and early 1960's is incentive travel. Such programs are widely used by large companies to reward their salesmen, agents, distributors, or dealers for attaining a specific objective, usually sales volume (or purchase commitments) in excess of some predetermined quota. Contemporary interest in incentive travel is not difficult to understand, owing to population mobility, world consciousn- ess, and air transportation facilities. As a rather typical example, a leading tire and rubber company in 1960 offered dealers with the highest percentage of sales over quota trips to the Far East, Europe, Hawaii, Mexico, or the Caribbean. Some 252 dealers earned trips on which they could take their wives. Dealer incentive trips are especially common in the household appliance industry, and often involve the mass movement of hundreds of dealers, with wives, to exotic places (e.g., Hawaii, Nassau, Bermuda, Las Vegas) by chartered aircraft. In many instances, social functions and recreation are intermingled with business sessions, dealer development activities, and the introduction of new product lines in a trade show atmosphere. Incentive travel has been widely used because experience has shown that, to a greater extent than equivalent monetary reward, it induces people to work harder to accomplish a specific goal, particularly when wives of salesmen or dealers are eligible who exhort their husbands to greater effort to attain such a reward.

Direct Consumer Stimulants

Manufacturers and distributors employ a number of techniques which are intended to stimulate more direct purchasing action than can ordinarily be effected through mass advertising and personal selling appeals. Illustrative are premiums, contests, coupons, special offer deals, samples, and store demonstrations.

Premiums

Premiums may be defined as articles of merchandise offered as inducements to purchase a product. While almost all types of consumer products have been promoted, at some time or another, by the use of premiums, they are most commonly employed by manufacturers of highly competitive products of low unit value and frequent purchase.

Contests

Contests in which the consumer is asked to write a sentence about a product, complete a verse, work a puzzle, or suggest a new use for a product are a very common method of direct stimulation. Great interest usually results from publicity accorded to the substantial prizes offered in such affairs. This interest is accentuated by the average person's natural desire to play or compete. Sales promotion experts generally regard about 500,000 entries with proof of purchase the minimum required to make a national contest a success. Owing to the large number of multiple entries, particularly by people who make a hobby of entering contests, as few as 100,000 to 200,000 present customers and new customer prospects may be involved in a contest with 500,000 entries.

Special-Offer Deals

Special-offer deals are promotions in which the manufacturer offers some special monetary inducement, other than an outright price reduction, to stimulate the purchase of his product during a specified period of time. Examples include "1¢ sales," which offer an item at 1 cent with the purchase of a specified number of the item at the regular price, 2-for-the-price-of-1 offers, and coupons, which are good for a specified reduction from the regular price. Trade sources indicate that more than a billion special-offer coupons are redeemed by consumers through food stores each year. Research conducted in connection with a limited number of products indicates certain relationships of marketing interest between consumer participation in special-offer deals and socioeconomic characteristics of households.

White families avail themselves of deals to a greater extent than nonwhite families. The tendency to purchase deals grows with increases in level of family income, size of household, and education of the head of household, and it declines with increases in the age of the housewife.

Samples

The use of samples is based on the idea that the best salesman for the product is the product itself. This obviously limits sampling to products of genuine merit. This method of promotion is also limited to products of low unit value and frequent purchase. Samples of high unit value products are too costly. If goods are not used or purchased frequently, the effect of the sample is forgotten before there is occasion to purchase such a product. Typical of items promoted by samples are cigarettes, cosmetics, drugs, prepared breakfast cereals, tooth paste and powder, baby food, and candy. Samples are often prepared in special packages, the size of which is determined by the minimum quantity that permits a reasonable trial of the item. Samples are distributed in a number of ways. Products of widespread use and very low unit value are often distributed free to all consuming units in selected areas, either through the mails or by house-to-house canvassers specially employed for the purpose. Another method of free distribution is through retail stores selling the product. Still a third method is publicizing the availability of the sample in advertisements. When this is done, a person desiring a sample has to take direct action in order to obtain it, with the result that distribution is restricted to those who show definite interest. In order to restrict distribution still further, a nominal charge is sometimes advertised in connection with the offer.

While an old form of sales promotion, sampling has grown greatly in importance, owing to an enlarging flow of new products. It is often combined with some other forms of sales promotion as, for example, the use of coupons providing a strong special-price incentive for actual subsequent purchase of the product which has been sampled.

Demonstrations

Demonstrations are often effective for products of a technical nature, for products having a variety of uses, or when the proper use or application of the product is not readily apparent. They vary in scope from elaborate field test demonstrations frequently conducted by farm implement manufacturers, to the free home demonstration of a television set for a limited trial period, or to the operation of hand wound mechanical toys on the variety store counter. In the cosmetics trade, use of manufacturer-trained and compensated demonstrators in retail stores has been a common practice. Such demonstrators are loaned to large department stores and are known as hidden demonstrators because their true employer is not usually known to the consuming public. The store benefits because it does not have to pay wages to the demonstrator but nevertheless realizes its normal gross margin of profit on all sales resulting from the demonstrator's efforts. The manufacturer benefits by having his own representative in contact with the consuming public in an influential retail establishment. The widespread use of manufacturer compensated demonstrators in large retail stores has resulted in a number of court cases brought under the provision of the Robinson-Patman Act that prohibits advertising allowances unless they are made available on proportionally equal terms to all customers.

When a seller makes demonstrators available to large retail stores, he must ordinarily provide smaller stores handling the line with some promotional service or allowance of proportionally equal value. Samples and demonstrations differ from premiums, coupons, and contests in their purpose which is that of educating the consumer in the use and value of the product. Emphasis is upon the merits of the merchandise rather than upon unrelated appeals.

Sales Promotion by Retailers

Retail sales promotion activities are motivated principally by the desire to attract patronage and secondarily by the intention of selling particular items of merchandise. Sales promotion activities, other than regular advertising in local media, are so numerous and diverse that they are very difficult to classify. For purposes of this brief discussion, it may be helpful to group them into two broad categories. First, there are many sales promotion efforts which are closely identified with the kind of merchandise or services offered by a store.

A few familiar examples include window and special interior displays of merchandise, fashion shows by apparel retailers, cooking schools by household appliance dealers, model homes decorated by furniture stores, and provision of special shopping services for male customers in women's stores during important gift buying seasons. When such activities are soundly conceived and administered, they are beneficial to merchants and are also laudable from a social viewpoint. They often build long-run good will for the sponsoring establishment as well as contribute directly to immediate sales volume gains. They also may be productive of consumer satisfaction by the utilization of merchandise that would not otherwise be purchased, or by the better utilization of merchandise or services thus promoted.

A second type of sales promotional activity embodies those which have no basic relationship to the store using them. Common illustrations include automobiles or other prizes given away as a result of drawings for which patronage is required for eligibility, free gifts of toys for children who visit an establishment in company with their parents, punch cards which entitle the customer to purchase non related merchandise items at a substantial discount after purchasing a certain volume of goods, and trading stamps redeemable in merchandise distributed by a stamp plan company. From an economic standpoint, activities in this class are almost altogether purely competitive in nature. Their success is largely dependent upon ability to divert patronage from other retailers or to hold patronage which would otherwise be lost to competing stores. Whether such activities have a significant long-run effect upon total consumption is debatable.

The soundness of many activities in this second group may be questioned from the standpoint of retailers. In extreme cases, they are attempts to win patronage by artifice or subterfuge. Large expenditures of managerial time and money for sales promotion devices that are not basically related to the merchandise offerings or character of a particular store may win patronage but on a precarious basis. While new customers may be enticed, they are also easily wooed away by similar stratagems of competitors.

Comparable expenditures in a well-conceived selling programme which is related to demonstrable advantages of the merchant are more productive of lasting benefits, but such a programme is difficult to develop in lines of trade where typical establishments are only weakly differentiated from each other. Such is commonly the case, for example, among gasoline service stations and supermarkets. The competitive character of some retail sales promotion activities may be illustrated with reference to *trading stamp plans* which were used on a wide scale in the depression of the 1930's, virtually disappeared from the scene with the coming of World War II, and experienced an extremely lusty revival in the 1950's.

As a general rule, trading stamps are purchased by retailers from trading stamp companies and distributed to consumers at the rate of one stamp for each 10 cents' worth of consumer purchases. The rate of distribution is such that the stamps cost the retailer about 2 or 3 cents for each dollar of sales. When the consumer accumulates a large quantity of stamps, which are usually pasted in books, they may be redeemed for miscellaneous merchandise and at a redemption value usually about two-thirds of the cost of the stamps. About one third of the stamp cost goes to the stamp company to cover the expenses of its operation and to provide it with a net profit.

When stamp plans are new in a community, the first participating merchants often experience a marked increase in patronage. When rivals retaliate with comparable stamp plans, the competitive advantage is lost and trade is likely to resume its former distribution. These effects are most easily visualized with reference to the grocery field where their use has been most common. It is rather obvious that the use of such stamps will not significantly increase total consumption of food products. When a number of major chain food organizations are involved in competitive stamp plans, it is not possible for them to increase their individual volume to the point that they can absorb the cost of the stamps.

Net profit margins among retail food chains are only about I or at most 2 per cent of sales, which is less than the typical cost of purchasing the stamps. Thus, it is inevitable that the cost of trading stamps, unless substituted for some other form of promotional activity which is eliminated, become an added expense of marketing which must be recovered by merchants in prices paid by consumers for goods sold in connection with trading stamp promotional activity.

The trading stamp industry has become an enormous marketing system in itself for premium merchandise distributed through some 1,600 redemption centre establish-ments operated by stamp companies. In 1960, it was estimated that sales of stamps to retailers were at an annual rate of some $600 million. Assuming a 90 per cent consumer redemption rate, this indicates an annual volume of about $540 million (retail value) of premium merchandise so distributed. The leading company in this field, Sperry & Hutchison (S & H Green Stamps), operated 600 redemption stores in 1960, and its stamps were distributed by some 70,000 retail outlets.

9

Transfer Pricing and Taxation

AN OVERVIEW

A small operation managed by a few individuals was the typical beginning of a large corporation with a hundred operating affiliates dispersed around the world. Decision making was highly centralized and lines of communication were short.

As the company grew, the founding management team found it more difficult to keep matters under control. This problem was greatly exacerbated when operations within the company became physically separated. Centres of activity in different locations called for a different style of management. Funneling of all decisions from diverse locations through a small group of individuals, who no longer possess the necessary intimate awareness of the circumstances surrounding each decision, is a surefire prescription for stifling growth.

Growth is the name of the game for modern corporations. Growth entails individual operating affiliates taking appropriate action to enhance productivity, market share, and the scope of a company's product line. It has been found that operating affiliates physically separated from the parent organization can best achieve these objectives under a decentralized style of management.

Responsibility now falls on the shoulders of the manager of an operating affiliate to make the necessary decisions that will lead to improved financial results, the universal measure of performance. The parent organization takes on a new role as coordinator and monitor of activities now that responsibility for operations has been transferred to the operating units. Far from playing a passive role, the parent organization focuses its attention on optimizing the performance of its semiautonomous operating affiliates.

To do this, the parent organization must establish, and articulate, a set of strategic goals and allocate limited corporate resources to the various operating affiliates to best achieve these goals. It must ensure that the short-term action plans of the operating affiliates are in accord with its long-term plans. Top management positions in the operating affiliates must be filled with individuals capable of leading their affiliates in the right direction and an incentive system must be set up to induce managers to orient their thinking to the goals of the company. Finally, the parent organization must set up a financial reporting and control system to monitor its global operations, to provide necessary information for the making of decisions and to evaluate the performance of the affiliate managers.

Although operating affiliates appear to be semiautono-mous units in that they are given a wide spectrum of decision-making responsibility in managing their local operations, they are not independent centres of corporate activity. They are often united in manufacturing and marketing a common product line, in the course of which they routinely buy and sell finished goods, components, or raw materials from one another. These intra company exchanges of goods, components, and raw materials require a transfer price. The parent organization sets the transfer price after considering various factors with an eye on optimizing corporate perfor-mance as a whole.

Transfer prices are often not negotiated and agreed on by the actual buyers and sellers of the goods and components being shipped between operating affiliates. Yet transfer prices directly affect the revenue and cost of goods sold, and therefore, the profitability of the operating affiliates. Because the affiliate managers are monitored by a financial reporting and control system that scrutinizes their financial results, one can expect that affiliate managers have an entirely different perspective on transfer pricing than the executives of the parent organization. Transfer pricing can easily embroil executives of the parent organization and the managers of operating affiliates in endless disputes. Some firms have even established an administrative panel for reviewing transfer prices to resolve sharp differences of opinion between those responsible for managing operating affiliates and those responsible for setting transfer prices.

TRANSFER PRICES AND TAXES

A global company with operations in many nations must deal with a new dimension of complexity in establishing transfer prices, which is not present when a company operates solely within the confines of a single nation. A company whose operations are within a single nation pays the same taxes on profits regardless of the transfer pricing policy. The consolidation process, whether for financial or tax accounting purposes, eliminates intra company transactions to arrive at either a book profit or a before-tax profit. When a company transacts business through affiliate companies in different nations, however, transfer pricing provides a mechanism for shifting taxable profits between tax jurisdictions.

Tax authorities in various nations are concerned with the notion that transfer pricing, often set by parent organizations outside their jurisdiction, is based on minimizing taxes paid in their jurisdictions. There certainly is an element of truth in this contention, but there are other considerations in administering transfer prices than minimizing taxes. The setting of transfer prices provides a way of moving funds internationally for a variety of purposes, of circumventing currency exchange controls that threaten to choke the operations of a company, of minimizing the deleterious impact of other artificial barriers to trade such as duties and tariffs, and of reducing currency risk exposure.

A transfer pricing policy attempts to satisfy a multiple set of objectives. Some of these objectives call for high transfer prices, whereas others require low transfer prices. A company must select what it considers to be an optimal transfer price, which is a compromise price for best achieving divergent objectives. This optimal transfer price may not be the one that minimizes taxes on profits. The selected transfer price may not be satisfactory both to the local tax authority and to the manager of an affiliate if it reduces the reported profitability of the affiliate. However, setting the transfer price is critical to optimizing the financial performance of the corporation as a whole, given the conditions that prevail at a point in time.

MINIMIZING TAXES

Tax authorities of most countries have guidelines or controls that are expected to be complied with in setting transfer prices. Management is not free to arbitrarily select transfer prices without having to substantiate their transfer price decisions. Nevertheless, there is still an element of choice where a selected transfer price may reduce the tax burden of a company. Suppose that a company consists of a parent organization and two operating affiliates—one in nation A, where the tax rate on profits is 30 per cent, and one in nation B, where the tax rate on profits is 40 per cent. The tax is applied to each affiliate's gross margin for illustrative purposes. The affiliate in nation A makes a product that is entirely sold through the affiliate in nation B. Two cases are considered—a low and a high transfer price.

Table. Case I-Low Transfer Price

	Nation A	Nation B	Consolidated
	Tax 30%	Tax 40%	
Sales	$2000	$3200	$3200
Cost of Goods Sold	1500	2000	1500
Gross Margin	500	1200	1700
Tax	150	480	630
Net Income	$350	$720	$1070

Everything made in a factory in nation A is sold through a marketing organization in nation B. Therefore, total sales in nation A, calculated on the basis of an administered transfer price, is also the cost of goods sold in nation B. Sales in nation B of $3,200 is the net consolidated sales for the company, because all goods produced in nation A are sold in nation B. The actual cost of manufacturing the goods in nation A is $1,500. Because nation B does not add value to the goods, the consolidated cost of goods sold for the company is also $1,500. The consolidated tax is the sum of the $150 and the $480 paid to the tax authorities of nations A and B, respectively. The consolidated net income is $1,070, the sum of the net incomes of the two affiliates.

Suppose that the transfer price is increased from $2,000 to $2,500 for goods shipped between the two affiliates. Consolidated sales, cost of goods sold, and gross margin are unaffected by the change in the transfer price, because it is netted out in the consolidation process. Taxes paid in each nation are no longer the same because of the change in the transfer price. In case II, the increase in the transfer price shifts the profit to Nation A, which has the lower tax rate. The affiliate in nation A earns more taxable income and pays more in taxes than in case I. The affiliate in nation B earns less taxable income and pays less in taxes in case II than in case I. The net effect, as seen by comparing case II with case I, is that the company as a whole is paying less in taxes, which increases its consolidated net income.

It is true that had the two nations the same tax rate, the total taxes paid by the company, and the consolidated net income, would not be affected by changes in the transfer price. Even so, transfer prices determine what portion of total taxes are to be paid to the tax authority in nation A and to the tax authority in Nation B. Although the parent organization may be relatively insensitive concerning to whom it pays taxes, needless to say, the tax authorities are very much concerned as to which is collecting taxes. The problem is compounded, from the point of view of a tax authority, because the transfer price is probably set by a parent organization not under its jurisdiction. The importance of transfer pricing to both managers and tax authorities can be appreciated when it is realised that between 40 per cent and 60 per cent of international trade involves goods moving between affiliates of the same company. Corporate decisions on transfer prices do have a meaningful impact on what a tax jurisdiction collects.

There are nations, islands, and localities where tax authorities exhibit little interest in transfer prices. Ireland, Puerto Rico, and other nations or areas designated as free trade zones or having special tax privileges may not tax corporate profits, or have a very low tax rate. These nations or locales are interested in companies building plants on their soil for the social benefits that accrue from employment of individuals who might otherwise be unemployed. Companies operating in such nations or locales can substantially decrease their overall tax rate. The effective reduction in tax rates depends on the transfer prices of imported components and semifinished goods and the transfer prices of exported finished goods. Granting tax concessions is one way for a nation to attract companies. At this time, eastern European nations offer tax incentives but do not have a prescribed accounting methodology to calculate profits, which makes it impossible to quantify the tax benefit. More than one company has set up an operation in eastern Europe to later discover that the government had a much different version in mind of the nature of the tax benefits than the investors anticipated. Such shortsightedness by government officials has a deleterious impact on attracting other companies.

Many nations are discovering that viewing business solely as a way to fill the public coffers may not be in their long-term best interests. Within the United States, states with high corporate tax rates have experienced companies moving to states with low corporate tax rates.

The higher they raise their corporate tax rates, the less they collect in taxes. As once companies moved from one state to another, now they move from one nation to another. In selecting a potential site, a businessman considers many factors, of which taxes are but one. Some of these are social and political stability; a system of commercial law to resolve disputes; a set of acceptable accounting practices (both to assess tax liabilities and evaluate tax incentives); a labour force with the requisite skills and will to work; and an infrastructure of transportation, communication, and utility and social (education, medical care) services. There are more locations that offer good potential sites for factories than before. Managers no longer feel that their factories must be anchored to one nation and have learned to manage far-flung operations.

Nations must now compete for factories. Tax authorities in developed nations are beginning to realise that they may end up collecting less tax revenue in their eagerness to collect more tax revenue by raising tax rates. The United States was forced to repeal a luxury tax on pleasure boats because pleasure boat construction virtually ceased with the passage of the new tax. New Jersey was forced to repeal a sales tax on trucks when truck selling companies moved their operations to nearby Pennsylvania. In both cases, tax revenues fell when tax rates were raised, and the tax authorities were forced to rescind tax increases. In a global economy, companies are mobile and will relocate to avoid especially burdensome taxes.

INTERNATIONAL FUNDING

Businesses operating in hard currency nations have the advantage of being able to transfer and convert currencies as necessary. Many nations, however, have currencies that lack convertibility, the so-called soft currencies. Transfer pricing provides a means of moving funds from one country to another, when direct currency convertibility is not possible.

If a nation has an affiliate that completes the manufacturing process and sells its output within that nation, funds can be moved out of that nation by increasing the transfer price for goods imported by the affiliate. The same objective can be accomplished by increasing the charges for services rendered by the parent organization to the affiliate, such as selling and administrative (SandA) fees, research and development (RandD) expenses, financial charges on transferred assets, and royalties for rights to patents and dividends. Sometimes currency exchange controls focus on the amount of dividends that can be paid by an affiliate to its parent. A quasi-dividend can be paid by raising the transfer price of goods moving into the nation or by increasing corporate fees, financial charges, and royalty payments. Some nations with severe restrictions on dividend outflows will permit increases in transfer prices and service fees. These quasi-dividend payments are allowed because the local government recognizes that few companies can afford the luxury of investing in a nation that prohibits the company from earning a return on its investment. However, actions such as these that drain funds out of a soft currency nation eventually result in some sort of currency exchange restriction. This often results in affiliate profits accumulating in a currency that may not be particularly desirable. Sometimes currency exchange restrictions can be bypassed by the affiliate making an investment, or lending funds, to an affiliate in another nation.

CONTROLLING REPORTED PROFITS

Shifts in transfer prices, corporate administrative fees, and other parent company charges to an affiliate are means of managing the affiliate's reported profitability. It may be in the interest of a parent organization to lower the reported profitability of an affiliate for reasons other than tax minimization.

These include deflecting union demands for higher wages, reducing political pressure to nationalize or expropriate a profitable affiliate, and dissuading potential competitors from entering the market. Lowering profitability is also a way to counter price controls that limit profitability. If a government has set price controls based on the cost of production plus a limited markup for profits, increases in the transfer price of goods sent to the affiliate lowers the profit margin of goods sold in that nation. This may permit goods to be sold at government decreed profit margins with the company as a whole still able to earn its normal profits.

A few nations have tax rates that are linked to profitability. The greater the profitability, the higher the tax rate. The logic behind this taxation policy is that there is a level of profits on investment that seems"excessive" to the government. Such excessive profitability should be punished by the government, and there is no greater punishment than taking away the excess profits through a higher tax rate. By increasing the transfer price of goods being imported into the nation, the degree of profitability is decreased, lowering the tax rate and, presumably, restoring respectability in the eyes of the government. Alternatively, it may be in the interests of the parent organization to enhance the profitability of an affiliate. This may be done by lowering the transfer price

of imported goods. One reason for enhancing the profitability of an affiliate is to provide sufficient financial resources to the affiliate for it to withstand price cutting by competitive companies. Improving an affiliate's profitability, even at the cost of paying more in taxes, may allow the affiliate to borrow needed funds for operation from local banks and other financial institutions, to improve its credit rating to qualify for lower interest loans and to fund capital outlays from its own resources.

CIRCUMVENTING EXCHANGE CONTROLS

Governments with soft currencies often limit the amount of their currency that companies operating in their nations can exchange for other currencies. Their motivation is to discourage the selling of the domestic soft currency and the buying of a hard currency, which would exert downward pressure on the value of the local currency. In other words, exchange controls are set up to keep a soft currency from becoming softer.

From the point of view of a parent organization, restricting hard currency outflows inhibits an affiliate's ability to pay for imported components or other items necessary for its operations. Transfer prices for the needed components can be kept artificially low to expand the volume of goods that are being imported into a soft currency nation. This sustains an affiliate's manufacturing operation without exceeding government decreed restrictions on converting soft currency to hard currency. But there is an adverse consequence because such a course of action results in a parent corporation accumulating even larger amounts of soft currency. These holdings of soft currency are constantly losing purchasing power through inflation.

The soft currency cannot be converted to a more desirable currency because of currency exchange restrictions and the soft currency, which has little value within the nation, has no value outside the nation. One of the knottiest problems associated with an operating affiliate in a soft currency nation is funding of hard currency imports necessary for its operation and obtaining a hard currency return on a hard currency investment.

Some companies will not set up an operation in a soft currency nation unless there is a prearranged means to earn hard currency to pay for hard currency imports and to provide a hard currency return on a hard currency investment.

Pepsi Cola struck a barter deal for producing its soft drink in the former Soviet Union. Its soft ruble revenue, net of soft ruble expenses, is exchanged for Russian built tankers, which are then sold for hard currencies. Oil companies will not set up operations in the Commonwealth of Independent States, and other soft currency nations, unless they receive a share of the output, which is shipped out of the nation and sold for hard currency.

The easiest way for a company to earn hard currency in a soft currency nation would be to export a portion of its output to hard currency nations. However, most soft currency nations do not permit the hard currency revenue to remain with the company. The hard currency revenue is exchanged for an equivalent amount of soft currency, which is then credited to the exporter's bank account.

In essence, the national government receives the hard currency revenue from exports and pays soft currency to the exporter. Sometimes international banks are at fault for imposing this condition on a nation as a means to guarantee repayment of international debt. Regardless of whether the nation or the international banks impose this condition, it is self-defeating because the economic development of a developing nation is held back by the inability of companies to earn sufficient hard currency to justify their investments.

MINIMIZING DUTIES AND TARIFFS

Duties and tariffs imposed on goods imported into a nation can be reduced by lowering the transfer price. This is the exact opposite of reducing taxes on profits by increasing the transfer price. Because the tariff rate is usually less than the tax rate on profits, lowering transfer prices to reduce import tariffs often results in a higher tax on profits.

In some nations, however, tariffs on certain imported goods and commodities are not set by a corporate-determined transfer price but by an internationally posted price. This can be done only for generic goods (steel) or commodities (oil), where there is an active market with published and verifiable prices. Sometimes tax authorities will reference costs not to a "transfer price" cost but to an internationally agreed standard. One example of this is tanker rates in the oil business. An oil company can manage the profitability, and therefore, the tax liability, of a refinery by the transfer price associated with international tanker transportation for moving oil to and from a refinery.

The tax authorities of many nations and the oil companies have agreed to a panel of experts determining a fair and representative tanker rate that is used for the computation of taxes independent of the transfer price, or internal cost, that oil companies charge for shipping oil among their affiliates. This eliminates arguments between tax authorities and oil companies concerning the appropriate shipping charge.

Determining the optimal transfer-pricing policy is further complicated when a nation in which an affiliate operates has an export subsidy programme or provides a tax credit on the value of exports. It may be advantageous to lower transfer prices to an affiliate whose output is exported to third parties or other affiliates in other nations to take advantage of these tax incentives.

The optimal transfer price depends on the nature of the export subsidy or tax credit, the volume of the affiliate's output that is exported from the nation, the relationship between taxes on profits and the generation of tax credits and on the capacity of the affiliate to utilize the tax credit or export subsidy. The nature of the taxes paid in a nation in the form of income taxes, duties and tariffs on imported goods, and export subsidies or tax credits on exported goods influence the setting of transfer prices.

There is no hard and fast rule on whether a high or a low transfer-pricing policy is best for a company. The particular circumstances of a company's operations in a nation and the nature of taxes and subsidies determine the best transfer-pricing policy.

A transferpricing system integrated into a financial reporting and control system should be capable of analyzing "what" if scenarios to evaluate the effect of different transfer-pricing policies.

REDUCING CURRENCY EXCHANGE RISK

Changes in currency exchange rates result in transaction and translation gains and losses. More importantly, they affect the competitive position of an affiliate. If an affiliate manufactures and markets its goods in a nation, and imports components from another nation, a revaluation of the currency where the finished goods are being sold relative to the currency of its purchased components reduces manufacturing costs.

This makes the affiliate more competitive and profitable. A devaluation, on the other hand, increases the cost of imported components, making the affiliate less competitive and less profitable.

Reality is much more complex than this simple example because affiliates may export and import components and finished goods to and from a variety of nations. Changes in exchange rates benefit some affiliates and hurt others, and it may not be obvious because of the nature of buying and selling of goods and services.

It is possible that a change in currency exchange rates that is adverse to a particular affiliate may be beneficial to the company as a whole because of the nature of the net exposure of the company to the affected currencies. Adjustments to transfer prices may affect currency holdings before an anticipated change in exchange rates takes place and may be able to restore a company's competitive position after the change has taken place.

Therefore, a financial reporting and control system should have the capacity to assess changes to both transfer prices and currency exchange rates to enable the parent organization to respond both to anticipated changes in currency exchange rates and to subsequent shifts in its competitive position.

TRANSFER PRICING AND JOINT VENTURES

A joint venture partner, a local partner owning a portion of an affiliate, and a minority shareholder are going to be as interested in transfer pricing as the local tax authority. Less often, a partnership is structured on the basis of a claim, or royalty, on revenue. More often, it is a claim on profits.

If one party to a venture or partnership can influence revenue, costs, and profitability through transfer pricing, then the other party or partner, or a minority shareholder, will be deservedly concerned. One way to manage transfer pricing with regard to having partners or minority shareholders is to formalize the setting of transfer prices in some verifiable manner such as a set markup above costs, another is to reference transfer prices to an observable market transaction.

Either way minimizes the opportunity for one party to a partnership or joint venture to manipulate transfer prices to its advantage. If the partners, participants, and minority shareholders feel that their interests are vulnerable by virtue of the other party to a business venture controlling transfer prices, then they may not contribute to the venture that which was expected of them.

Avoiding these problems can be more easily said than done. Some years ago, Ford Motor Company purchased the minority shares of its partially owned subsidiaries because the company felt that it could not administer transfer pricing in a way that was fair to all concerned.

Some managements have made the strategic decision not to enter into joint ventures, or have local partners or minority shareholdings in corporate affiliates, where they can manage the profitability of the venture through transfer prices. Sometimes, the solution for a problem is to avoid the problem.

TRANSFER PRICING AND MANAGERIAL PERFORMANCE EVALUATION

It may be in the interest of the corporation as a whole to transfer in components that are more highly priced than those an affiliate can purchase from other sources. It may be in the interest of the corporation as a whole to transfer goods made in one affiliate to another affiliate for less than what the affiliate can sell them for to third parties. Although the corporation may gain by such a set of transfer prices for goods moving among affiliates, it does not serve the interests of the affiliate managers if they are subsequently judged on profitability. This dichotomy of purpose in establishing a transfer-pricing policy for the good of the whole company, yet holding managers of affiliates accountable for profits that are contaminated, so to speak, by transfer prices has not been successfully addressed when transfer prices are different from market prices.

In fact, this is one potent argument in favour of companies having transfer pricing policies based on the market price for comparable goods. If transfer prices are set at the price for goods exchanged between unrelated parties, then there is no dichotomy of purpose in setting transfer prices and measuring performance. Managers of affiliates can be judged in an unbiased fashion on the profitability of their operations because they are buying and selling at market prices—the same prices that would prevail if they were independent companies.

The disadvantage of letting the market set transfer prices is that the parent corporation can no longer utilize transfer pricing as a means to pursue the overall optimization of the financial performance of the corporation. One possible approach to the dysfunctional aspects of setting transfer prices at other than market prices and measuring management performance of affiliates is to isolate and separately state the amount of inter company "profit" or "loss" that each affiliate is experiencing in its transactions with other affiliates. This approach provides the parent organization with information on whether an affiliate is suffering from unwarranted decreased profitability or enjoying unwarranted increased profitability because of transfer pricing.

SETTING TRANSFER PRICES BY COST OF PRODUCTION

There are two general approaches for setting transfer prices: the cost of production and market prices associated with third party, or unrelated, transactions. The cost-of-production approach bases the price of goods to be transferred between affiliates on the variable cost of production, an allowance for fixed costs that are general in nature and are apportioned over the entire product line, and an allowance for fixed costs that can be apportioned among the individual products.

This latter category usually includes research and development costs and selling and administrative costs. The remaining components may include financial fees and royalties associated with tangible and intangible assets to be apportioned to individual products and the selection of an appropriate profit margin.

The variable cost of production includes labour, material, and other direct costs that are consumed in the production of an item. If the policy of the company is to hire and fire (lay off) factory workers as production rises and falls, then labour is a variable cost. If a company is reluctant to let go of their workers when sales decline, then factory labour should be considered part of fixed costs. Factory labour costs are usually part variable and part fixed. Other variable costs can be the unit financing and utility costs associated with machinery and processes used in the manufacture of a particular product and unit shipping costs. These costs can also be treated as fixed costs depending on how the company's cost accounting system is set up.

Fixed costs are all costs not included in variable costs. Fixed costs are the financing or depreciation costs of the factory; the overhead costs of marketing, accounting, and supervision; the cost of inventories, warehouses, insurance, utilities, communication, property taxes, and other non-variable cost items.

Fixed costs may not be entirely fixed in that there is some variation as production levels change. For instance, bonuses, which would be considered part of the fixed costs of having an executive suite, rise and fall with profits, which are related to production levels. The number of staff personnel in marketing, accounting, engineering, and other overhead functions can vary with the production level. Some elements of fixed costs are allocated in the transfer price setting mechanism in a way that fairly apportions the fixed cost burden among the various products. Other elements of fixed costs can be apportioned more on the basis of the benefit derived by an individual product. One of these is research and development, where the allocation can be made over a product line in proportion to the degree of RandD expenditures associated with the development of an individual product.

Although there is general agreement that this is a fair way to apportion RandD expenses of successful undertakings, there is lack of agreement on how to apportion RandD expenses for failed projects.

Some maintain that the allocation of expenses associated with failed RandD projects should be apportioned to all products on the basis that every product should bear the risk of failed RandD efforts. Others object on the grounds that had the RandD effort succeeded, a particular product might not have benefited. Therefore, it makes no sense for the transfer price to contain the cost of a failed RandD effort, which, had it succeeded, would not be part of the transfer price of the product.

The question as to the proper treatment of failed RandD projects is not an internal accounting matter. Tax authorities are interested in who takes the write off of a failed RandD project. In the United States, the Internal Revenue Service (IRS) is concerned whether a transfer price contains a provision for failed RandD expenditures.

If a transfer price contains only that portion of RandD expenditures that were successful with regard to a particular product, then failed RandD projects of a U.S. corporation are being written off solely against U.S. income. A portion of the tax loss write-off is passed on to the tax authority of another nation by including an element of failed RandD expenditures in the transfer price.

Another fixed cost element that can be separated and apportioned in a different manner than general fixed costs are services provided to an individual product.

These may be coordination and control expenses associated with a product; costs for enhancing the efficiency of operations for manufacturing the product or expanding the scope of its market; and the costs of recruiting and training of management and operations personnel associated with manufacturing, marketing, and repairing or servicing the product. The allocation of these service costs to individual products provides another element in deriving their transfer prices.

The derivation of the transfer price also includes elements for tangibles and intangibles associated with a product. Tangibles are the plant, equipment, and other physical assets dedicated to the manufacture of the product. Part of the transfer price provides a financial return for tangibles based on their value. Intangibles represent the technical knowledge and expertise and applicable patents that can be allocated to a particular product. The transfer price also contains an element that provides a company with a return on intangibles.

Intangible costs within a transfer price cannot be capriciously determined by management because intangible costs affect taxable profits. For this reason, the IRS has established guidelines for determining the intangible cost element in a transfer price.

An intangible cost element must be present if there are intangible costs associated with the manufacture or marketing of a product and must be so identified. Intangible costs can be proportioned in relation to the income attributable to the intangibles by units of production, sales, net or gross profits, or other reasonable methods. The fee for intangible property incorporated in a transfer price must be similar to what would have been arranged with an independent third party.

The last part of the cost approach in setting transfer prices is determining the proper profit margin on the goods made by one affiliate and shipped to another. This may be the average profit margin for the company as a whole or a profit margin associated with a specific product line. Regardless, the stipulated profit margin must be reconciled in some manner with the profitability of the company or a product line to satisfy the tax authorities.

The need for reconciliation of the profit and the various cost elements of the transfer price with the tax authorities sometimes results in the tax group within the finance department of a company being responsible for administering transfer prices.

However, this choice may hinder general management from using transfer prices as a means to achieve corporate objectives. The chief advantage of the cost of production approach for setting transfer prices is that the costs are available and are subject to quantification. For this reason, the production cost approach has been more common in the past than the market price approach.

The chief disadvantage is that there is no real incentive for an affiliate to improve its manufacturing process, to enhance its efficiency, or to take steps to lower costs. Mistakes, errors, inefficiencies in manning or machinery, management inattention to detail, worker carelessness, and excessive remuneration of white and blue collar workers alike may all be incorporated in the determination of costs and passed on to the affiliates in the transfer price. Another disadvantage is that both the tax authority and the affiliates may object to the nature of the apportionment of RandD, SandA, tangibles, and intangibles among the various products and the assigned profit margin.

SETTING TRANSFER PRICES BY MARKET PRICES

The disadvantages associated with the cost-of-production method of setting transfer prices can be mostly avoided by referencing transfer prices to third party transactions for identical, or nearly identical, products.

If an affiliate can obtain the item being purchased from a third party for a certain price, then that price can be the basis for setting the transfer price. The proponents of market-oriented transfer prices maintain that letting the market set the transfer price is inherently more fair than a production-cost-based system because one affiliate is not supporting the inefficiencies of another.

If an affiliate receives only the global competitive price for its products, then there is an incentive for it to take whatever actions are needed to correct the inefficiencies in its operations that are resulting in higher costs.

In a truly decentralized operation, managers are expected to make their decisions on an independent basis, and unrelated companies are permitted to compete for the business of an affiliate, along with other affiliates. The parent organization does not set transfer prices and has little or no influence over the decisions made by the managers of the affiliates. No favour or special consideration is shown to fellow affiliates in the competitive process of selecting suppliers for components and goods. The hope, of course, is that everyone is kept on his or her competitive toes to produce salable goods at the lowest possible cost.

This managerial philosophy, where each affiliate is treated as an independent company, is sometimes referred to as the small business unit (SBU) management philosophy. The disadvantage is that, although each affiliate is focused on optimizing its operations, the end result may be suboptimal performance of the corporation as a whole. Suppose that affiliate X produces all of a component (part X) for a number of widget manufacturing affiliates. Total demand for part X is 2 million per year.

Affiliate X has $10 million in fixed annual costs, which include a profit margin on the investment in manufacturing facilities plus a return on the RandD investment for the development of part X. The variable costs for manufacturing part X is $5. The transfer price based on the fixed and variable costs of affiliate X supplying all other affiliates with part X is $10.

Table. Volume Of Sales: 2,000,000

Fixed Costs	$10,000,000
Variable Costs at $5 per Unit	10,000,000
Total Costs	$20,000,000
Transfer Price Based on Cost of Making 2,000,000	$10.00

Affiliate A is free to cut its best deal and obtains a quote of $9.50 from another company. Affiliate A does what is best for maximizing its profits and purchases 200,000 part X's from a third party for $9.50 rather than pay $10 to affiliate X. Affiliate X has lost a contract for 200,000 part X's and now operates on a basis of a sales volume of 1,800,000 per year.

Table. Volume Of Sales: 1,800,000

Fixed Costs	$10,000,000
Variable Costs at $5 per Unit	9,000,000
Total Costs	$19,000,000
Transfer Price Based on Cost of Making 1,800,000	$10.56

The remaining affiliates must pay a higher price because there is less sales volume to cover the fixed costs of affiliate X. The increase in transfer price to cover the fixed and variable costs is essentially equivalent to treating fixed costs as a component of variable costs, which it is not. Nevertheless, affiliate X must cover all its costs. When affiliate X announces the increase in price, affiliate B concludes a deal with a third party at $9.75 causing another loss of 200,000 for affiliate X.

Table. Volume Of Sales: 1,600.000

Fixed Costs	$10,000,000
Variable Costs at $5 per Unit	8,000,000
Total Costs	$18,000,000
Transfer Price Based on cost of Making 1,600,000	$11.25

Now it's time for affiliate C to say goodbye to affiliate X, as it maximizes its profit by reducing the cost of part X by paying $10.50 to another outside source. This is higher than the $10 price that applied when all the affiliates received part X from affiliate X. It is clear from the continuation of this exercise that, as each affiliate maximizes its profits by cutting costs, the corporation as a whole is being sub optimized. Even if the various affiliates do not pay more than an average price of $10 per unit for part X in purchasing all part X's from outside sources, the global company is stuck with an affiliate with no sales and a fixed annual cost of $10 million that represents, in large measure, financing costs on plant and equipment.

It is highly likely that the fixed costs in affiliate X contain an allowance for RandD expenses and product development that have to be recouped in the operation of a company, but do not have to be recouped by another company if it is essentially manufacturing a copy of part X. Copying is fairly common in global commerce because patent protection is limited to the nation issuing the patent. Global companies often obtain patents in a number of nations, but this may not be possible for all nations.

A company may manufacture a copy of a product in one of these nations. Although it is true that affiliate X is free to pursue patent infringement action against sales in a particular nation where it has patent protection, the time involved in enforcement proceedings and the legal expenses may make such protection prohibitively expensive. Furthermore, there is no internationally recognized legal structure to handle patent infringements.

In addition to RandD expenses, the fixed costs of affiliate X may also contain a service element for the benefit of the affiliates purchasing its output that may not be provided by third parties. By each affiliate "doing its own thing," the RandD and service costs cannot be covered. One principal problem associated with using market reference points for transfer pricing is that the affiliates may be shipping components and parts that are not readily available from other firms.

Most components and parts are specifically designed for a company's product line and are not available from third parties unless contracted for by an affiliate. Market prices for similarly designed components that cannot be actually used in the company's product line may not be relevant. Moreover, the quality inherent in third-party quotes for similar parts may not be up to the standards imposed on products made within a global corporate family.

There is no easy answer as to which approach for determining transfer prices should be followed. Both have their adherents and detractors. Either approach restricts transfer prices to something related to third-party, or market, transactions or to the cost of manufacture. Surveys have shown that nations seem to exhibit cultural preferences as to which approach to follow and as to what motivates companies in setting transfer prices.

Companies in some countries favour costbased transfer prices, whereas companies in other nations favour market-based transfer prices. U.S. based corporations have historically preferred setting transfer prices by the cost approach because the necessary data is available, whereas the necessary data for setting transfer prices on the basis of market transactions may not be available. Oftentimes, market quotes for uniquely designed parts and components may have to be derived rather than observed because there are no market transactions for the precise item.

Should General Motors set its transfer price on carburetors being shipped to Europe based on its cost of production or on what Toyota charges its U.S. transplants? The two carburetors are not the same and do not have the same cost of production. Furthermore, there may not be a data base available for prices for carburetors sold between related and unrelated parties from which to derive a market price.

Preferences change with time. Surveys done in the 1970s indicated that the preponderance of U.S. companies were motivated by tax minimization in setting transfer prices. More recent surveys indicate that companies are more interested in setting transfer prices on the basis of measuring the performance of affiliate managers and of providing reliable and unbiased information for the making of decisions.

This change in attitude in U.S. companies may be the result of the United States becoming a relative tax haven compared to other nations. Its corporate tax rate of 34 per cent, plus state taxes, is less than in many other industrialized nations, where tax rates range between 40 per cent and 55 per cent. A U.S. company's total tax bill may, in fact, be reduced by allocating more profits to the United States. Regardless of changes in attitudes as to what is important in setting transfer prices, the essential point is that there is no unanimity on which approach to use and on what motivates companies in setting transfer prices.

Up to this point, an important assumption has been that the parent company has real control over transfer prices to manage corporate cash flows and the profits reported by affiliates and to overcome artificial barriers to trade in the form of custom duties, currency exchange, and price controls. Some recent surveys suggest that competitive forces and market conditions within a nation seem to be more important in setting transfer prices than decisions made by a parent organization. If transfer prices are being set by exogenous commercial forces, then the presumption that a parent organization is able to achieve optimal financial performance of a global family of affiliates through the careful orchestration of transfer pricing is being challenged.

TAX CONSIDERATIONS

Taxation and transfer pricing are intimately entwined, because transfer pricing of goods, parts, and components moving in and out of a nation has a direct impact on taxes on profits and on the amount of duties and tariffs paid to the tax authority. The discussion on transfer pricing based on the cost-of-production approach shows an intimate involvement with the tax authority in the methodology for calculating various elements of the transfer price. There is little uniformity on taxation among nations. Taxes range from taxation of a corporation's activities to the "water's edge" or on its global earnings, the so-called "unitary tax." The state of California invented the unitary tax in the 1930s when movie companies in California began moving out of the state to avoid state taxes. A unitary tax was applied against the global earnings of a company and the tax was determined by the proportion of a company's sales, property, and payroll within the state to its global sales, property, and payroll. The resulting tax had no relation to the degree of profitability of a company's operation in California. A company could operate at a loss in California and still pay a tax based on its global profits.

Needless to say, both foreign governments and multinational companies have vigourously fought the unitary tax. A number of court decisions confirmed or restricted unitary taxation over the years. Ultimately, opposition to the unitary tax succeeded. In November 1991, Alaska was the last state to abandon having a company's state tax liability based on the global earnings of the company. The unitary tax still exists in a truncated form, where earnings are restricted to the "water's edge." The state tax is calculated on the portion of a company's activities within a state as compared to its activities within the United States.

Although most other countries limit their assessment on what is to be taxed to the operations of a company within their jurisdiction, there is no universal agreement as to what constitutes revenue and expenses in the calculation of taxable income and no uniformity on tax rates. Every nation decides what is subject to taxation and the applicable tax rates. The complexity of tax regulations, in general, and the diversity of tax laws among nations are such that it is necessary for an affiliate to retain the technical expertise necessary to understand and comply with local tax regulations. The parent organization must retain the technical knowledge for its own tax jurisdiction and have sufficient knowledge of tax matters elsewhere to coordinate tax planning among the various affiliates.

The vigour with which tax payments are enforced varies among nations. Some countries with seemingly high tax rates permit an underground economy to flourish without much in the way of enforcing tax payments. The other side of the coin is the willingness of companies to adhere to tax laws. In some nations, a businessman who scrupulously follows the tax laws and pays what is owed to the tax authority will find himself at a competitive disadvantage.

NATURE OF TAXES

Taxes can be direct or indirect. The United States relies more on direct taxation, which is applied to each taxable entity. A U.S. corporation is taxed at 34 per cent on its profits. If a corporation pays a dividend to its shareholders, then the next taxable entity, the individual, pays a tax, which may be 28 per cent or more. This is double taxation. Some nations, such as Germany, have two corporate tax rates on profits—one for retained profits and the other for distributed profits in the form of dividends. A lesser tax rate applies to profits that are distributed to shareholders to reduce the degree of double taxation.

Europe relies more on indirect taxes—particularly, the value added tax (VAT). The VAT is basically a tax applied to each stage of the production process and is not directly associated with the degree of profitability. Indeed, only a small portion of a VAT is associated with profits. Suppose that a company's manufacturing operations has the following financial results.

Wages, rents, interest, profit	$400,000
Outside purchases of goods and services for which VAT has already been paid	600,000
Total sales	$1,000,000

The additive method is to apply the VAT rate, say 10 per cent, to all costs associated with the production of goods, including profit and excluding purchases of goods and services from third parties for which the VAT has already been paid. In this case, $400,000 of a company's activities falls into this category resulting in a VAT of $40,000. A simpler method of calculation is to take the gross sales of the company ($1,000,000), subtract all purchases of goods and services for which VAT has already been paid ($600,000), and apply the VAT rate to the balance ($400,000). Either method yields the same result. The VAT is essentially equivalent to a national sales tax, because every company associated with the production and marketing of goods and providing services pays a tax on whatever value it adds to the goods or services. The value added tax, like a sales tax, is a tax on consumption, whereas U.S. taxes are on income and profits.

Value added tax rates vary widely from country to country and according to the nature of the business. Certain European countries have low VAT rates (5 per cent) for business transactions associated with food and high VAT rates (40 per cent) for luxury products. Others attempt to have one rate that applies to most forms of commerce. Because the VAT is not paid on items that have already been exposed to a value added tax, and with the European economy becoming more integrated, there is a powerful incentive for the European Community to harmonize VAT rates and coordinate the handling of VAT payments for products or components shipped between members of the European Community.

The amounts of value added by a company are frequently disclosed in European financial statements. In the excerpt from the British company, the company had gross revenues of 3,213 million pounds in 1987 of which 919.1 million pounds represents added value by the company. Of the total of 919.1 million pounds of added value, 496.8 million pounds was paid to the company's employees, 157.1 million pounds was paid in taxes to government tax authorities, and the remainder was paid to the internal and external providers of capital.

U.S. TAXATION OF GLOBAL COMPANIES

Nations have different ways of taxing global companies domiciled within their jurisdiction. If a parent corporation is domiciled in the United States, it does not pay taxes in the United States on profits earned by incorporated affiliates in other nations, unless the nation is considered a tax haven. This, in the United States, is known as Subpart F income, which will be discussed later under rein voicing centres. Unlike an incorporated affiliate, a branch of a U.S. company located in a foreign nation is taxed directly on its earnings regardless of whether the earnings are remitted to the home office or not. The taxes paid on remitted and unremitted earnings are not the same, in that unremitted earnings have to be translated to U.S. dollars before a tax liability can be assessed, and therefore, are influenced by changes in currency exchange rates. Taxes can also be calculated on the basis of the increase in the net worth of the branch, which can also be affected by changes in currency exchange rates. Sometimes a U.S. company will first open a branch operation in another country to permit startup losses to flow back to the parent organization. When the branch becomes profitable, it may be reorganized as a wholly owned subsidiary, reducing the company's overall tax liability.

U.S. based companies usually operate in the global market through operating affiliates whose stock is owned by the parent corporation. The parent corporation pays U.S. taxes only on the profits generated from dividends, royalties, and other service payments and fees paid by a non-U.S. domiciled affiliate to the parent organization. Taxes paid on profits by affiliates in their nations of domicile can be treated either as a tax credit or a tax deduction by the parent organization in the calculation of its U.S. taxes. To the degree that a tax paid on profits to a foreign government is treated as a tax credit, the net effect of a company paying taxes on its profits in a foreign country is that these taxes are essentially paid for by the U.S. government foregoing an equivalent amount of U.S. source based tax revenue.

Obviously, taxes paid to foreign governments must pass certain criteria set forth by the Internal Revenue Service to be considered for a tax credit. Foreign tax credits apply to taxes paid on foreign source profits calculated in a conventional way as U.S. source profits. Tax credits are also available for foreign government withholding taxes on dividends, interest payments, and royalties paid by a foreign-based affiliate to a U.S. parent company. There is a maximum permissible limit on tax credits linked to the ratio of foreign source income to total worldwide income multiplied by the tax liability of U.S. operations. This effectively limits the foreign tax credit to the U.S., not the foreign, tax rate. A company doing business in a nation with a higher tax rate on profits than in the United States does not receive a tax credit equal to the taxes paid to the foreign government. The tax credit is based on the U.S. tax rate. With U.S. tax rates being lower than in most other industrialized nations, U.S. based global companies are not being fully compensated by tax credits on foreign income taxes. This may provide an incentive to shift taxable income back to the United States through changes in transfer prices.

The U.S. tax authorities permit a credit for taxes paid on profits to other nations under the notion of tax equity and tax neutrality. The principle of tax equity implies that a U.S. taxpaying entity with an operation in another nation should not pay more in taxes than having the operation domiciled in the United States.

Were the equity principle absolutely true, a U.S. taxpaying entity would be indifferent, or neutral, to whether the operation was located in another nation or in the United States. Some maintain that the U.S. tax code does not adhere to the tax neutrality principle because a company doing business in New York City does not obtain a tax credit on its federal taxes for taxes paid to the state and city of New York on profits made in their jurisdiction.

A company with an affiliate in another nation not only receives a tax credit, which neutralizes its foreign and U.S. income taxes, but does not have to pay U.S. taxes on its foreign source earnings until those earnings are remitted to the parent in the form of a dividend, a royalty payment, or an equivalent thereof.

As long as foreign source profits remain in the coffers of the affiliate, no taxes are due to the U.S. government, even though, under special circumstances, the affiliate may lend these funds to the parent company. Deferral of dividend payments is essentially an interest-free loan made by the U.S. government to the foreign affiliate of a U.S. parent company on the amount of U.S. taxes due if, and when, these funds are repatriated to the U.S. parent. The principles of equity and neutrality built into the U.S. tax code were designed to provide an incentive for U.S. firms to invest overseas as part of the national policy of rebuilding war-torn nations. U.S. companies would be better off confining their activities within the United States, and would not invest in foreign affiliates, if the profits of these foreign affiliates were exposed to double taxation. Qualified foreign taxes, which cannot be utilized as tax credits, may be used as a tax deduction. A tax deduction is not as valuable as a tax credit. Tax deductions apply when there is not sufficient U.S. taxes to be shielded by tax credits, or where the overall limitation on tax credits has been exceeded. Tax deductions can be carried back or carried forward, whichever is more useful.

REIN VOICING CENTRES

Some companies have set up rein voicing centres to manage all intra company trading of products. A rein voicing centre is at a single location, buying the output of the manufacturing affiliates and selling it to the marketing affiliates. Each affiliate receives or pays in its own currency, thus concentrating all intra company transaction currency exposure at the rein voicing centre. The centre possesses the necessary data to assess the net currency exposure of intra company transactions and can enter into appropriate currency hedges. The centre may also receive better quotes from currency exchange dealers because all intra company currency exchange transactions are done at one location.

The rein voicing centre can mark up the price of all products flowing through the centre to cover its administrative expenses. If there is little or no profitability associated with the operations of a rein voicing centre, it does not matter where the rein voicing centre is located from a tax viewpoint. However, it is possible to increase the markup to the point where corporate profit can be diverted from the nations where the goods are manufactured and marketed to the nation where the rein voicing centre is located. Now the location of the rein voicing centre is critical from a tax viewpoint.

In the 1960s, the U.S. government became concerned with the accumulation of profits in rein voicing centres located in tax havens. Tax havens were characterized as nations imposing no, or a very low, tax on profits, having a high degree of bank secrecy, and little or no currency controls. These nations consider financial activities of importance to their economy, provide modern communication facilities, and promote themselves as offshore financial centres. Bahamas, Bermuda, Cayman Islands, Liberia, Panama, and Vanuatu have been identified as tax havens.

It is possible to "run" a rein voicing centre through these nations without a physical presence of personnel or products. Profits can be easily diverted to tax havens by increasing the markup on selling prices, thus reducing tax liabilities to the nations where the products are manufactured and marketed. If the criteria for determining a tax haven is satisfied, then the income earned by a rein voicing centre, or any corporate entity in the declared tax haven, is deemed Subpart F income. This income flows directly to the U.S. parent corporation and is taxed as though the income was earned in the United States.

TAXATION IMPACT ON TRANSFER PRICING

Companies operating in the United States are guided by Section 482 of the Internal Revenue Code when setting transfer prices. Specifically, the IRS, through the Secretary of the Treasury, has the right to "distribute, apportion, or allocate gross income, deductions, credits, or allowances... between or among... businesses, if he determines that such distribution, apportionment, or allocation is necessary in order to prevent evasion of taxes. The IRS has been granted wide latitude to do whatever it wants if the IRS deems that dealings between a U.S. parent and its affiliates do not meet its standards. For instance, the IRS can reallocate income and deductions if loans have been made between a parent corporation and an affiliate at an unrealistic interest rate.

Unrealistic interest rates are those that would not occur for similar transactions between unrelated third parties. This also applies to charging for services and use of property, and transfers of tangible and intangible property including lease payments and royalties. A reference to IRS guidelines has already been made in discussing RandD and intangible costs in setting transfer prices by the production cost approach. Basing transfer pricing on published data rather than corporate derived prices is another example of the close working relationship, voluntary or not, between tax authorities and managers responsible for transfer prices.

In general, the IRS standard for determining transfer pricing, and other dealings between a parent and its affiliates, is whether it is an "arm's-length" transaction—one that would occur between a company and a third party having no affiliation other than the commercial transaction under consideration. This is independent of whether the transfer price is based on the cost of production or on market prices. If the transfer price between affiliates is seemingly out of line with a price that would have been charged to an unrelated party, then the IRS has the right to reallocate income or deductions according to what it feels to be the appropriate transfer price.

The IRS specifies various methods for establishing an appropriate transfer price. The preferred one is the comparable uncontrolled price method where prices are the same for goods sold to affiliated and to nonaffiliated companies. The price for goods sold to an unrelated third party establishes the transfer price for goods transferred to an affiliate.

This method does not work when goods are not sold to third parties, but are totally transferred between affiliates. Under these circumstances, the second method for setting the transfer price is the resale price method. This is the price for which the company would sell the item to an unspecified third party. The third party would add the same comparable value as the affiliate and sell the completed product with an appropriate markup. By netting the market price of the appropriate markup and the value added to the product by an affiliate, one can "back into" an appropriate transfer price from the point of view of the tax authority. The third method is the "cost plus" method, where the IRS permits three different ways of allocating costs (full absorption, direct cost, and incremental cost). All these methods leave some margin of discretion as to what is the appropriate transfer price.

If all these fail, as they frequently do for high-technology products, customised components, or subassemblies, then so-called fourth methods are permitted, such as determining transfer pricing on the basis of a predetermined profit for the foreign firm's operations and, through a netting process of accounting for applicable costs, establishing an appropriate transfer price.

Regardless of the methodology, the burden of proof in supporting a transfer price is with the taxpayer, not the IRS. To confuse matters more, there have been occasions when the tax courts have rejected the notion of arm's-length transfer pricing in settling tax disputes between corporations and the IRS.

OTHER NATIONS' POLICIES CONCERNING TRANSFER PRICING

The tax authority in Canada views transfer pricing of goods similar to the way the United States does. Transfer pricing for services differs in that it is based on a pro rata sharing of actual incurred costs between the parent corporation and its affiliate, and not necessarily at an arm's-length price.

Tax authorities in Japan follow a system comparable to that of the United States. German tax code provisions permit the reallocation of domestic source income if revenue or income has been shifted to another nation through a transaction that is different from those that would have been entered into by unrelated parties. In other words,

transfer pricing should be arm's-length, although the code is not specific in defining arm's-length pricing. The United Kingdom is similar to Germany in not specifically defining arm's-length pricing. The Inland Revenue may adjust taxable income based on fairness and arm's-length criteria. Disputes between corporations and Inland Revenue agents are frequently settled by negotiation, resulting in some sort of compromise between the two parties. This is unlike in Germany, where the adjustments made by the tax authorities are considered final, and unlike in the United States, where adjustments are litigated in tax courts.

Tax authorities in many nations are currently taking a much closer look at transfer pricing practices. Recently, the U.K. Inland Revenue recast the accounts of one non-British company operating in the United Kingdom and assessed back taxes of nearly 2 billion pounds. In the United States, there is growing political pressure for the IRS to take more vigourous action against foreign-owned companies operating through U.S. based affiliates.

This pressure stems from the realization that the aggregate expenses for foreign-owned businesses operating in the United States exceed aggregate revenues. This means that, in the aggregate, foreign-owned subsidiaries are claiming to operate at a loss, although individual foreign-owned subsidiaries may be paying taxes on profits. Some foreign-owned affiliates operating in the United States have a twenty-year string of consecutive losses. This is not considered a realistic appraisal of performance because there are few profit-motivated foreign-based parent companies that would support twenty years of successive losses were they real.

Poor or nonexistent profits for foreign-based affiliates operating in the United States are blamed on transfer pricing. Transfer price manipulation is felt to have resulted in tax underpayments of between $12 and $50 billion. Legislation was passed in 1989 to require foreign-owned businesses in the United States to keep records, in English, of transactions with foreign related parties. Much of this legislation has to do with substantiating transfer pricing on either a cost or arm'slength transaction with an unrelated third party. A growing risk associated with manipulating transfer prices for the purpose of tax minimization.

The risk is that the tax authorities will recast the company's statements with their own version of the proper transfer price, thus exposing a company to the risk of double taxation. Most nations have entered into tax treaties with various other nations with regard to taxing of affiliates of parent organizations domiciled in the treaty nations. These treaties determine withholding taxes on dividends, interest, and royalties; relief from double taxation; and the types of taxes and organizations covered by the treaty. Overall exposure to taxation can be reduced by judicious structuring of the legal corporate entities of a parent company and its affiliates in accordance with the provisions of these treaties.

Some of these treaties contain formal agreements for the mutual examination of the tax returns of affiliates of a parent company. The tax returns of affiliates and parent organizations are exchanged and examined by the tax authorities to determine correct tax liabilities, detect tax avoidance maneuvers, scrutinize trans- fer pricing practices, and exchange information useful to the tax authorities. These treaties also provide a forum for one tax authority to complain about the actions taken by another, when these actions are deemed detrimental to its interests.

Recent developments in international cooperation of tax authorities include the establishment of a formal agreement on transfer prices. The mutual agreement of various nations to reference a published source for tanker rates in determining oil company tax liabilities is an example of this. Australia and the United States are attempting to grant "advance determinations" of the proper transfer price for Australian companies dealings with their U.S. affiliates. A recent survey has shown that about half of IRS tax examinations of multinational companies involve transfer prices. If a mutually agreeable methodology could be arranged between a company and the IRS, many of these tax examinations could be eliminated.

The IRS is attempting to develop a procedure whereby a company and the IRS would mutually agree to a transfer-pricing agreement covering the distribution of finished goods, sales of raw materials and components, general and administrative expenses, and managerial and technical services. If the taxpayer develops an acceptable transfer-pricing methodology, then the taxpayer and the IRS would enter into an advance-pricing agreement. The IRS would limit its examinations to an audit to ensure that the taxpayer has complied with the agreement.

However, the taxpayer is obliged to submit pricing data of independent transactions, or an adequate substitute, to show that the transfer price possesses the necessary attributes of an arm's-length transaction. The taxpayer is also responsible to show that the agreed transfer-pricing methodology is generating acceptable transfer prices from an arm's-length perspective.

The preference of tax authorities in many nations for arm's-length transfer pricing may act as an inducement to switch from the cost-of-production to the market price approach in setting transfer prices because, presumably, they are one and the same. The financial and taxation departments of multinational, or global, companies must deal daily with what are considered to be the most pressing issues in international accounting today. Those involved with transfer pricing must measure the consequences of their transfer-pricing decisions both on corporate profits and on current and potential tax liabilities. Potential tax liabilities, stemming from tax authorities rejecting management's transfer price decisions, and substituting their own, are enormous. This must weigh heavily on the shoulders of those responsible for setting transfer prices.

10

Inventory Management

MANAGEMENT INVENTORY

Inventory is a list for goods and materials, or those goods and materials themselves, held available in stock by a business. Inventory are held in order to manage and hide from the customer the fact that manufacture/supply delay is longer than delivery delay, and also to ease the effect of imperfections in the manufacturing process that lower production efficiencies if production capacity stands idle for lack of materials.

BUSINESS INVENTORY

The Reasons for Keeping Stock

There are three basic reasons for keeping an inventory:

1. *Time*: The time lags present in the supply chain, from supplier to user at every stage, requires that you maintain certain amount of inventory to use in this "lead time"
2. *Uncertainty*: Inventories are maintained as buffers to meet uncertainties in demand, supply and movements of goods.
3. *Economies of scale*: Ideal condition of "one unit at a time at a place where user needs it, when he needs it" principle tends to incur lots of costs in terms of logistics. So Bulk buying, movement and storing brings in economies of scale, thus inventory.

All these stock reasons can apply to any owner or product stage.

- Buffer stock is held in individual workstations against the possibility that the upstream workstation may be a little delayed in long setup or change-over time. This stock is then used while that change-over is happening. This stock can be eliminated by tools like SMED.

These classifications apply along the whole Supply chain not just within a facility or plant. Where these stocks contain the same or similar items it is often the work practice to hold all these stocks mixed together before or after the sub-process to which they relate. This 'reduces' costs. Because they are mixed-up together there is no visual reminder to operators of the adjacent sub-processes or line management of the stock which is due to a particular cause and should be a particular individual's responsibility with inevitable consequences. Some plants have centralized stock holding across sub-processes which makes the situation even more acute.

Special Terms used in Dealing with Inventory

- Stock Keeping Unit (SKU) is a unique combination of all the components that are assembled into the purchasable item. Therefore any change in the packaging or product is a new SKU. This level of detailed specification assists in managing inventory.
- Stockout means running out of the inventory of an SKU.
- "New old stock" (sometimes abbreviated NOS) is a term used in business to refer to merchandise being offered for sale which was manufactured long ago but that has never been used. Such merchandise may not be produced any more, and the new old stock may represent the only market source of a particular item at the present time.

Inventory Examples

While accountants often discuss inventory in terms of goods for sale, organizations - manufacturers, service-providers and not-for-profits - also have inventories (fixtures, furniture, supplies,) that they do not intend to sell. Manufacturers', distributors', and wholesalers' inventory tends to cluster in warehouses. Retailers' inventory may exist in a warehouse or in a shop or store accessible to customers. Inventories not intended for sale to customers or to clients may be held in any premises an organization uses. Stock ties up cash and if uncontrolled it will be impossible to know the actual level of stocks and therefore impossible to control them.

Whilst the reasons for holding stock are covered earlier, most manufacturing organizations usually divide their "goods for sale" inventory into:

- *Raw materials*: Materials and components scheduled for use in making a product.
- *Work in process, WIP*: Materials and components that have begun their transformation to finished goods.
- *Finished goods*: Goods ready for sale to customers.
- *Goods for resale*: Returned goods that are salable.
- Spare parts

MANUFACTURING

A canned food manufacturer's materials inventory includes the ingredients to form the foods to be canned, empty cans and their lids (or coils of steel or aluminum for constructing those components), labels, and anything else (solder, glue,) that will form part of a finished can. The firm's work in process includes those materials from the time of release to the work floor until they become complete and ready for sale to wholesale or retail customers.

This may be vats of prepared food, filled cans not yet labelled or sub-assemblies of food components. It may also include finished cans that are not yet packaged into cartons or pallets. It's finished good inventory consists of all the filled and labelled cans of food in its warehouse that it has manufactured and wishes to sell to food distributors (wholesalers), to grocery stores (retailers), and even perhaps to consumers through arrangements like factory stores and outlet centers.

LOGISTICS OR DISTRIBUTION

The logistics chain includes the owners (wholesalers and retailers), manufacturers' agents, and transportation channels that an item passes through between initial manufacture and final purchase by a consumer. At each stage, goods belong (as assets) to the seller until the buyer accepts them.

Distribution includes four components:

- *Manufacturers' agents*: Distributors who hold and transport a consignment of finished goods for manufacturers without ever owning it. Accountants refer to manufacturers' agents' inventory as "matériel" in order to differentiate it from goods for sale.
- *Transportation*: The movement of goods between owners, or between locations of a given owner. The seller owns goods in transit until the buyer accepts them. Sellers or buyers may transport goods but most transportation providers act as the agent of the owner of the goods.
- *Wholesaling*: Distributors who buy goods from manufacturers and other suppliers (farmers, fishermen, etc.) for re-sale work in the wholesale industry. A wholesaler's inventory consists of all the products in its warehouse that it has purchased from manufacturers or other suppliers. A produce-wholesaler (or distributor) may buy from distributors in other parts of the world or from local farmers. Food distributors wish to sell their inventory to grocery stores, other distributors, or possibly to consumers.
- *Retailing*: A retailer's inventory of goods for sale consists of all the products on its shelves that it has purchased from manufacturers or wholesalers. The store attempts to sell its inventory (soup, bolts, sweaters, or other goods) to consumers.

High Level Inventory Management

It seems that around about 1880 there was a change in manufacturing practise from companies with relatively homogeneous lines of products to vertically integrated companies with unprecedented diversity in processes and products. Those companies (especially in metalworking) attempted to achieve success through economies of scale - the gains of jointly producing two or more products in one facility. The managers now needed information on the effect of product mix decisions on overall profits and therefore needed accurate product cost information. A variety of attempts to achieve this were unsuccessful due to the huge overhead of the information processing of the time. However, the burgeoning need for financial reporting after 1900 created unavoidable pressure for financial accounting of stock and the management need to cost manage products became overshadowed.

In particular it was the need for audited accounts that sealed the fate of managerial cost accounting. The dominance of financial reporting accounting over management accounting remains to this day with few exceptions and the financial reporting definitions of 'cost' have distorted effective management 'cost' accounting since that time. This is particularly true of inventory.

Hence high level financial inventory has these two basic formulas which relate to the accounting period:

- Cost of beginning inventory at the start of the period + inventory purchases within the period + cost of production within the period = cost of goods
- Cost of goods – cost of ending inventory at the end of the period = cost of goods sold

The benefit of these formulae is that the first absorbs all overheads of production and raw material costs in to a value of inventory for reporting. The second formula then creates the new start point for the next period and gives a figure to be subtracted from sales price to determine some form of sales margin figure.

Manufacturing management is more interested in inventory turnover ratio or average days to sell inventory since it tells them something about relative inventory levels. Inventory turn over ratio (also known as inventory turns) = cost of goods sold/Average Inventory=Cost of Goods Sold/((Beginning Inventory + Ending Inventory)/2) and its inverse. Average Days to Sell Inventory=Number of Days a Year/Inventory Turn Over Ratio=365 days a year/Inventory Turn Over Ratio

This ratio estimates how many times the inventory turns over a year. This number tells us how much cash/goods are tied up waiting for the process and is a critical measure of process reliability and effectiveness. So a factory with two inventory turns has six months stock on hand which generally not a good figure (depending upon industry) whereas a factory that moves from six turns to twelve turns has probably improved effectiveness by 100%.

This improvement will have some negative results in the financial reporting since the 'value' now stored in the factory as inventory is reduced. Whilst the simplicity of these accounting measures of inventory are very useful they are in the end fraught with the danger of their own assumptions. There are in fact so many things which can vary hidden under this appearance of simplicity that a variety of 'adjusting' assumptions may be used. These include:

ACCOUNTING PERSPECTIVES

THE BASIS OF INVENTORY ACCOUNTING

Inventory needs to be accounted where it is held across accounting period boundaries since generally expenses should be matched against the results of that expense within the same period. When processes were simple and short then inventories were small but with more complex processes then inventories became larger and significant valued items on the balance sheet. This need to value unsold and incomplete goods has driven much new behaviour into management practise. Perhaps most significant of these are the complexities of fixed cost recovery, transfer pricing, and the separation of direct from indirect costs. This, supposedly, precluded "anticipating income" or "declaring dividends out of capital". It is one of the intangible benefits of Lean and the TPS that process times shorten and stock levels decline to the point where the importance of this activity is hugely reduced and therefore effort, especially managerial, to achieve it can be minimised.

ACCOUNTING FOR INVENTORY

Each country has its own rules about accounting for inventory that fit with their financial reporting rules. So for example, organizations in the U.S. define inventory to suit their needs within US Generally Accepted Accounting Practices (GAAP), the rules defined by the Financial Accounting Standards Board (FASB) (and others) and enforced by the U.S. Securities and Exchange Commission (SEC) and other federal and state agencies. Other countries often have similar arrangements but with their own GAAP and national agencies instead.

It is intentional that financial accounting uses standards that allow the public to compare firms' performance, cost accounting functions internally to an organization and potentially with much greater flexibility. A discussion of inventory from standard and Theory of Constraints-based (throughput) cost accounting perspective follows some examples and a discussion of inventory from a financial accounting perspective. The internal costing/ valuation of inventory can be complex.

Whereas in the past most enterprises ran simple one process factories, this is quite probably in the minority in the 21st century. Where 'one process' factories exist then there is a market for the goods created which establishes an independent market value for the good. Today with multi-stage process companies there is much inventory that would once have been finished goods which is now held as 'work-in-process' (WIP). This needs to be valued in the accounts but the valuation is a management decision since there is no market for the partially finished product. This somewhat arbitrary 'valuation' of WIP combined with the allocation of overheads to it has led to some unintended and undesirable results.

Financial Accounting

An organization's inventory can appear a mixed blessing, since it counts as an asset on the balance sheet, but it also ties up money that could serve for other purposes and requires additional expense for its protection. Inventory may also cause significant tax expenses, depending on particular countries' laws regarding depreciation of inventory, as in Thor Power Tool Company v. Commissioner. Inventory appears as a current asset on an organization's balance sheet because the organization can, in principle, turn it into cash by selling it. Some organizations hold larger inventories than their operations require in order to inflate their apparent asset value and their perceived profitability.

In addition to the money tied up by acquiring inventory, inventory also brings associated costs for warehouse space, for utilities, and for insurance to cover staff to handle and protect it, fire and other disasters, obsolescence, shrinkage (theft and errors), and others. Such holding costs can mount up: between a third and a half of its acquisition value per year. Businesses that stock too little inventory cannot take advantage of large orders from customers if they cannot deliver. The conflicting objectives of cost control and customer service often pit an organization's financial and operating managers against its sales and marketing departments. Sales people, in particular, often receive sales commission payments, so unavailable goods may reduce their potential personal income. This conflict can be minimised by reducing production time to being near or less than customer expected delivery time.

This effort, known as "Lean production" will significantly reduce working capital tied up in inventory and reduce manufacturing costs role of a cost accountant on the 21st-century in a manufacturing organization. By helping the organization to make better decisions, the accountants can help the public sector to change in a very positive way that delivers increased value for the taxpayer's investment. It can also help to incentivise progress and to ensure that reforms are sustainable and effective in the long term, by ensuring that success is appropriately recognized in both the formal and informal reward systems of the organization. To say that they have a key role to play is an understatement.

Finance is connected to most, if not all, of the key business processes within the organization. It should be steering the stewardship and accountability systems that ensure that the organization is conducting its business in an appropriate, ethical manner. It is critical that these foundations are firmly laid. So often they are the litmus test by which public confidence in the institution is either won or lost. Finance should also be providing the information, analysis and advice to enable the organizations' service managers to operate effectively.

This goes beyond the traditional preoccupation with budgets - how much have we spent so far, how much have we left to spend? It is about helping the organization to better understand its own performance. That means making the connections and understanding the relationships between given inputs - the resources brought to bear - and the outputs and outcomes that they achieve. It is also about understanding and actively managing risks within the organization and its activities.

FIFO VS. LIFO ACCOUNTING

When a dealer sells goods from inventory, the value of the inventory is reduced by the cost of goods sold (CoG sold). This is simple where the CoG has not varied across those held in stock; but where it has, then an agreed method must be derived to evaluate it.

For commodity items that one cannot track individually, accountants must choose a method that fits the nature of the sale. Two popular methods exist: FIFO and LIFO accounting (first in - first out, last in - first out). FIFO regards the first unit that arrived in inventory as the first one sold. LIFO considers the last unit arriving in inventory as the first one sold. Which method an accountant selects can have a significant effect on net income and book value and, in turn, on taxation.

Using LIFO accounting for inventory, a company generally reports lower net income and lower book value, due to the effects of inflation. This generally results in lower taxation. Due to LIFO's potential to skew inventory value, UK GAAP and IAS have effectively banned LIFO inventory accounting. In computer science, FIFO and LIFO correspond to the queue and stack data structures, respectively. In fact, the acronyms are commonly used to denote the corresponding data structures.

STANDARD COST ACCOUNTING

Standard cost accounting uses ratios called efficiencies that compare the labour and materials actually used to produce a good with those that the same goods would have required under "standard" conditions.

As long as similar actual and standard conditions obtain, few problems arise. Unfortunately, standard cost accounting methods developed about 100 years ago, when labour comprised the most important cost in manufactured goods. Standard methods continue to emphasize labour efficiency even though that resource now constitutes a (very) small part of cost in most cases. Standard cost accounting can hurt managers, workers, and firms in several ways.

For example, a policy decision to increase inventory can harm a manufacturing managers' performance evaluation. Increasing inventory requires increased production, which means that processes must operate at higher rates. When (not if) something goes wrong, the process takes longer and uses more than the standard labour time.

The manager appears responsible for the excess, even though s/he has no control over the production requirement or the problem. In adverse economic times, firms use the same efficiencies to downsize, rightsize, or otherwise reduce their labour force. Workers laid off under those circumstances have even less control over excess inventory and cost efficiencies than their managers. Many financial and cost accountants have agreed for many years on the desirability of replacing standard cost accounting. They have not, however, found a successor.

THEORY OF CONSTRAINTS COST ACCOUNTING

Eliyahu M. Goldratt developed the Theory of Constraints in part to address the cost-accounting problems in what he calls the "cost world". He offers a substitute, called throughput accounting, that uses throughput (money for goods sold to customers) in place of output (goods produced that may sell or may boost inventory) and considers labour as a fixed rather than as a variable cost. He defines inventory simply as everything the organization owns that it plans to sell, including buildings, machinery, and many other things in addition to the categories listed here. Throughput accounting recognizes only one class of variable costs: the operating expenses like materials and components that vary directly with the quantity produced. Finished goods inventories remain balance-sheet assets, but labour efficiency ratios no longer evaluate managers and workers.

Instead of an incentive to reduce labour cost, throughput accounting focuses attention on the relationships between throughput (revenue or income) on one hand and controllable operating expenses and changes in inventory on the other. Those relationships direct attention to the constraints or bottlenecks that prevent the system from producing more throughput, rather than to people - who have little or no control over their situations.

- *National Accounts:* Inventories also play an important role in national accounts and the analysis of the business cycle. Some short-term macroeconomic fluctuations are attributed to the inventory cycle.
- *Distressed Inventory:* Also known as distressed or expired stock, distressed inventory is inventory whose potential to be sold at a normal cost has or will soon pass. In certain industries it could also mean that the stock is or will soon be impossible to sell. Examples of distressed inventory include products that have reached its expiry date, or has reached a date in advance of expiry at which the planned market will no longer purchase it (*e.g.* 3 months left to expiry), clothing that is defective or out of fashion, and old newspapers or magazines. It also includes computer or consumer-electronic equipment that is obsolescent or discontinued and whose manufacturer is unable to support it.

IMPACT ON FIRMS' PERFORMANCE

A firm is required to maintain a balance between liquidity and profitability while conducting its day to day operations. Liquidity is a precondition to ensure that firms are able to meet its short-term obligations and its continued flow can be guaranteed from a profitable venture. The importance of cash as an indicator of continuing financial health should not be surprising in view of its crucial role within the business. This requires that business must be run both efficiently and profitably.

In the process, an asset-liability mismatch may occur which may increase firm's profitability in the short run but at a risk of its insolvency. On the other hand, too much focus on liquidity will be at the expense of profitability and it is common to find finance textbooks begin their working capital sections with a discussion of the risk and return tradeoffs inherent in alternative working capital policies. Thus, the manager of a business entity is in a dilemma of achieving desired tradeoff between liquidity and profitability in order to maximize the value of a firm. Small businesses are viewed as an essential element of a healthy and vibrant economy. They are seen as vital to the promotion of an enterprise culture and to the creation of jobs within the economy. Small Medium-Sized Enterprises (SMEs) are believed to provide an impetus to the economic progress of developing countries and its importance is gaining widespread recognition.

Equally in Mauritius the SMEs occupy a central place in the economy, accounting for 90% of business stock (those employing up to 50 employees) and employing approximately 25% of private sector employees. Storey (1994) notes that small firms, however, they are defined, constitute the bulk of enterprises in all economies in the world. However, given their reliance on short-term funds, it has long been recognized that the efficient management of working capital is crucial for the survival and growth of small firms. A large number of business failures have been attributed to inability of financial managers to plan and control properly the current assets and current liabilities of their respective firms. Working capital management (WCM) is of particular importance to the small business. With limited access to the long-term capital markets, these firms tend to rely more heavily on owner financing, trade credit and short-term bank loans to finance their needed investment in cash, accounts receivable and inventory. However, the failure rate among small businesses is very high compared to that of large businesses. Studies in the UK and the US have shown that weak financial management - particularly poor working capital management and inadequate long-term financing - is a primary cause of failure among small businesses.

The success factors or impediments that contribute to success or failure are categorized as internal and external factors. The factors categorized as external include financing (such as the availability of attractive financing), economic conditions, competition, government regulations, technology and environmental factors. While the internal factors are managerial skills, workforce, accounting systems and financial management practices. Some research studies have been undertaken on the working capital management practices of both large and small firms in India, UK, US and Belgium using either a survey based approach to identify the push factors for firms to adopt good working capital practices or econometric analysis to investigate the association between WCM and profitability.

Specific research studies exclusively on the impact of working capital management on corporate profitability of the small manufacturing companies are scanty, especially for the case of Mauritius. The financial management of small firms in developing countries and in particular, Mauritius, a small island developing state is altogether an ignored area of research. Keeping this in view and the wider recognition of the potential contribution of the SME sector to the economy of developing countries, our study is a modest attempt to measure and analyse the trend of working capital investment and needs of small manufacturing firms. This study, therefore, attempts to assess the impact of WCM on profitability of a sample of small manufacturing companies and its results are expected to contribute to the existing literature on working capital and SMEs.

The study objectives are to examine the working capital management of the sample firms, and in particular to:

- To examine the impact of accounts receivables days, inventories days, accounts payable days and cash conversion cycle on return on total assets; and
- To analyse the trend in working capital needs of firms and to examine the causes for any significant differences between the industries.

Nature and Importance of Working Capital

The working capital meets the short-term financial requirements of a business enterprise. It is a trading capital, not retained in the business in a particular form for longer than a year. The money invested in it changes form and substance during the normal course of business operations. The need for maintaining an adequate working capital can hardly be questioned. Just as circulation of blood is very necessary in the human body to maintain life, the flow of funds is very necessary to maintain business. If it becomes weak, the business can hardly prosper and survive. Working capital starvation is generally credited as a major cause if not the major cause of small business failure in many developed and developing countries.

The success of a firm depends ultimately, on its ability to generate cash receipts in excess of disbursements. The cash flow problems of many small businesses are exacerbated by poor financial management and in particular the lack of planning cash requirements. The Management of Working Capital While the performance levels of small businesses have traditionally been attributed to general managerial factors such as manufacturing, marketing and operations, working capital management may have a consequent impact on small business survival and growth. The management of working capital is important to the financial health of businesses of all sizes. The amounts invested in working capital are often high in proportion to the total assets employed and so it is vital that these amounts are used in an efficient and effective way.

However, there is evidence that small businesses are not very good at managing their working capital. Given that many small businesses suffer from undercapitalization, the importance of exerting tight control over working capital investment is difficult to overstate. A firm can be very profitable, but if this is not translated into cash from operations within the same operating cycle, the firm would need to borrow to support its continued working capital needs.

Thus, the twin objectives of profitability and liquidity must be synchronised and one should not impinge on the other for long. Investments in current assets are inevitable to ensure delivery of goods or services to the ultimate customers and a proper management of same should give the desired impact on either profitability or liquidity. If resources are blocked at the different stage of the supply chain, this will prolong the cash operating cycle. Although this might increase profitability (due to increase sales), it may also adversely affect the profitability if the costs tied up in working capital exceed the benefits of holding more inventory and/or granting more trade credit to customers. Another component of working capital is accounts payable, but it is different in the sense that it does not consume resources; instead it is often used as a short term source of finance.

Thus it helps firms to reduce its cash operating cycle, but it has an implicit cost where discount is offered for early settlement of invoices. Review of previous studies Although working capital is the concern of all firms, it is the small firms that should address this issue more seriously. Given their vulnerability to a fluctuation in the level of working capital, they cannot afford to starve of cash. The study undertaken by revealed that small firms tend to have a relatively high proportion of current assets, less liquidity, exhibit volatile cash flows, and a high reliance on short-term debt. The recent work of Howorth and Westhead (2003), suggest that small companies tend to focus on some areas of working capital management where they can expect to improve marginal returns. For small and growing businesses, an efficient working capital management is a vital component of success and survival; i.e both profitability and liquidity. They further assert that smaller firms should adopt formal working capital management routines in order to reduce the probability of business closure, as well as to enhance business performance.

The study of Grablowsky (1976) and others have showed a significant relationship between various success measures and the employment of formal working capital policies and procedures. Managing cash flow and cash conversion cycle is a critical component of overall financial management for all firms, especially those who are capital constrained and more reliant on short-term sources of finance. Given these peculiarities, Peel and Wilson (1996) have stressed the efficient management of working capital, and more recently good credit management practice as being pivotal to the health and performance of the small firm sector. Along the same line, Berry *et al* (2002) finds that SMEs have not developed their financial management practices to any great extent and they conclude that owner-managers should be made aware of the importance and benefits that can accrue from improved financial management practices. The study conducted by De Chazal Du Mee (1998) revealed that 60% enterprises suffer from cash flow problems. Narasimhan and Murty (2001) stress on the need for many industries to improve their return on capital employed (ROCE) by focusing on some critical areas such as cost containment, reducing investment in working capital and improving working capital efficiency. The pioneer work of Shin and Soenen (1998) and the more recent study of Deloof (2003) have found a strong significant relationship between the measures of WCM and corporate profitability.

Their findings suggest that managers can increase profitability by reducing the number of day's accounts receivable and inventories. This is particularly important for small growing firms who need to finance increasing amounts of debtors. Mauritius provides a good case study for this paper as it looks at the small and medium sized enterprises operating in the manufacturing sector of a small island developing state. Most of the previous studies on working capital management and financial management of small firms have focused on the US, UK and some other developed countries like Belgium and Australia.

Methodology

The primary aim of this paper is to investigate the impact of WCM on corporate profitability of Mauritian small manufacturing firms. This is achieved by developing a similar empirical framework first used by Shin and Soenen (1998) and the subsequent work of Deloof (2003). We extend our study by also analysing the trends in working capital need of firms and to examine the possible causes for any significant differences between the industries. Our study focuses exclusively on the small manufacturing firms operating in five major industry groups which are both registered and organised as proprietary/ private companies. This restriction places a limit on the number of firms qualifying for the study and is further narrowed down following the revised Companies Act of 2001 which requires firms with a given turnover threshold to file only an aggregated financial statements.

Thus the empirical study is based on a sample of 58 small manufacturing companies. The data has been collected from the financial statements of the sample firms having a legal entity and have filed their annual return to the Registrar of Companies. The sample was drawn from the directory of Small Medium Industrial Development Organisation (SMIDO), a database for registered manufacturing firms operating in diverse activities and for which data was available for a 6 years' period, covering the accounting period 1997-98 to 2002-03. The companies qualified for the two conditions are further grouped into industries based on the classification as listed in the 2003 directory. Thus the data set covers 58 firms from five industry sub-sectors: food and beverages, leather garments, paper products, prefabricated metal products and wood furniture. This has given a balanced panel data set of 348 firm-year observations for a sample of 58 firms. For the purpose of this study, profitability is measured by Return on Total Assets (ROTA), which is defined as profit before interest and tax divided by total assets. The operating income measure of profitability used in the study of Deloof (2003) is not appropriate for this study. The SMEs is characterised by a low fixed assets base and relied to a large extent on accounts payable to fund its gross working capital.

Thus a comprehensive measure of profitability is best captured by computing the return on total assets which is equal to the total liabilities of the firms, made up mainly of equity capital and current liabilities. Some firms have significant fixed financial assets and were thus excluded from the calculation of ROTA.

The Explanatory Variables

The efficiency ratios, namely accounts receivable, inventory and accounts payable have been computed. The Cash Conversion Cycle (CCC) is used as a comprehensive measure of working capital as it shows the time lag between expenditure for the purchases of raw materials and the collection of sales of finished goods. The longer the cycle, the larger the funds blocked in working capital. The return on assets is a better measure since it relates the profitability of the business to the asset base. There are many ways of managing return on assets but, in principle, key levers are, of course, profit increase and assets reduction. The latter has become more important to many businesses as the former becomes more elusive.

Control Variables

In order to account for firm's size and the other variables that may influence profits, sales a proxy for size (the natural logarithm of sales), the gearing ratio (financial debt/total assets), the gross working capital turnover ratio (sales/current assets) and the ratio of current assets to total assets are included as control variables in the regressions. The regressions also include the ratio of current liabilities to total assets to measure the degree of aggressive financing policy, with a high ratio being relatively more aggressive. Return on total assets is on average 5.6% with paper products industry having the highest return of 11%. The leather and garments industry reported a negative operating profit margin, which could be explained by their high foreign exchange risk exposure and the high labour costs.

Typical to the SME sector, the firms have relied mostly on short-term financing, with the metals industry being more aggressive, with an average of 82%. On average firms collect their receivables after 65 days while they take on average 116 days to pay suppliers. The average CCC is 105 days, implying that typical to the manufacturing sector firms turnover their stocks on an average of 3.3 times a year. This shows the influence of leather and garments, metals products and wood and furniture industries holding inventories for more than 150 days, with a maximum value of 1688 days. Mean sales value for the sample companies is 10 million rupees, with only the paper products industry having a value twice the amount. On average about 22% of all assets are financed with financial debt. It is also noteworthy that the average firm in the sample has a gross working capital turnover ratio of 3.1, thus indicating a lower operational efficiency.

WORKING CAPITAL ANALYSIS

The major components of gross working capital include stocks (raw materials, work-in-progress and finished goods), debtors, cash and bank balances. The composition of working capital depends on a multiple of factors, such as operating level, level of operational efficiency, inventory policies, book debt policies, technology used and nature of the industry. While inter- industry variation is expected to be high, the degree of variation is expected to be low for firms within the industry. A comparison of inventory composition of industries over the years shows only slight improvement for the food and beverages and the paper products industries. It is interesting to note the consistent improvement in trade debtors share of current assets in all the industries and except for the food and beverages, it represents less that 30% of total current assets.

Thus it can be deduced that the companies have monitored the accounts receivable reasonably well and this could be partly due to their need for generating funds from the operating activities instead of relying from outside funds. Except for the paper products, the other four industries have a greater reliance on short-term funds and this is even more in 2003. The prefabricated metal product is financing 85% of its assets out of current liabilities and this over-reliance may be a threat to the industry's survival.

In terms of liquidity, all the four industries, food and beverages, garments, metal products, wood and furniture are having less liquid assets to meet their current obligations and if this becomes permanent, it may affect supplies of materials and thus production. The proportion of liquid assets to total assets is above 70% for the wood and metal industries, indicating a low fixed assets base. This implies that these two industries can operate with a relatively low investment in fixed assets as compared to the other industries like printing and garments where the production tend to be heavily mechanised. Another plausible reason could be that the Mauritian small manufacturing firms have been more concerned about current operations than about longer term issues like capacity and technology. Weinraub and Visscher (1998), also report industry-wise differences in the level of aggressiveness with respect to working capital investment over time. Pearson correlation coefficients for the variables used to assess the impact of working capital management on profitability, measured by return on total assets. ROTA is significantly positively correlated with OPM and capital-turnover ratio, but negatively correlated with the measures of WCM, except for the cash conversion cycle. This positive relation for CCC is consistent with the view that resources are blocked at the different stage of the supply chain, thus prolonging the operating cycle. This might increase profits due to increase sales, especially where the costs of tied up capital is lower than the benefits of holding more inventories and granting more trade credit to customers. Also the small manufacturing firms may be able to obtain trade credit from the suppliers and this is supported by the higher proportion of current liabilities to total assets for all the industries except for the paper products. However, care must be exercised while interpreting the Pearson Correlation coefficients because they cannot provide a reliable indicator of association in a manner which controls for additional explanatory variables. Examining simple bivariate correlation in a conventional matrix does not take account of each variable's correlation with all other explanatory variables.

Our main analysis will be derived from appropriate multivariate models, estimated using fixed effects framework and pooled OLS. The different analyses have identified critical management practices and are expected to assist managers in identifying areas where they might improve the financial performance of their operation. The results have provided owner-managers with information regarding the basic financial management practices used by their peers and their peers attitudes towards these practices. The working capital needs of an organization change over time as does its internal cash generation rate.

As such, the small firms should ensure a good synchronization of its assets and liabilities. This study has shown that the paper and printing industry has been able to achieve high scores on the various components of working capital and this has positively impact on its profitability. On this premise this industry may be referred as the 'hidden champions' and could thus be used as best practice among the SMEs. Further, this research concludes that there is a pressing need for further empirical studies to be undertaken on small business financial management, in particular their working capital practices by extending the sample size so that an industry-wise analysis can help to uncover the factors that explain the better performance for some industries and how these best practices could be extended to the other industries. This would also assist policy-makers and educators to identify the requirements of, and specific problems faced by small firms in Mauritius, especially as more emphasis is placed on the sector by the government.

This study has come at an opportune time where the Mauritian government is deploying resources to help the SME sector so that the latter can positively contribute to the Mauritian economy. This analysis has been constrained by the sample size and the nature of the data, which could have well affected the results. Further studies will aim at increasing the sample size for still better and consistent panel estimates. Many pharma could focus on increasing sales and investing in new markets, without worrying too much about housekeeping. Times have changed and in future, domestic economies will play a far greater part in maintaining profitability in the industry. One area where pharma could create value is in working capital management. Marc Loneux from working capital consultancy REL, the largest US and European pharrna companies have up to US$25 billion tied up in working capital that could be liberated through better management.

The same companies could a further billion by reducing costs and implementing better business practice. His comments are based on research conducted by REL on pharma's practices in this field. Like performance management, working capital management has been a priority for older industries with lower margins, but has been largely ignored by pharmaceutical companies. However, it is now widely recognised that operating efficiencies will be a major contributor to the long-term value growth in the industry. At the end of 2004, the net operating working capital of the 18 largest pharmaceutical companies in the world (by sales, 13 US and five European) was US$79 billion. US firms had between US$6.4 billion and US$16 billion tied up in working capital.

European companies have between US$4.6 billion and US$0.3 billion that could be liberated. Dealing with this excess would increase the market value of the US companies by between (0.8 per cent and 2.1 per cent. Of the European firms included in the survey, better capital management could increase their value by between 0.9 per cent and 1.8 per cent. The smallest pharma companies in the US, together with Roche in Europe, offer the greatest potential for creating market value, says REL. Although there is a specific working capital model for every business sector, there are general principles that can be applied everywhere, says Loneux. One of The largest US and European pharma companies have up to US$25 billion tied up in working capital these is close collaboration between producers, sellers and wholesalers.

This creates a win-win situation, giving manufacturers a better view of demand, and allowing both parties to manage their inventories more effectively. The automotive industry, in particular, has provided good collaborative models, as has the computer manufacturer Dell, which produces computers only when they are ordered and has negotiated very good payment terms with its suppliers. Pharma has begun to implement better inventory-management practice over the past two years, with some firms entering inventory management agreements with their wholesalers. As a result, sections of the industry have levelled the quarterly volume fluctuations that once made it difficult to streamline production and reduce inventories.

Improving working capital management also creates savings elsewhere. "We are talking about improved collection, improved logistics and supply chain, further consolidation, more efficient buying and so on," says Loneux. When you implement best practice in working capital, you can cut the number of collectors and people involved in wholesaling and logistics. You can also reduce write-offs in receivables because your inventories are lower. A more general strategy for pharma, says Loneux, is "optimising the commercial". Focusing better on the product mix, ensuring that companies make the most of what they have out there, withdrawing or postponing launches in order to maximise the model.

Such strategies could prove a problem with governments and other healthcare providers, who are seemingly ready to oppose what they regard as manipulation of the market. It appears that pharma industry leaders are increasingly focused on engaging with external agents - governments, healthcare providers and patients - to develop a more collaborative working model. Loneux acknowledges these difficulties, but thinks public-private collaborations pioneered by the likes of Bill Gates and GlaxoSmithKline are the way forward, ensuring people get medicines they can afford with a decent return for pharma. Asked about the cost-effective ness of outsourcing admin, sales and marketing roles, Loneux is sceptical. He believes this will have a negligible impact on costs and that possible savings in R&D are limited by the quality constraints placed on pharma manufacturing - companies can't place the work just anywhere.

Moreover, he says, outsourcing is often done to serve local demand. Although many companies are opening up in India, where there is a growing market, demand is still largely concentrated in Europe and the US. "There is some outsourcing in India by the big ones," he says, "but I wouldn't say it was a priority." After the research was carried out, REL showed its work to some of the major pharma companies. Loneux comments "Big Pharma recognises that it is something it has just started to address, that there is clearly room for improvement.

11

Inventory Control

A simple function relating the volume passing through a facility (e.g., warehouse throughput) to the inventory level is used as an integral part of facility location analysis to estimate inventory levels at various stocking points. It allows inventory levels at the facilities to be approximated as customer demand is allocated to them.

Once inventory levels are known, inventory carrying costs can be computed. Trade-offs can then be considered involving production/purchase; transportation; and facility fixed, handling, and storage costs. The sum can then be minimised. The function has additional utility as an evaluative tool for inventory policy. It is an expression of a company's inventory policy application and provides a means for comparing performance.

That is, various inventory policies can be represented by the turnover curve from which the resulting inventory levels can be compared to existing levels. The magnitude of the differences are determined that can serve as the basis for improvement.

Incomplete data and misapplication of policy can require that the function be established from the nature of the inventory policy itself. This requires that the relationship of inventory policy to the inventory turnover curve be understood.

It is the intent of this chapter to develop the turnover curves resulting from various inventory policies applied under a variety of item characteristics, uncertainty conditions, and fill rates. Thus, by knowing basic information about item cost, demand, lead time, and inventory control methodology, a normative inventory turnover curve can be expressed.

INVENTORY POLICY

Inevitably, product flows in a supply channel must be moved to meet demand simply because product is not available at the time and place desired. Depending on the strategy that a firm adopts to manage the flows, some inventories will accumulate at various facilities in the channel or in the transportation system. A supply-to-demand, or just-in-time, strategy attempts to avoid inventories by matching supply to demand as demand occurs. On the other hand, a supply-to-stock strategy includes inventories with the objective of balancing them with product availability requirements. It is the control of these planned inventories that is considered in this research.

Planned inventories are controlled in numerous ways. Ford Harris attempted to optimise inventory levels as early as 1913 with the development of the Economic Order Quantity (EOQ) model for determining replenishment order size in perpetual demand inventories. Subsequently, the EOQ became an integral part of reorder point and periodic review inventory control methodologies for controlling the combination of regular and safety stocks when demand and lead time are uncertain.

Although demand is assumed constant and perpetual, practical application usually involves forecasting demand with one of the popular forecasting methods, such as exponential smoothing or moving average. The reorder point and periodic review methodologies are well described in most operations, logistics, and supply chain management textbooks; however, for reference, they are repeated.

Less discussed, but very popular with companies, is the stock-to-demand approach to inventory management. With this method, inventory levels are directly related to the demand forecast. The objective is to maintain inventory items at the level of, for example, 6-weeks demand or of a specific inventory turnover ratio. It is a form of the periodic review method, since inventory levels are examined at specified time intervals, perhaps monthly in conjunction with a forecast, except that replenishment quantities are not based on the EOQ and the review period is not economically determined and optimised. The method's popularity probably comes from its simplicity of understanding and application.

These previous methods are "pull" methods, meaning that stocking decisions are made locally to the inventory. In contrast, many companies prefer a "push" methodology. Under the latter, inventory decisions are made at the source point level in the channel based on the demand at more than one downstream stocking location. Stocking quantities shipped to the inventory locations are determined from the combined forecasted demands, the period for replenishment of all stocking points, and product lot sizes or vendor order minimums.

Except for demand being forecasted from multiple stocking locations, the "push" method is similar to the stock-to-demand methodology. As a practical matter, variations of these basic control methods are used. For example, orders from the same source may be composed of multiple product items, order quantities may be determined by vendor deals and quantity discounts, and there may be different policies applied to different stocking locations.

Although there may be many possible inventory policies applied to specific situations, the analysis here will be limited to these popular methods for perpetual demand inventories. Just-in-time, or supply-to-demand, methods are not considered since their intent is to eliminate inventories rather than manage them. The "pull" methods are more likely to be applied by those members of the supply channel that experience perpetual item demand and regular demand patterns, namely retailers and distributors, but are not limited strictly to these.

The conversion of inventory policy to the inventory turnover curve format is necessary when empirical data do not produce a true representation of a firm's inventory policy, when there are inadequate data to accurately construct the turnover curve, or when a different inventory policy from an exiting one is to be represented for which there are no data. Otherwise, developing the turnover curve directly from empirical data would be reasonable.

THE TURNOVER CURVE

The inventory turnover curve perhaps finds its greatest usefulness in supply chain network planning, although it is useful for projecting inventory levels of individual items or all items collectively under various inventory policy scenarios. Numerous researchers such as Baumol and Wolfe; Magee, Copacino, and Rosenfield; Ballou; Bender; Ho and Perl; Shapiro; and Daskin, Coullard, and Shen recognised that inventory costs should be an integral part of location analysis because inventory levels change with the number of facilities and the demand allocated to them.

A major problem with including inventory cost directly in location analysis rather than adding it after a solution is found is that inventories are temporally oriented whereas location is spatially oriented. It is difficult to merge the two into a single analysis because of the dimensional dissimilarities. However in location analysis, it is possible to estimate inventory levels in the aggregate by approximating them from facility throughput rather than through more traditional approaches involving lead times, demand levels, and relevant inventory costs.

The inventory turnover curve serves the purpose, although others have used the square root law that associates inventory levels with the number of stocking points in a distribution network. The turnover curve is preferred because it combines both cycle and safety stock. If applied to empirical inventory data, no assumption needs to be made about the underlying control policy. The development and application of the turnover curve has been described on several occasions.

As stated, this relationship has several limitations not inherent in the inventory turnover curve. First, it is assumed that the throughput is the same for all stocking points. Second, it is constructed from an EOQ-based inventory policy. Third, demand variance/forecast errors are the same and independent among stocking points; however, the utility of the formulation has been extended by empirically determining a. Based on practice, Bender's suggestion is for a to be between 0.4 and 0.6. Varying a allows for some safety stock or the effect of inventory control methods other than EOQ-based ones, although there was no attempt to relate the value of a to either of these.

The turnover curve concept can be used to estimate inventory levels at a single location as well. Although the turnover curve can be determined for a single inventoried item, it is perhaps most useful for estimating inventories in the aggregate, i.e., a collection of multiple items. By establishing the turnover curve for a group of items, it is then possible to project the effect of policy changes on overall inventory levels. Top managers are concerned with the overall investment in inventories, and network planning involves the location of broad classes of inventoried items.

The process to establish the turnover curve is to relate the shape factor a to the type of inventory policy used to control inventory levels. Then, once; is known, the curve can be fitted to the known inventory level for a particular group of inventoried items. What is not known is how the shape factor relates to inventory policy. Therefore, one of the objectives of this research is to determine the relationship.

Specifically, the policies to be evaluated are:

Reorder point (ROP)

- Order quantities optimally determined
- Specified order quantities

Periodic review (PR)

- Review time optimally determined
- Specified review times

Stock-to-demand (STD)

- Pull
- Push

These policies were selected because they are the ones most frequently described in the literature and observed in practice for perpetual demand patterns that are projected in the short run from historical time series.

Each inventory control policy was evaluated under a variety of inventory situations.

These were:

- Items of varying values
- Perpetual demand with varying coefficients of variation
- Lead times of various lengths
- Customer service represented with various item fill rates
- Multiple items managed simultaneously within the same fill rate

A Monte Carlo type computer simulation was used to accurately establish the inventory levels that occur under various fill rates, cost, and demand-lead time conditions. Using simulation is especially appropriate as a research methodology (compared with calculating the inventory levels from theoretical formulations) because fill rates and, in some cases safety stocks, can only be determined approximately through calculation.

Simulation allows the action of an inventory policy to mimic, over time, actual inventory performance. The simulator used was SCSIM in the LOGWARE supplement to Ballou (2004) for a single supply chain echelon.

Simulation is an experimental methodology whereby complex problems, such as the inventory policies described previously, cannot be solved accurately using analytical techniques, usually because of the limiting assumptions required to achieve an analytical solution.

When the problem contains probabilistic elements, such as random demand and lead times as in this case, random numbers and probability distributions are used to create a trial, which represents a specific level of demand on a given day or the lead time for a particular replenishment order. A trial is a specific outcome, which is an inventory level in our case. Multiple trials are averaged to generalise the outcomes, and the variation from multiple trials is expressed statistically. If different random numbers cause a substantial difference in the outcomes, repeating the simulation a large number of times may be needed to assure results that can be generalised. Determining the correct probability distributions and the often lengthy time required for building a simulation model can be a disadvantage. If the simulation closely mimics the problem in practice, testing various scenarios with a simulation can be a real economic advantage, since testing the scenarios under actual conditions that interrupt on-going operations can be avoided.

Each of the noted inventory policies were simulated using one-day increments for a period of 10 years. Demand was randomly generated from normal distributions for a single-location inventory. A variety of seed numbers used to initiate the simulation processes were tested to see if outcomes changed significantly due to the number selected. Although the outcomes generally changed little (less than 1 %) when using different seed numbers, there was some increased variability in the outcomes from seed numbers as lead times increased, but this may not be statistically significant.

Since the results were consistent for a given seed number and the variation in outcomes was not great, the same seed number was used throughout the study. Various run lengths were tested so as to ensure stable results. The first two simulated years were omitted from the results to eliminate start up aberrations in the simulation process; then, the results for years 3 through 10 were averaged. Run lengths beyond a 10-year simulated period made no significant difference in the results. A base case for item characteristics, demand, lead time, forecast smoothing constant, fill rate, and inventory related costs was established from which changes were made for testing purposes.

This base case is outlined as follows:

- *Item value (C)*: \$3 per unit
- *Procurement cost (S)*: \$50 per order
- *Inventory carrying cost (I)*: 25% per year of item value
- *Item demand (d)*: 100 units per day
- *Demand variability (sa)*: 10 units per day
- *Lead time (L)*: 1 day order filling and 4 days in transit
- *Item fill rate*: 99%

- *Forecasting method*: Simple exponential smoothing with a smoothing constant of 0.2

This base data case was the author's attempt to represent an inventoried item having medium to low value with a reasonable level of demand and demand variability. Other costs and factors were set at what would likely be experienced in practice.

It was recognised that no single product description can be representative of all items in a variety of inventories so key factors were varied over a wide range to test many situations that might occur. Average demand was varied from a low of 100 for the base case to high of 20,000 units per day. The forecast error ranged from zero to a coefficient of variation of 0.3, since larger values would violate the assumption of normality and the time series would be lumpy rather than perpetual. If larger forecast errors were to be experienced, a supply-to-demand policy rather than a supply-to-inventory policy would be more appropriate for lumpy demand. Lead times were assumed to be certain in this study. It is this author's experience that, in practice, lead time variability is rarely measured when planning inventories.

Experimentation shows that, along with demand variability, the effect on inventory levels is difficult to portray with a single variable. Also, theoretical formulations involving both demand and lead time uncertainty were of questionable accuracy. As a practical matter, managers will increase desired in-stock probabilities or increase average lead times for the purpose of setting inventory levels as a way of compensating for not knowing lead time variability. Thus, the lead time variability effect is accounted for when managers take such actions. For testing purposes, average lead times ranged from 2 days to 800 days, or over two years.

Item value, procurement cost, inventory carrying cost, exponential smoothing forecast method with a smoothing constant of 0.2 (a typical range is 0.05 to 0.3 according to Flowers 1982) were set at nominal values, although items values were varied up to $10 per unit for validation checking purposes. Testing variations in their values is not needed since they don't affect the shape of the turnover curve, although the forecasting method can affect the degree of uncertainty in an inventory planning problem. However, the effect is captured within demand variability and is not tested further.

Knowing average demand, the forecast error expressed as a standard deviation, and the average lead time for an inventoried item or groups of items, the shape factor can be estimated for a particular inventory control policy. The methodology is to run the simulation multiple times varying demand, lead times, fill rates, and other item characteristics to determine the average inventory levels. From each series of runs where demand is the primary variable, all other variables are held constant; a power function is fitted to the inventory level data to find the shape factor 1. With repeated simulation runs, curves are developed that allow the shape factor a to be found for a variety of item characteristics.

BASIC EFFECTS

The simulated results using the base data case show that there are economies of scale to be expected with reorder point and periodic review policies when the EOQ formula is used to find the order quantities and review times. These scale economies are not present with a stock-to-demand policy since review time parallels forecasted demand.

There is certainty in both demand forecasting and lead times, which allows the performance of the different policies (as calculated from theory) to be seen as they actually might perform in practice (as simulated). Formulas that represent inventory policy are based on assumptions such as constant demand, fill rate, and the distribution of the demand during lead time that need not be made in the simulation; thus, a more accurate representation of reality is expected from the simulation against which theoretical results may be compared.

The curves in the figure result from fitting a power function to the simulation results without the complications of demand uncertainty. However, the periodic review policy formulation is approximate and the simulated results reflect that fact. Although not specifically shown in a graph, when demand is held constant while lead times are varied, inventory levels increase but at a decreasing rate with increases in lead time. This is true for both reorder point and periodic review policies whose order quantities are determined through EOQ calculation.

The economies of scale are not seen for the stock-to-demand policy where safety stock is determined from demand levels and not lead times. This is also true when the reorder point and periodic review policies are fixed. Demand uncertainty, as represented by the coefficient of variation of demand, has a significant effect on the inventory levels as demand changes for an item, for a reorder point policy and a fill rate (FR) of 99%. Greater demand uncertainty or poorer forecasting has the effect of flattening the curve, thus resulting in fewer scale economies with increasing throughput. The same phenomenon holds for the periodic review policy, except that there is slightly more inventory held under this policy than with the reorder point policy.

Stock-to-demand, reorder point with a specified order quantity, and periodic review with a specified order interval is polices that show inventory levels to be proportional to demand levels, regardless of the degree of uncertainty. The increased linearity of the inventory turnover curve with greater demand uncertainty is a result of safety stock becoming a higher proportion of total stock (regular plus safety) for a known lead time and a given fill rate. Whether the inventory levels are simulated or calculated from theoretical formulas, the estimates are similar. The STD policy will show similar results as long as safety stocks are determined from a square root function of the lead time, e.g., as in Equations A4 and A8. There are economies of scale as safety stocks increase at a decreasing rate with increasing lead times.

Regular (cyclical) stock remains constant. The scale effect diminishes for lower fill rates and when safety stock is tied to demand levels rather than to lead time. In all cases, calculating inventory levels is satisfactory for the purposes here.

DETERMINING THE SHAPE FACTOR

Now that the basic effects of inventory policy on inventory levels have been established, attention is directed toward developing the turnover curve for inventory estimating purposes. It is possible to generalise the shape factor a for a given inventory policy and then k can be determined from a specific inventory situation.

Once the simulated shape factors were known for FR = 99%, the shape factors for FR = 99% were determined mathematically by calculating the inventory levels for various demand levels and fitting a power function to these results. A smooth curve through the computed a values showed a reasonable approximation to the simulated results. With this good correspondence between simulated and calculated results for the FR = 99% case, similar shape factor curves confidently can be calculated for other FRs without the need for further simulations, which saves time-consuming simulations and allows curves for fill rates not shown to be easily approximated.

The shape factors for a periodic review policy where the order interval is optimally computed. The PR simulated results do not track as well with the computed results as they did for the ROP policy. On the other hand, the shape factor curve varies little over a wide fill rate range. Because the simulated results likely are more accurate than the calculated ones due to the approximations within the theoretical PR formulations and the marginal difference caused by variations in fill rate levels, the simulated shape factor curves represented by the bold line for FR = 99% are preferred.

The second bold line for FR = 85% is approximated by extrapolating from the position of the calculated FR = 85% line to the calculated FR = 99% line. Shape factors for the stock-to-demand policies of both push and pull are known to be 1 and are therefore not plotted. That is, inventory levels directly follow demand levels. Although different fill rates will change the overall inventory level, they will not cause the shape factor to deviate from 1. When the order quantity in the ROP policy is specified to be in proportion to item demand and the order interval in the PR policy is specified, the shape factor for these policies will be 1 as well.

For a given lead time, none of these policies will show inventory levels that increase at a decreasing rate with increasing demand levels.

AGGREGATING ITEMS

The theoretical formulations for inventory policies are for individual items. The concept of the turnover curve is to estimate inventory as a collection of items that form an item classification. Items within a classification are likely to have the same fill rate, inventory carrying cost, and order processing cost but will differ according to demand rate, demand variability, lead time, and item value.

VALIDATION

The accuracy of projecting inventory in the aggregate using various inventory control policies and the turnover curve needs to be established. Forty-two tests were conducted where two items having the base case characteristics had average demand levels of 100 and 200 sales units per day respectively. Five inventory policies were used: ROP with the order quantity calculated from the EOQ, ROP with the order quantity specified as a fraction of demand, PR with the order interval calculated from the EOQ, PR with a specified order interval, and STD with the order interval and the safety stock as a fraction of demand.

For some policies, the shape factor is known to be 1 and requires no lookup from a graph. After the shape factor was determined, the k parameter in the turnover curve was found, given the average inventory level AIL for the combined products. This combined inventory level was established from the theoretical estimates for AIL. After changing demand variability (10% to 30% of average demand), average lead time (60 to 120 days), fill rate (90 to 99%), and product value ($3 to $10 per unit), demand for the two items was decreased by 50% or increased by 100%. By comparing the inventory level from theoretical formulas with that determined from the turnover curve, an estimate of the expected deviation was projected. Test results showed that the aggregate inventory projected from a ROP policy with a calculated Q will have an average difference of 8.3% with a range of 3.4% to 17%.

Using the same policy but with Q as a fraction of demand showed no difference between the two approaches. For the PR policy with a calculated T, the average difference using the turnover curve was 9.5% with a difference range of 2.8% to 14.8%. If the T interval was specified, the average difference was 4.5% with a range of 1.3% to 8.5%. There was no error using a STD policy. Overall, the average expected difference was 4.6% using the turnover curve approach to aggregate inventory estimation rather than summing the inventory levels as determined through theoretical calculation.

USING THE RESULTS

The use of the results is now illustrated in two ways: estimating the inventory level changes as the number of stocking points is changed and estimating the effect of an inventory control policy change. Additional uses of the turnover curve include comparing theoretical control policy results with current inventory performance, approximating inventory levels where there currently is no inventory, developing an inventory estimating relationship when only one inventory point exists, and projecting inventory level changes as critical factors such as demand, lead time, and fill rate are changed.

INVENTORY SPLIT BETWEEN TWO LOCATIONS

In a practical situation, many items make up inventory. First, the items are to be separated into a class where the fill rate is the same, such as A items, B items, or C items, if a classification scheme is used second, because many items typically will be in a class, the items will be sampled to be representative of all items in the class. For illustrative purposes, three items are used that are assumed to represent 90% of the items having a fill rate of 95% (the B items). The control policy is ROP with EOQ-determined order quantities.

The inventory is to be divided between two locations, where 60% of the demand is allocated to one location and 40% to the other. How much inventory can be expected in the two locations versus one? This kind of question might be the raised when designing a supply chain network.

POLICY CHANGE

A firm currently has inventory at three locations and uses a STD control policy that produces the linear relationship of inventory level to annual demand. The product characteristics are the same and three items are taken as representative of the entire B-class inventory and are 80% of total class inventory. The same item mix is stocked at all locations. Will a policy change to PR with an optimised order interval T perform better than the current policy? The application of the inventory turnover curve rests on several assumptions. First, demand is perpetual, that is, non-terminating over the planning horizon. Second, it is expected that the items in inventory that are the subject of this application are in the middle stages of their life cycles. Third, demand is expected to show a "regular" pattern whereby its variability is not great relative to its average. Fourth, demand is reasonably forecasted from historical patterns. Fifth, lead times do not vary greatly from one stocking location to another, which is probably reasonable where transportation time is not a high proportion of total replenishment cycle time. Sixth, lead times are constant although lead time variability can be accounted for by increasing the fill rate level.

Seventh, demand forecasting error is approximately normally distributed. It is not expected that each of these conditions will be precisely met in every application; however, the robustness of the methodology suggests that reasonable results can be achieved in most applications. It has been the intent of this research to develop a process whereby aggregate inventory levels can be estimated from individual product characteristics and the inventory policy that controls them. The inventory turnover curve with the form AIL = kV;1 is used as the medium in which to relate policy to inventory levels.

Its major benefit is that the combined inventory levels of multiple items can be projected without the need to calculate and then sum the inventories for many individual items, which can be time consuming for many items stocked at numerous locations. Once the turnover curve is constructed, inventory levels can be projected in situations where none exist.

For many top-level managers, financial control of inventory levels in the aggregate is of more interest than the control of individual items; and for strategic planning, projection of overall inventory levels is preferred to that of single items.

This aggregate control, and the inventory turnover curve, is useful in the following applications:

- Planning supply chain networks
- Evaluating inventory policy change
- Comparing theoretical inventory control policy with current inventory performance
- Approximating inventory levels where there now is no inventory
- Estimating inventory levels for a range of circumstances when only one inventory point currently exists
- Projecting inventory level changes as critical factors such as demand, lead time and fill rate change

Three classes of inventory policies were examined: reorder point, periodic review, and stockto-demand. It cannot be assumed that theoretical formulations of inventory policy would produce the inventory levels experienced in practice even when the policy was faithfully and precisely applied.

At least one policy is approximate and the relationship between fill rates and inventory levels for all policies cannot be stated exactly. Therefore, the inventory policies were replicated through Monte Carlo simulation to better approximate actual inventory levels and to relate them to the inventory predicted by theory. Through this process, the shape factor a in the turnover equation was estimated, which relates directly to the type of inventory policy used.

Then, from known inventory levels, the k factor was found to complete the turnover curve formulation. It was found that the turnover curve can be a reasonable substitute for theoretical estimation.

The average difference between turnover curve estimation and theoretical calculation was 4.6% when tested under a variety of item characteristics and inventory control policies. Future research might well centre around relaxing the assumptions made in this analysis.

These would include:

- Treating variable lead times exactly;
- Testing non-normality distributions for demand forecast error and lead time;

- Using forecasting methods other than exponential smoothing such as collaborative forecasting or regression analysis;
- Testing the robustness of the turnover curve when demand is not "regular" and predictable; and
- Evaluating inventory policies not contained in those identified here.

Approximating the k coefficient in the turnover curve when no inventory exists would be particularly useful. Finally, reporting on applications of the turnover curve in a variety of situations would help to establish its accuracy and utility.

Within the logistics function, companies face many challenges and responsibilities. The challenges often deal with cost reduction considerations. Efficiency in cost reduction is one of the major driving forces in logistics. New technologies have become available that allow management to better understand and control company performance in the various logistics functions.

Since the mid-1970s, one such function that has had its pulse closely monitored is that of inventory management. With erratic swings in the cost of money over the past two decades, and new pressures put on asset productivity, inventories have been closely watched. The interest in such methodologies as Just-in-Time, MRP, and DRP is evidence of the importance being placed on inventory levels.

Just how well have companies been able to control inventories? One could safely speculate that some degree of improvement has been made over the years in the levels of inventories maintained by companies as the cost of money and operations has risen.

However, as a general hypothesis, it is validated only by national composite inventory averages. The purpose of this chapter is to focus on inventory management, and to attempt to obtain a clearer understanding of how four selected industries have responded to meet the challenges and opportunities in this area.

Specifically, the results of the research show that definite trends can be identified in inventory levels between 1970 and 1987. The per centage of total inventories at fiscal year end compared to total annual sales was chosen as the primary metric for this study. It is believed the use of this ratio over the 18 years of the study will provide consistency and identify any trends that have developed.

Four industries were chosen for inclusion in this study. Over time, the chemical, electronics, food, and pharmaceutical industries have established themselves as being on or near the cutting edge of logistics practices. They have been the subject of many studies, and have often set the benchmarks of logistics systems' performance measurements.

This chapter will first analyse the changes that have occurred in the area of inventory management between 1970 and 1987. Next several questions developed to drive this research will be discussed, followed by the interpretation and presentation of the data. Managerial implications of this study are briefly surveyed, followed by a summary of the research results and final comments.

It is hoped that the information and research findings that follow will assist logistics executives in their understanding of inventory management patterns over the past two decades, as well as offer some insight into the potential for future opportunities.

INVENTORY MANAGEMENT DEVELOPMENT

Inventory management, as it is known today, has been evolving only since the mid-1970s. Before then, dating back as early as the 1950s, companies managed the flow of materials with excess inventories. Due to the relatively low cost of money in that era, companies used inventories to buffer against the uncertainty and variance found in each of the three segments of the material flow process: procurement, manufacturing, and distribution.

In procurement, uncertainty and variance factors are introduced by quality considerations ("buy enough to cover the defective units"). In manufacturing, variance is seen in work-in-process waiting for inspection ("can't shut down the line"). In distribution, uncertainty is always present due to varying customer needs ("increase safety stock to cover our varying customer requirements").

In the mid-1970s, however, the cost of money began to increase. As a result, the financial investment in inventories mandated that closer controls be instituted. The days of"filling the cracks" with inventories were over. Technology to track and measure data was becoming increasingly available and affordable. The ability to tap into accessible technology enabled companies to begin the work of breaking down the problems associated with uncertainty and variance. Information flow throughout and between logistics channels has aided companies in better coordinating both internal and external control over inventories.

As the cost of money rose, and has subsequently stayed relatively high, management concern over asset productivity increased. Of the three asset bundles managed (fixed assets, labor, and inventory), inventory is the easiest to change. As a result, emphasis was focused on the area of inventory control. While the problems associated with too much inventory (financial costs. obsolescence, storage costs, insurance, taxes, etc.) have focused efforts on overall reduction, the process is not a one-way street. The problem of not enough inventory looms on the horizon with each reduction made in inventory levels. Stock-out costs can be extremely high and affect all three segments of material flow mentioned earlier. These costs not only show up in increased administrative, production, and processing costs, but also result in customer dissatisfaction and loss of future sales.

In reducing inventory levels, and thus eliminating the buffers, management has been able to identify where problems exist within a system.

In order to overcome these problems, it is essential that total system coordination be continuously nurtured and fine-tuned. Management appears to have accepted the challenge and responsibility necessary to properly approach the area of inventory control.

The following study is intended to show the results of efforts made in this area. To guide this study and keep it focused, it was necessary to establish a set of desired goals and outcomes; therefore a set of research questions was formulated.

The questions are presented below with a brief description regarding their importance to the study:

- How have inventory levels dropped over the past two decades in the four industries studied? Rising costs have resulted in an increased awareness for greater inventory efficiencies. National inventory to sales averages show that inventory levels have dropped. Yet, industry specific data is not available and the question remains as to what the four industries in this study have accomplished in this area.
- What effect does the size of a company have on its inventory levels? Do the largest companies maintain higher or lower levels of inventory when compared to smaller companies within the same industry? This question is included to see if any differences exist that would show that sales volume dictates an identifiable difference in inventory levels. In order to better understand which companies are most effectively controlling inventory levels, this question will help to show if size plays a noticeable factor in a company's ability to improve its inventory position.
- Does the level of a company's inventory affect its profitability? Is profitability directly correlated with inventory levels, and do the more profitable companies within an industry maintain lower levels of inventory? These questions are derived from the belief that well-run, profit-driven companies strive to achieve the greatest efficiencies possible in their inventory management. Therefore, would one expect to see lower inventory levels kept by the most profitable companies within each industry? Is there a competitive advantage to be gained by increased control over inventory levels?
- Have companies been able to control inventories as a strategic-management tool? Reaching profit goals is paramount in any company. Further, it seems fair to conclude that during the time period of this study, customer service emerged as a very powerful market requirement. Clearly, reducing inventory levels without adversely affecting customer service will, in itself, improve a company's profit picture. Thus, maintaining customer service goals and controlling costs is the challenge managers take on as they attempt to gain more control over inventory levels.

Between 17 and 20 companies were studied in each industry. It was felt that this sampling would provide an adequate information base from which to draw conclusions to the research questions mentioned above. The 1985 list of Fortune 500 companies provided by Fortune magazine was used to determine the participants of each industry to be included in this study. Fortune broadly groups various industries together in their classifications. Thus companies grouped in the same industry may be very diverse in their revenue generating markets. However, it is important to keep in mind that this study was undertaken to view various industries' trends. Specific detailed comparisons by company are not the objective. The annual"Fortune 500" issues of Fortune from 1971 to 1988 were also referenced. For each company, individual annual reports were examined for each year to obtain the necessary data. The sales data was taken directly from the income statements as reported, and inventories were grouped as a whole, due to the lack of consistency in the reporting of the various inventory segments (i.e.. raw materials, work-in-progress, and finished goods).

While some data was not available, more than 98% of the 2,592 separate pieces of information sought were located. The lack of complete data is attributed to several factors. First, in some instances, data was not available in the information sources being used. Secondly, some companies (as they are known today) began doing business after 1970, and their early data is not available. Lastly, there has been a big increase in the number of mergers and buy-outs. The inclusion of data from 1986 and 1987 update the initial study, which examined results between 1970 and 1985. With the inclusion of 1986 and 1987 data, the impact of these mergers and buy-outs was evident. The base year for establishing company size rankings and for inclusion in the study was kept at 1985.

While conclusions will be drawn from the data. It should be noted that many factors are involved in the make-up of inventory levels. Information that is not known, and was not within the scope of this study, include the fact that the inventory levels presented were possibly affected by changes in a company's manufacturing process. Also, new product introductions are another influence on inventory levels. There are a number of reasons that could affect the data. However, it is believed the information base is sufficiently broad to allow for comparisons and analysis of both the individual industries and of the four industries as a group.

RESULTS AND INTERPRETATIONS

Once the available data was compiled, it was grouped together by industry. In order to develop the analysis, each industry's results are presented individually. This section focuses on the improvements made in regard to inventory management. Later sections look at the other questions of size and profitability, and also examine the four industry groups together. In this section, the data for each industry was compiled in the same manner.

For each company, the data accumulated and compiled includes annual sales, inventory levels (at fiscal year end), and inventories as a per centage of sales. The tables of data are quite extensive and lengthy. Due to space limitations, all tables compiled are not included in this text. A sample is shown for the chemical industry, which is the first group whose results are discussed. (A complete set of study results is available on request.)

For each industry, yearly averages of inventories as a per centage of sales were computed. The yearly industry averages were determined by giving equal weight to each company within the industry. This was done to give a better feeling for each industry trend without skewing the data in the direction of the larger companies within each group. For comparative purposes, the graphs for each industry are plotted on the same scale.

For the chemical industry, one can see that, on the average, the inventory to sales ratio dropped from a level of 20.1% in 1970 to 12.6% in 1987, for a 37.3% decline. The correlation coefficient for these data is -.964. The general trend for the chemical industry was consistently downward, with the exception of the over-stockpiling that resulted from the inventory shortages of 1972-1973, and slight increases in 1981 and 1986.

Overall, the data for the chemical industry is quite dramatic. To fully understand the industry's results, the types of chemical companies are identified by group according to Value Line classes of basic, diversified, and specialty. In examining the individual company's ratios over the time of the study, no identifiable patterns developed to distinguish these three groups.

For the electronics industry, the inventory-to-sales ratio dropped from a level of 21.3% in 1970 to 15.6% in 1987, for a 26.8% decline. Again, the trend was definitely downward with the exception of four years, and the correlation coefficient is -.916. In 1973-1974, a sharp increase is seen. This increase is also observed in the chemical industry results. Yet an interesting result for this industry is that five years later, in 1979, a sharp increase occurred again. Lastly, in 1994, again five years later, another minor increase occurred.

The interesting point to be made here is to note how the"spikes" in the data soften as we progress through the years. Technology can be credited as playing a big factor in this. As technology advances, new types of inventory control systems allow for much more responsiveness in minimizing the"whip" effect, and inventories reacted more quickly to changes in business and economic factors. (Prior to increased technological tracking methods, downturns and upswings in business activity would not be reflected quickly in inventory level adjustments. The"whip" effect is the term used to describe this situation.)

When trying to draw conclusions about the electronics group, it is important to point out again that this group has been defined by Fortune magazine. When Value Line was referenced, it had two electronics classifications: electronics and electrical equipment. Only 5 of the 17 companies studied were classified by Value Line as being in either one of these groups.

This leads one to believe that this group includes a large number of electronics-related companies, and as a result will be the least homogeneous industry under consideration.

For the food industry, the industry average dropped from 14.4% in 1970 to 11.1% in 1987, for a 22.9% decline. The correlation coefficient for this industry is -.725. As with the two previous industries, the food industry figures jumped in 1973 and 1974. Like the electronics industry, the food industry also was up in the 1979 and 1984 eras. The overall curve for the food industry does not have the same slope as the two previous industries, yet a definite trend does exist.

For the pharmaceutical industry, the inventory to sales average dropped from 21.3% in 1970 to 14.9% in 1987 for a 30% decline. An interesting note about this group is that from 1970 to 1979, not much progress was made in inventory reductions, but from 1979 to 1987, consistent and broad cuts were made. The overall correlation coefficient is -.748. In summarizing these individual results, each industry exhibits a definite downward sloping curve. While the chemical industry made the largest declines from 1970 to 1987, the pharmaceutical companies studied lowered levels the most from 1979 through 1987.

COMPANY SIZE RESULTS

To answer the question,"Does the size of a company have any bearing on the levels of inventory maintained?", the five largest and five smallest companies in each industry are grouped together, and an average"big" and"small" company yearly inventory level is generated. For the chemical industry, one can see that size does not by itself provide a means of differentiating inventory levels. The two averages cross each other on three occasions.

However, it is interesting that the bigger companies do not have the big swings in inventory levels seen with the smaller companies. Size appears to have a stabilizing influence in regard to inventory levels, which may be a simple result of the difficulty of changing larger inventory levels quickly. Or, it may be that the larger companies are more diversified, which would tend to have a smoothing effect on overall inventory levels. For the electronics industry, the larger companies clearly run at consistently lower relative levels of inventory than do the smaller companies in the study.

Again, the spikes in inventory levels are present for the smaller companies, but less dramatic for the larger companies. For the food industry, no conclusions can be drawn regarding size. This graph clearly illustrates the spike phenomenon. Note how the smaller companies follow the same trends as their larger counterparts, but at greater extremes.

The graph for the pharmaceutical companies shows that the larger companies ran at consistently lower relative inventory levels with the exception of 1987. To summarize, while two of the graphs (electronics and pharmaceuticals) suggest that larger companies run at lower inventory levels than their smaller competitors, two of the other graphs (chemical and food) do not support this conclusion. Keep in mind that the"small" companies included in this study are still Fortune 500 companies. A true study of"small" businesses might provide more insight into this research question.

COMPANY PROFIT RESULTS

To determine if inventory levels can be tied to company profits the five most profitable companies and the five least profitable companies for each year were grouped together and compared. By looking at the graphs, one can see that no conclusions can be drawn regarding this question.

For three of the industries, the graphs repeatedly weave across each other. Only the graph for the food industry provides any differentiation in the curves. It shows that for the food industry, the more profitable companies maintained higher levels of inventory than their less profitable counterparts.

CROSS-INDUSTRY COMPARISONS AND INTERPRETATIONS

Attention is now turned to comparisons of all four industries to determine how each performed in this period in relation to the others. By viewing the data this way, one can see that broad differences do exist in the inventory to sales ratio of the four industries. Yet the ratios for the four industries did converge in the latter years.

Except for a brief period from 1971 to 1973, and again in 1987, when the electronics and pharmaceutical industries reversed positions, each industry has maintained the same relative overall inventory to sales ratio ranking (i.e., the food industry running at the lowest ratios and the pharmaceutical industry running at the highest ratios).

An interesting pattern in the data is identifiable and warrants discussion. First, consider the landmark customer service study presented to the National Council of Physical Distribution Management in 1976 by LaLonde and Zinszer. In their presentation, they showed that as a per centage of sales, total transportation and warehousing costs for the four industries in question were:

- Food Industry 11.6%
- Chemical and Plastics Industry 9.6%
- Electronics Industry 6.4%
- Pharmaceutical Industry 2.6%

If the inventories to sales per centages are listed for the same four industries for the same year as the study (1976):

- Food Industry 12.6%
- Chemical and Plastics Industry 17.5%
- Electronics Industry 20.6%
- Pharmaceutical Industry 21.6%

One can see that the per centages are inversely related (i.e., the food industry had the highest total transportation and warehousing cost and the lowest inventory levels. etc.) Next, consider the 1985 Physical Distribution Cost and Service Database compiled by Herbert W. Davis and Company.

Once again, aside from the exclusion of the electronics industry from the Davis Report, the numbers are inversely related. In fact, this finding presents an interesting possibility. It appears as if companies within each industry either consciously or subconsciously are performing some form of trade-off analysis or "total acceptable logistics costs" analysis. This notion suggests that logistics managers have an idea of what is viewed as acceptable logistics cost, and plan their logistics system around that concept.

Consider the following two scenarios for the extreme industries in regard to these figures. First, with their relatively low transportation and warehousing costs, pharmaceutical logistics managers do not feel as compelled to keep as close a watch on inventory levels. Due to demanding customer service requirements, higher levels are maintained. Even with additional inventory costs, total distribution costs as a per centage of sales remain quite low, and thus are considered to be at an acceptable level.

Contrast this with the situation facing food logistics managers. With transportation and warehousing costs very high, these managers know that inventory levels must be kept lean. Thus, their levels of inventory are necessarily squeezed to minimal levels in order that total logistics costs, while still very high, can be defended as being at minimal levels. Likewise, similar scenarios can be generated for the chemical and electronics industries in varying degrees.

As the cost of money skyrocketed in the mid-1970s, those companies with this natural slack saw inventory costs rising quickly and were forced into reduction measures. As pressures have mounted for inventory reduction measures, more attention has been directed at utilizing the inventory management tools that technology has made available. Inventory data are now readily accessible due to the computer systems in place at most companies.

MANAGERIAL IMPLICATIONS

Upon examining the data that have been collected in this area, anyone with an interest in inventory management cannot help but be impressed with the strides made in reducing inventory levels. This study, while unfortunately not drawing conclusive ties to inventory levels and profits, shows us that great advances have been made in the management of inventories. What is really quite impressive is the short time span over which the results were accomplished within these four industries. Knowing what has been accomplished will most surely make any aggressive logistics manager encouraged about future potential gains in this area. If the notion of"total acceptable costs" is a valid concept, one cannot help but wonder what minimum levels of inventory could be achieved if given the proper attention. This is not to imply that inventories can be manipulated and trimmed with ease. On the contrary, an inventory network is a complex system, and positive change can only come about through commitments to such desired results.

If one concedes that this theory of"total acceptable costs" may be valid, then one also concedes that there definitely exists further levels of efficiency to be achieved. Considering the new technologies and methodologies being studied and implemented today, this research could help create a new sense of excitement and curiosity about the future among logistics-minded individuals. Also, there are some interesting trends that are observable in the data.

The convergence of the industry groups indicates that inventory control techniques are being applied effectively by most companies within each of the industries. The smoothing of inventory swings over the period of the study makes a strong statement about the role of computerization and forecasting in controlling inventory levels.

Lastly, this study provides good benchmark figures for all types of companies. For those companies within each industry studied, it provides direct comparisons with competitors and offers insight into how they measure up against their industry's trend.

For companies in industries other than those studied, it provides a means of greater understanding of how inventory levels in general have been managed. There were four research questions presented at the beginning of this chapter aimed at focusing the direction of the data analysis.

The conclusions reached from these questions are now discussed:

- How have inventory levels dropped over the past two decades in the four industries studied? This first question brought the most dramatic offering from the analysis. Each industry made significant reductions in the levels of inventory held during the time period of the study. Inventories declined a minimum of 22.9% for the food industry, to a high of 37.3% for the chemical industry. Obviously, a great deal of attention and resources were given to reducing inventory levels throughout each industry.
- What effect does the size of a company have on its inventory levels? No clear-cut conclusions can be drawn from the data with respect to this question. The data gathered showed that in two industries (electronics and pharmaceuticals), the larger companies operated with lower relative levels than did their smaller counterparts. However, the other two groups (chemical and food) do not support the same conclusion.
- Does the level of a company's inventory affect its profitability? Again, no definite conclusions can be drawn from the data. The only group that exhibited any clear pattern was the food industry, whose more profitable members held higher inventory levels than their less profitable competitors.

- Have companies been able to control inventories as a strategic-management tool? The three previous questions were aimed at statistically measuring the issues raised about inventory control methods of the past two decades. The most striking data is produced by the research done on the first question. This much is true: management has been able to reduce the levels of inventories held. The issues of size and profit established in the other two questions are not answered by this research.

With the declines in inventory levels shown in this study one can conclude that management has successfully turned inventory control into a strategic tool. The realization of this notion has given managers increased options in the operation of their business units.

In an era of increased customer service awareness, inventory levels have been substantially reduced. As such, management's perception of inventory should reflect this attitude. By no means has a static necessity, inventory management become a dynamic tool.

To logistics executives, this research may bring about an increased awareness of potential gains that may not yet have been realised. The companies in the four industries studied suggest how inventories can be managed more effectively, and have thus moved toward making themselves much stronger companies.

Not only have their inventory costs decreased, but the additional information and increased responsiveness provided by new technological inventory applications is invaluable. Further, the comparison of industry results with distribution cost information presents interesting evidence that indicates there is room for improvement in the area of inventory control. While this may seem obvious to most, this research should help to reinforce the notion.

Thus, it is hoped that at the minimum, the findings presented by this study will accomplish two goals: first, to confirm for those who are committing their time to the improvement of inventory control measures that they are indeed pursuing a worthwhile cause, and secondly, to convince others that further time and effort allocated to the area of inventory control will in return provide the potential for great dividends.

12

Distribution Policies

Some of the distribution policies guiding business enterprises have already been discussed in appropriate parts of this book. For example, a fairly detailed treatment of the nature of distribution channels, their vertical and horizontal aspects, and the various factors involved in a proper choice for a given type of merchandise. Similarly, throughout the parts dealing with retailing and wholesaling institutions, each principal type was examined in the light of its advantages and limitations and possible use as part of a channel of distribution for certain goods. There remain, however, several important questions of distribution policy that have not been previously covered. One of these relates to the number of outlets to be used in a given channel or on a given level of distribution. Another has to do with the service policies that are related to distribution policies. A third deals with leasing as a distribution policy or strategy.

GENERAL VERSUS LIMITED DISTRIBUTION

Following the selection of a channel or channels of distribution for a given product or line of merchandise, it remains to be determined, by way of policy, whether the distribution should be effected through the largest possible number of outlets on a given level or plane or through a highly selected group of such outlets. The first policy involves what may be termed as "general distribution" or blanket coverage of the entire market; the second type of policy may take the form of selective distribution or exclusive agency arrangement. On the surface it might appear best for a seller to obtain the widest possible distribution for his product or line of merchandise and thus secure for it the maximum exposure to ultimate consumers or business buyers.

This would obviously call for a policy of general distribution. Actually, however, such a policy is quite limited in application, partly because of the cost factor and partly on account of the nature of the goods and the buying behaviour of consumers and other customers. In the field of consumer goods, widespread or general distribution is confined almost altogether to convenience goods, and even there it is limited to the leading brands of the most widely used and most frequently replaced or purchased items on a convenience basis by the vast majority of the consuming public. In this category are such items as cigarettes, candy bars, matches, toothpaste, bread, and aspirin tablets all of which are sold through a multiplicity of channels with both vertical and horizontal variants. For such products maximum sales can be realized best in this manner. In the long run, the costs involved and the buying pattern of consumers determine the kinds and numbers of outlets and the relative importance of each outlet type through which a given product will be distributed.

This applies to wholesale as well as to retail types of outlets, the latter determining the former. For example, a product sold through drugstores is also likely to be handled by wholesale drug firms that normally serve the retail outlets. It follows that if more than one type of retail outlet is used, the same would tend to be equally true of the wholesale level of distribution. That is why some cosmetics and toilet goods are sold not only through drug wholesalers, but also through wholesale grocers, tobacco jobbers, dry goods wholesalers, sundry wholesalers, and others in order to reach drugstores, grocery stores, dry goods and department stores, confectionery establishments, and general stores.

In the industrial market, a policy of general distribution is adopted only for commodities that are highly standardized and that have a horizontal market. Illustrative are small hand tools, cleaning preparations, and other standard supplies.

POLICIES OF LIMITED DISTRIBUTION

While a policy of general distribution is appropriate under the circumstances indicated above, the great majority of manufactured items are marketed through a selected or limited number of outlets on the retail or wholesale level of distribution, or on both such levels. An extreme form of this policy is known as the *exclusive agency method of distribution,* while a more liberal application of similar concepts gives rise to what is known as *selective distribution.*

Exclusive Agency Method of Distribution

An exclusive agency arrangement presupposes a definite agreement between principal and agent, each assuming certain obligations. The relationship is exclusive in the sense that the vendor agrees to sell his goods or services within a certain territory only through a single dealer or through a limited number of such representatives. The agreement not to sell to any representative other than the one to whom the privilege is granted results in a relationship known as a single, unlimited, exclusive agency. The term joint exclusive agency, although somewhat of an incongruity, is often used to designate a situation where more than one representative is selected to serve a given territory. Both the size of territory to be covered and the number of representatives appointed depend upon the type of commodity or service to be sold and the density of the market, judged usually by the number and size of potential customers in the case of industrial goods and by the extent of the population in the case of consumer goods. In the marketing of automobiles, for example, one representative dealer may suffice for the Lincoln or Cadillac in a community of about 300,000; but several dealers are required to handle Chevrolets, Plymouths, or Fords in the same community if the territory is to be covered intensively.

The number of prospects to be cultivated for the latter cars exceeds by far the number of possible purchasers for the more expensive product. When paints and varnishes are distributed on this basis, it is usually advisable to have a number of dealers handle the product in different parts of a large city. Well-known lines of men's clothing, on the other hand, are more often distributed through a single retailer in a community. Not infrequently a manufacturer combines the two methods, appointing single exclusive agents for areas with a sparse population and two or more agents for large metropolitan areas.

While the term agent or agency is commonly used in connection with an exclusive dealing arrangement, actually there is no agency relationship in the legal sense. The dealer having the so-called agency does not act for a principal. Since he purchases the goods outright and takes full title to them, he acts on his own behalf in the conduct of the business and not as an agent for someone else. As such he is an independent businessman with full dominion over the goods in which he deals and over his operating methods. His actions as an "authorized agent" are subject only to certain price and other restrictions as mutually agreed upon by a cancelable arrangement.

Exclusive agencies are sometimes granted by manufacturers to wholesalers who may, in turn, be required to select retail outlets in their respective territories or to sell the line to all dealers who qualify financially and otherwise. When agencies are given to wholesalers of consumer goods, as is common in the musical instrument field, the electrical trade, and the automotive accessories industry, or to industrial distributors, exclusive territories are naturally wider than when such agencies are extended to retailers and tend to correspond with the wholesale trading area of the city in which a distributor is located. The exclusive agency is, however, most common in lines which are generally distributed directly to retailers.

Exclusive Agency Agreements

Exclusive agency agreements may be formal or informal. Some manufacturers have no written contracts with their wholesalers or dealers, preferring to operate in this manner because they believe that it affords greater flexibility. When, however, the manufacturer's line of goods constitutes all or a very large share of the dealer's total sales volume, and possible misunderstandings about responsibilities of the parties may become matters of serious concern to either, it is common to spell out all pertinent matters in a written contract. Such contracts are sometimes called franchise agreements, and the expression franchised dealer or franchised distributor is often used to designate the retailer or wholesaler who has signed such an agreement with a manufacturer. The specific points covered in contracts vary considerably, but a clearer understanding of the nature of exclusive agency relationships can be gained from considering some of the items commonly covered in them, as indicated in the following list.

- The contract may enumerate exactly what *products* are *covered* by the agreement, which is especially important in cases where the manufacturer does not desire to distribute all of his products through exclusive agents.
- The agreement may be limited to certain *classes or types of customers.* The manufacturer sometimes retains the right to sell direct to some customers such as large industrial users or national chain store organizations that purchase through central buying offices.
- The *territory* in which the agent has exclusive rights of sale may be defined. Sometimes this is supplemented by an agreement to the effect that the agent shall not make any sales outside this area, although this is becoming less common, as indicated by certain legal implications discussed at a later point.
- The dealer may agree to maintain adequate *inventories* of specified items covered by the franchise. In the case of consumer durables and industrial equipment, this may also be broadened to include repair parts and the types of *installation and repair services* which the agent is to provide for his customers.
- *Prices* to be paid to the manufacturer and to be charged to the agent's customers are often specified. Even though it may not be practical to incorporate specific selling prices in the agreement, the basis for price determination is often indicated. For example, in a contract used by a wholesale distributor for a line of furnaces, the retail dealer is granted in the franchise a quantity discount according to a schedule based on the dealer's annual volume of purchases. It is sometimes required that the dealer agree to maintain the manufacturer's resale prices.
- In return for the privilege of becoming an exclusive agent, the dealer is sometimes expected to meet a *sales quota.* Some minimum level of dollar or unit purchases may be specified in the contract, or some method of arriving at annual quotas may be defined. For example, an exclusive wholesale distributor for a line of major household appliances may have to agree to obtain a total sales volume within his territory which is determined by applying a percentage to the national sales objective of the manufacturer. The percentage may be ascertained on the basis of the number of wired homes within the distributor's territory as a per cent of the total number of such

homes throughout the country. Failure of the agent to obtain the level of quota sales may be a cause for terminating, on due notice, the franchise agreement.

- *Advertising and sales promotional* obligations of both parties may be indicated. This may include some statement about the quality or ethical standards to be maintained in local dealer advertising. The amount of advertising to be placed by the dealer or distributor and the degree to which the manufacturer will cooperate in payment for it may also be specified.
- It is sometimes provided that the agent shall deal only in products furnished by the manufacturer or, if the agent carries a diversified product line, that he shall not deal in any products that are directly competitive with those of the manufacturer. As explained in a later section, such *exclusive dealing covenants* may involve complex legal questions. It is, therefore, more common for manufacturers to obtain exclusive dealing arrangements by other means-by oral agreements (which may also be found illegal on the basis of intent or effect), by refusing to grant exclusive agency contracts to prospective dealers who handle a competitive line, or by terminating contracts with dealers who take on a competitive line.
- The *duration* of the contract is usually specified. Such agreements are normally for a period of one year, but contain a *provision for renewal.* As a rule, *termination* can be effected by the agent on reasonably short notice, say 30 days, or by the manufacturer; but in the latter case termination may be limited to certain causes which are stated in the agreement. In the contracts used by one of the leading automobile manufacturers, the dealer may arrange for anyone who is active in his business to succeed him as the franchise holder in event of death or incapacity. Furthermore, since the passage of the Automobile Franchise Act (1956) some companies have announced agreements for an initial period of three to five years, all subject to renewal.

Advantages and Disadvantages to Manufacturers

Manufacturers often desire to retain close control over resale prices, kind of selling, and servicing standards. When it is not possible for a manufacturer to sell direct to business users or ultimate consumers, the exclusive agency plan is an alternative means of effecting such control. By limiting distribution to exclusive agents, thus providing each of them with a reasonably large sales and profit potential, the manufacturer may expect special and concentrated sales effort from his distributive organization. Once agencies have been established, there is little need for ordinary personal selling effort on his part. His salesmen can devote more time to educational activities, service work, and dealer development programs. When quotas are incorporated in the contracts, it is easier to count on a certain amount of business in advance. It is thus possible to develop a regular and economical schedule of manufacturing. Use of exclusive agencies holds to a minimum the number of accounts with which the manufacturer must do business. This tends to reduce certain expenses involved in physical distribution and in communications, such as credit investigations, shipping, accounting, and correspondence.

When the number of outlets for a manufacturer's product is very limited, there is the disadvantage that exposure to sale and perhaps actual sales may also be unduly limited. The problem of selecting an adequate number of the most desirable outlets is usually rather complex. Often the most desirable outlets in the trade are already pre-empted as exclusive agents for competitive products. If mass market advertising is used, some circulation may be wasted because the network of distributing organizations does not always provide full market coverage. When a particular agent does not do a good selling job, the manufacturer's sales are likely to suffer greatly in a given market area. While the manufacturer has the right to terminate contracts with unsatisfactory agents, he is often reluctant to do so because of difficulties in locating more satisfactory agents, or because of a fear of developing antagonism among other agents who are doing a satisfactory job. To illustrate, in the automobile industry in the mid-1950's leading manufacturers disenfranchised a considerable number of well-established dealers who were unable to meet their sales quotas in the face of competition from large new retail agencies that operated on a high-volume, low-overhead, aggressive advertising approach.

Termination of such franchises was one of a number of practices carefully investigated in a 1956 Congressional study of marketing practices in the automobile industry and particularly of certain alleged monopolistic implications attributed to the bigness of the General Motors Corporation. It was also a condition that promoted considerable unrest among automobile dealers, led them to make unified and persistent demands upon manufacturers, and resulted in various liberalizations in customary franchise agreements and in the enactment of the Automobile Franchise Act.

Advantages and Disadvantages to Middlemen

Several benefits may accrue to wholesalers and retailers who receive exclusive rights to sell a line of goods in a given area. Parallel lines may be eliminated, thus facilitating both a concentration of sales effort and a more rapid rate of stock turn. Manufacturer as well as dealer promotional effort should be reflected directly in larger sales volume, with little of the beneficial effects carried over to the business of competitors in the area. Closer cooperation and more concessions can be expected from manufacturers than would otherwise be possible. A profitable margin is easier to maintain because there is no competitor in the area to cut prices on identical goods. As the product is exclusive, the consumer has little opportunity to shop around and compare prices on the identical item. If the line gains consumer acceptance, repeat sales are assured because the customer will seek out the dealer handling the particular brand. As a matter of fact, good will created for the exclusive line may result in increased trade for other items carried by the retailer or distributor.

This method of distribution is not without disadvantages to middlemen. Sales volume may be adversely affected where strong brand preferences have been developed in competing lines. There is always a possibility of overstocking, because quotas set by manufacturers are frequently larger than can be absorbed by the market which the agent serves. It may become more difficult to meet competition from price cutters handling similar lines, since manufacturers operating on this basis usually stipulate resale prices from which it is inadvisable to deviate. The policy often invites increased competition from exclusive agents selling parallel lines. The principal disadvantage, however, consists in possible termination of the arrangement on the initiative of the manufacturer. An agency is sometimes withdrawn from one agent and transferred to another who is supposedly better qualified to render satisfactory service. The exclusive agency plan is sometimes used by a manufacturer as a means of breaking into the market and securing initial distribution. Once the line becomes well established in the public mind, the exclusive privilege may be withdrawn. The agent who has spent time, money, and effort in his pioneer attempt to build up patronage will then find several dealers in the community taking advantage of the situation.

Some Specific Possibilities and Limitations

From what has been said above, it should be apparent that exclusive agencies cannot *normally* be used at the retail level in the distribution of convenience goods which consumers desire to purchase at the nearest stores, nor for many items of shopping goods where consumers make comparisons in several stores, which circumstance indicates the need for more than one retail outlet. Exclusive agencies are used by many manufacturers under certain conditions. The more usual of these may be listed for convenience as follows:

- In the marketing of specialty goods which have a sufficient attraction to induce consumers to put forth unusual effort to visit the one establishment where they are sold.
- In introducing new goods or in breaking into new markets. Such a circumstance often prompts the use of an exclusive agency even for convenience or shopping goods as an introductory device, especially when the agents selected for this purpose are large chain organizations or department stores that are in a position to provide substantial advertising and sales promotion support and which can practically insure a significant volume of sales during an introductory period.

- When dealers must make a large investment in order to carry a representative stock of the line produced by a manufacturer. This is often true of such items as men's suits and major household appliances.

Where special installation or repair services must be made available in connection with the sale of a product. Farm tractors, automobiles, household air conditioning equipment, and furnaces are illustrative in the field of consumer goods. Among types of industrial or business goods meeting this criterion and commonly sold on an exclusive agency basis by distributors are barber chairs, hospital operating room equipment, road construction machinery, industrial trucks for materials-handling purposes, and certain types of lathes and drilling equipment.

The exclusive agency method of marketing has tended to diminish somewhat in importance owing to several circumstances discussed elsewhere and at other places in the book. First, the emergence of new discount retailing companies has provided many manufacturers with a desired type of outlet not previously available in many market areas. Second, the growth of scrambled retailing, or merchandise line diversification by many kinds of traditional retailers, has led manufacturers to seek retail outlets in multiple kinds of business classifications. Third, the development of central service facilities, especially in the household appliance trade, has reduced the need for the manufacturer to depend upon dealers with service departments. Fourth, as rising levels of more evenly distributed purchasing power have created a more homogeneous consumer market, many articles once considered luxuries have become common needs, thus causing some manufacturers to seek more widespread distribution. For these and other related reasons, formal exclusive agency arrangements have tended to give way to selective distribution in many industries.

Selective Distribution

This is a policy of *selecting only those distributors or outlets that are able best to serve the manufacturer or wholesaler making the selection.* It is similar to the policy of distributing through exclusive agencies but differs in that several dealers or distributors are often used in a single trading area, and arrangements are usually less formal and not as restrictive. It can be applied to convenience, shopping, or specialty goods, except that a larger number of outlets must be chosen for the first-named class of goods. The policy results in eliminating sales to dealers or wholesalers whose orders are so small as to make their business unprofitable or who, because of a bad credit standing, a reputation for making too many returns, or for asking too much service, are not deemed profitable customers.

Manufacturers who follow a policy of selective distribution do so in order to obtain most of the advantages that can be realized through an exclusive agency policy, but to accomplish this objective without unduly restricting the number of customers. A selective distribution policy is often feasible under conditions when it would be unthinkable to follow a policy of exclusive agency distribution.

Some Illustrations

A drug wholesaler formerly employed a large staff of salesmen who called on all drugstores in his trading area. Although some retailers purchased most of their requirements from this wholesaler, others gave him only occasional or token orders. From a sales analysis it was learned that about 80 per cent of total sales volume was accounted for by orders received from only 24 per cent of the total number of customers.

This meant that about three-fourths of total selling effort in terms of sales calls was devoted to the group of customers that contributed only one-fifth of the sales volume. As a result of additional studies, the wholesaler concluded that it was not ordinarily worthwhile to continue soliciting business from a drugstore unless sales to it amounted to about 40 per cent or more of the store's requirements for types of merchandise handled by the wholesaler. By discontinuing sales calls upon outlets that fell far short of meeting this criterion, and by having salesmen spend a larger amount of time per call on customers who bought a large share of their requirements from the house, it was possible to help retailers with sales training and promotional work and thereby increase their purchases at any one time and in total.

A manufacturer of a wide line of standardized rubber industrial products has potential users in almost all types of manufacturing industries. To reach such users, the company sells through a large number of industrial distributors in a variety of trade classifications. Attempts are made to limit distribution to firms that will devote special attention to the line. In doing so, it is easier to insure that each distributor will have a reasonable opportunity to obtain an adequate volume of profitable sales, provided proper selling effort is used. When it appears that a given market area has sufficient potential to justify an increase in the number of distributors in it, additional wholesale outlets are carefully selected.

As a basis for the selection, information is obtained from complete credit investigations of prospective distributors obtained from a national credit agency, correspondence with other manufacturers of noncompetitive products that sell through the distributors to determine the quality of services they provide to suppliers, interviews with selected industrial purchasing agents in the area to determine the standing of distributors among customers, and personal visitations at each distributor's place of business to ascertain the quality of his sales and inside personnel, the number and types of items handled, extent of the trading area served, adequacy of physical facilities, financial condition of the firm, and other relevant matters.

Application of the Policy

Manufacturers and wholesalers who seek to change from a policy of general to more selective distribution have a number of problems to solve before it can be placed in effect. The principal ones relate to the cost of serving different classes of buyers and those who buy in varying quantities. It is thus necessary to analyse distributive expenses in order to know the costs of selling under varying conditions. When this is done it is often found that, in some lines, only those buyers who purchase in original packages are profitable for wholesalers. In some cases the minimum point may be a dozen or a hundred packages or a certain volume in dollars. In other cases, study may disclose that it is not profitable to sell to certain entire classes of buyers. Distribution cost analyses give distributors or manufacturers a definite idea as to how large an average order must be to justify servicing an account on a profitable basis. They may also disclose that certain classes of customers should be omitted from the sales plan. Yet it is not always feasible to restrict calls to profitable accounts. Sometimes new accounts must be cultivated at a loss for an initial period, with the hope that they will ultimately develop into profitable outlets. Many manufacturers feel that although some classes of customers are not profitable when measured by direct selling costs, the volume which they contribute is an essential part of the entire production plan of the factory, and therefore a greater loss might be incurred were this portion of the sales volume eliminated. It also depends upon prevailing economic conditions. Selective distribution is favored in a sellers' market or when competition compels strict attention to economy of operation.

Service Policies and Policies of Limited Distribution

Policies with respect to installation and repair services have an important bearing upon the degree to which it is feasible or desirable to limit distribution to exclusive or selected outlets. In the marketing of major appliances, the maintenance of adequate consumer service has always been an important problem related to distribution channel questions. Traditionally, service was supplied by the franchised appliance dealer who, in typical situations, maintained a separate repair department employing from one to three or four persons. For many years service was an extremely important patronage motive among consumers. Manufacturers tended to limit the distribution of major appliances largely to dealers who could provide a strong personal selling organization and satisfactory installation and repair service facilities. Since the mid1940's, the market for appliances has been substantially enlarged, but not nearly to the extent that manufacturing capacity in the industry was over-optimistically increased. This generated great internal economic pressure for most manufacturers to increase sales volume and created much more aggressive competition among them. As a result of failure of marginal manufacturing firms, product quality improvements by survivors, and mass media advertising, a number of existing brands are acceptable to most consumers. A substantial segment of the consuming public relies less upon the reputation of the store in which it buys and more upon attitude toward the manufacturer's line as created by his advertising programme and as derived from hearsay information among consumer associates. Under such conditions, the sale of appliances by retailing organizations without service facilities has become much more common.

The consumer, nevertheless, demands some kinds of service after sale. Often this has been provided only with great reluctance by regular dealers in cases where they did not make the original sale. Such dealers, moreover, have found it difficult to keep pace with technological progress as related to service problems in the industry. Substantial investments in capital are required for shop equipment to service properly television sets, freezers, and home laundry equipment, all of which are manufactured with increasingly complex automatic features or attachments. It is difficult to realise a profitable return on the investment in such equipment unless a large and regular volume of service business is developed and is also well managed.

Because of the growing importance of sales of appliances through discount houses and other dealers who may not provide services, and because of consumer dissatisfaction with the type of service provided by some smaller dealers without properly trained personnel or with inadequate equipment, a number of manufacturers have established central service organizations in major metropolitan areas. General Electric Company and Westinghouse Electric Corporation, for example, have provided central service facilities of their own or those managed by their wholesale distributors in a large number of metropolitan areas with over 100,000 population. Some of these facilities have as many as 100 service employees and may do as much service work as the aggregate of 100 or more independent dealers operating small-scale service shops. Obviously, only a large metropolitan area will support such a centralized service arrangement. In small market areas, service is still handled almost wholly by dealers who must necessarily be selected with a view to their ability to render needed installation and repair service.

Maintenance of a central service organization in a large city obviously tends to insure satisfactory servicing of appliances at probably lower costs. In addition, it reduces the need for confining distribution to carefully selected and decidedly limited numbers of outlets. A manufacturer's line of products that is pre sold to some extent through aggressive advertising and other types of sales promotion may thus be placed in a much larger number of diverse types of outlets, approaching a more general or broadly selective method of distribution.

Legal Implications

Applications of exclusive agency or selective distribution policies pose several questions as to legality under the antitrust laws. One relates to the right of a manufacturer to prohibit a dealer from handling competitive products, a second has to do with the right to confine a distributor's sales to a defined territory, a third has to do with the right to force a dealer to carry a full line, and a fourth is concerned with the right to refuse to sell to a dealer who may desire to purchase from another manufacturer. Under varying conditions, these might be subject to one or more of three federal laws—the Sherman Antitrust Act, the Clayton Act, and Federal Trade Commission Act under Section 5.

Exclusive Dealing

The first question is governed mainly by Section 3 of the Clayton Antitrust Act of 1914 which provides, in part, as follows: It shall be unlawful for any person engaged in commerce to lease or make a sale or contract for sale of goods... on the condition, agreement, or understanding that the lessee or purchaser thereof shall not use or deal in the goods... of a competitor of the lessor or seller... where the effect of such lease, sale, or contract... may be to substantially lessen competition or tend to create a monopoly in any line of commerce.

After the enactment of this law, the courts have consistently condemned contracts between manufacturers and dealers which excluded the sale of competitive goods by the latter when the volume of the manufacturer's sales was a significant proportion of the total volume for the type of product in question, or when the effect was to exclude competitors from a substantial part of a market.

An important case in point is that of the Standard Oil Company of California, ruled upon by the Supreme Court in June of 1949. It was shown that the company's sales of petroleum products constituted 23 per cent of the total in a group of "western" states of which sales by company owned stations represented 6.8 per cent, sales by independent stations with exclusive agency contracts accounted for 6.7 per cent, and sales to industrial users constituted the remainder. Operators of 5,937 independent stations had signed exclusive agency contracts which required the dealers to purchase all of their requirements of one or more products from the company. The court ruled the contracts illegal because "competition has been foreclosed in a substantial share of the line of commerce affected," and further, that "Standard's use of the contracts creates just such a potential clog on competition as it was the purpose of Section 3 to remove wherever, were it to become actual, it would impede a substantial amount of competitive activity." Another important illustrative case is that of Dictograph Products, Inc., ruled upon by the Supreme Court in 1955. In an industry in which there were about 1,000 retail dealers for hearing aids, Dictograph had exclusive dealing contracts with 220 of them. These contracts contained provisions for mutual termination, but with the requirement that the distributor shall not engage in the hearing aid business in the same sales area for one year if he becomes unwilling to continue the sale of Dictograph hearing aids exclusively. The court upheld the Federal Trade Commission in the ruling that these agreements tended to foreclose a substantial portion of the market to competitors and denied competitive opportunities to Dictograph dealers. A substantial volume of business was affected and, it was ruled, there was a tendency to substantially lessen competition in violation of Section 3 of the Clayton Act. On the other hand, in a number of cases it has been held that contracts involving small or insignificant proportions of the business in a particular line do not come within the scope of this provision.

For example, in a case involving a manufacturer who sold about 1 per cent of the national production of oleomargarine and who made contracts with wholesalers that prohibited them from handling competing brands (even though it gave each wholesaler exclusive selling privileges in a certain territory), and where some 20 other manufacturers had similar contracts and the largest producers did not use exclusive contracts, it was held that the contracts did not have an actual or potential effect to substantially lessen competition. There is, however, no hard and fast rule that may be applied to determine in advance the legality of such a proposed exclusive dealing policy. The question depends upon the volume of business involved, the practices of competitors, and other considerations in a particular industry or line of trade that may be considered by the Federal Trade Commission or by the courts in order to evaluate the effects of such agreements upon the actual or potential amount of competitive activity.

Exclusion features are perfectly legal when they are not related to competition. For example, the court upheld the right of oil companies to prohibit the sale of competing brands of gasoline in pumps and storage equipment supplied to the dealer by the manufacturer. It was ruled that the purpose of this agreement was not to restrict competition, but to prevent the confusion of the gasoline of the contracting oil companies with competing products and substitution, without knowledge by the ultimate consumer, of one brand for another.

Right to Confine a Dealer's Sales Territorially

As early as 1916 it was well established that manufacturers have the legal right to sell through one dealer in a given territory. Both state courts and Federal Trade Commission rulings have held that once a manufacturer designates an exclusive dealer in a given territory he may require the dealer not to sell his products outside of the territory assigned, and that such agreements are not per se in violation of the Sherman Antitrust Act, the Clayton Act, or state antitrust legislation. They become illegal, however, in cases where it can be shown that they have been used in such a manner that the effect was or tends to restrain competition or to monopolize commerce in the commodity. In Department of Justice cases brought in recent years against exclusive territorial distributor systems, all have involved two factors:

- Their use by very large or leading manufacturers and
- Government allegations that the exclusive territorial arrangement was part of an attempt to monopolize, illegally restrain competition, or fix resale prices.

A number of such cases have been settled by consent decree. In one illustrative case, the Philco Corporation was enjoined from engaging in a number of so-called restrictive practices including entering into or enforcing any contract, agreement, or understanding "limiting or restricting, directly or indirectly, the persons to whom or the territory within which any wholesale distributor or retail dealer may choose to sell Philco products." It was clearly specified, however, that Philco had the right "to designate geographical areas in which such distributors shall respectively be primarily responsible for wholesaling Philco products and to terminate the franchise of distributors who do not adequately represent Philco and promote the sale of all Philco products in areas so designated as their primary responsibility.

Full-Line Forcing

Requirements that a retailer or wholesaler handle a full line of a manufacturer's goods is not an illegal practice, as long as there is no requirement that the dealer shall not handle competitive products. To illustrate, in one important case brought under the Clayton Act, the government contended that the company required each of its dealers to handle the full line of its farm machinery as a condition of receiving the contract to handle any of its products.

It was asserted that this practice tended to exclude the dealer as an outlet for competitive lines of machinery. The court pointed out that "merely because a dealer handles one full line he is not disabled from handling another full line. In any event, a mutual arrangement between the farm machinery manufacturer and its dealer that it is for the best interest of both for the latter to handle a full line of the manufacturer's output, *without any restriction imposed upon the dealer,* is not violative of any law." There is an inference in this ruling and in other cases that a policy of full-line forcing which had the effect of excluding competitors from doing business with the dealers involved would be illegal, provided a substantial share of commerce in the commodity was involved.

Right to Refuse to Sell

A number of cases have been brought before the courts by the Federal Trade Commission and the Department of Justice, alleging that refusal to sell to dealers who desire to purchase constitutes a violation of the Sherman Act which prohibits contracts, combinations, or conspiracies in restraint of trade or monopolies or attempts to monopolize trade or commerce. The guiding principle in such cases is that stated in the famous Colgate case, decided by the Supreme Court in 1919, and in which the court ruled that the Sherman

Act "does not restrict the long recognized right of a trader or manufacturer engaged in an entirely private business, freely to exercise his own independent discretion as to parties with whom he will deal. And, of course, he may announce in advance the circumstances under which he will refuse to deal."

In another case a wholesale distributor brought suit against the Ronson Art Metal Works, Inc., for alleged violations of the Clayton Act, because of Ronson's refusal to continue to take orders from the wholesaler. Ronson had written to the wholesaler, in part, as follows: "At the present time we are reducing our distribution in most sections of the country and in your market area we find that we are very well covered with distribution by other distributors. We therefore regret that we shall be unable to ship any further Ronson merchandise to you. This move is consistent with our current policy of reducing our distributors in all territories where we already have adequate coverage." The court ruled that Ronson had the right to do business with whom it pleased; that, as a private trader in interstate commerce, it could refuse to sell its merchandise to anyone, and by so doing it would in no way violate the antitrust laws.

Not only does a seller have the undisputed right to choose his customers in the first place, but such right extends to his choice of whether to continue dealings. The latter applies even when a contract is in existence, so long as such contract is terminable and does not contain any provision prohibiting the customer from dealing in the products of a competitor (which would make the contract illegal and unenforceable). In another case it was ruled that the manufacturer has the right to stop dealing with a distributor who is acting unfairly toward his products, so long as this right is exercised in good faith and in a manner that will not "substantially lessen competition" or "tend to create a monopoly" in any line of commerce.

The right to refuse to sell may not be used as a matter of policy to attain illegal or monopolistic ends. A manufacturer may not refuse to sell to a dealer *solely* because the dealer refuses to enter into a price-fixing agreement, unless the agreement is legal under resale price maintenance legislation. Vertical price maintenance agreements or understandings which do not come within the scope of the socalled Fair Trade laws are illegal *per se*, regardless of the reasonableness of the price which may be set. In the historically significant Eastman Kodak case, the Supreme Court branded as an attempt to monopolize the discontinuance of photo supplies to a competitor who had previously resisted Kodak's attempts to buy him out in a plan for monopoly control. Much more recently, the Supreme Court similarly condemned a newspaper's policy of turning down advertisers who utilized a competing radio station, as part of a pattern of "bold, relentless, and predatory commercial behaviour" designed to stifle competition in local communication media.

This entire matter has become somewhat confused as a result of a later Supreme Court decision in which the *Colgate* doctrine has been modified, in fact substantially so according to the opinion of the three dissenting justices.

It was ruled in 1960 that the *Colgate* decision of 1919 still holds and that a manufacturer, having announced a price maintenance policy, may bring about adherence to it by refusing to deal with customers who do not observe that policy.

In the particular case before the court, however, it was decided that the company in question so entwined the wholesalers and retailers in a programme to promote general compliance with its price maintenance policy as to go beyond mere customer selection and to create combinations or conspiracies, in violation of Sections I and 3 of the Sherman Act, to enforce resale price maintenance. The dissenting justices disagreed with the majority opinion ruling on this question and concluded that, "It is surely the emptiest of formalisms to profess respect for *Colgate* and eviscerate it in application." It remains for the future for this obviously controversial question to be resolved.

LEASING AS A DISTRIBUTION POLICY

Nature of Leasing Arrangements

Under the lease method of marketing, the manufacturer or distributor gives possession of equipment or other articles to the customer. The manufacturer or distributor, commonly designated as the lessor, retains title and receives remuneration in the form of lease or rental payments made by the customer who is the lessee. Such a marketing policy is similar in many respects to that used in connection with instalment selling under the conditional sales agreement. A fundamental distinction is that under leasing there is usually no intention of passing title to the customer. Exceptions are encountered, however, in leasing contracts which provide that rental payments may be applied against a specified purchase price, on an instalment sale basis, if the lessee decides at a later date to make an outright purchase rather than continue the leasing arrangement.

Common Uses

In several industries, leasing is an extensively used distribution policy. Much of the machinery used in shoe, glass container, and textile manufacturing is distributed in this manner as are also many kinds of industrial trucks and conveyors for materials handling, container-filling machinery, and various types of special purpose machinery used for riveting, sawing, or welding. Many of the more complex types of business machines and tabulating equipment have been leased under a service plan that affords valuable advisory, training, and maintenance aids for the user's executive and other employees. In the transportation field, leasing is common in the case of rolling stock for railroads, trucks for intercity freight haulers and local users, tires for bus companies, and fleets of automobiles for executives and salesmen. Many items of major construction equipment are so distributed.

An interesting new development in 1960 consisted of programs announced by several manufacturers of appliances to lease equipment to owners of apartment houses. According to a plan in use by some manufacturers, the owner may lease all kinds of appliances needed for a multiple dwelling building for a set period of time, say five years. Full repair service is included in the contract. At the expiration of the contract period, the owner of the building may purchase the appliances if desired, or the contract will be renewed by replacing all used items with new models. Used items, in the latter case, would be marketed by the lessor through dealers as second-hand appliances.

Manufacturers of supplies and of consumer goods have in some cases expanded their markets and have secured exclusive patronage or preferable point-of-sale display positions by leasing equipment in conjunction with the sale of the basic product. Even in dealing with ultimate consumers, renting or leasing is important for such products as floor sanders, paint sprays, automobile trailers, and other items of fairly high unit value used only irregularly or periodically.

Principles Governing Leasing

Leasing policies have been in use for a sufficient period of time and under such a variety of circumstances that it has been possible to formulate a number of principles which govern the adoption of such a policy and which indicate the conditions under which it may be employed advantageously.

A fundamental principle is that leasing facilitates the securing of a fair profit return from a limited market. There are a number of kinds of highly technical and very costly production equipment for which the number of potential customers is very limited. Engineering and tooling costs in such cases may best be recovered by charging a royalty or rental fee. In this manner some part of any cost savings realized by the user may be returned to the manufacturer of the equipment. The major alternative would be to fix a price so high that the product might be out of reach of some of the few available customers.

Second, leasing is of significance to the user principally as a financing arrangement. While leasing does not actually involve an investment in fixed assets from a strict accounting standpoint, it does make possible the acquisition of fixed assets for use purposes on the basis of what amounts to a 100 per cent mortgage. Since no new fixed or long-term liability appears on financial statements of the user in many situations, he does not impair his credit standing with customary suppliers or sources of cash funds.

Any alternative method of financing an investment in equipment ordinarily involves the requirement for at least some down payment. From a tax standpoint, a genuine lease is the equivalent of greatly accelerated depreciation. In other words, an item of equipment that would have to be depreciated over a period of ten years for Internal Revenue requirements might be acquired and charged off as business expense in a much shorter period of time under leasing. Leasing often permits more rapid expansion because of other financial implications of income taxation. For example, payments for the outright purchase of new equipment are made from funds available *after* taxes, out of net profits, but lease payments for the use of equipment are business expenses charged *before* taxes. In most cases the aggregate monetary outlay for the use of equipment acquired on a lease basis is greater, over the period of the lease, than under any alternative form of financing. When tax implications are considered, and due account is given to alternative uses made of funds that might otherwise have been tied up in ownership of fixed assets, the *net* cost of leasing is commonly less than that of any alternative method, and hence it is most attractive to customers with heavy needs for working capital.

Legal Limitations to Leasing

In contrast to outright sale, leasing enables the lessor to impose a number of restrictions upon the use of his product. Most of the contract provisions cover the basic privileges and obligations of both parties, but there is often a possibility that some of the limitations may be in violation of the antitrust laws. Under Section 3 of the Clayton Act, as explained in a preceding section, it is illegal to lease commodities on the condition that the lessee shall not use machinery or supplies offered by a competitor, where the effect may be substantially to lessen competition or tend to create a monopoly. As further explained in connection with the cases cited in the discussion of exclusive dealing, legality depends not upon precise objective criteria, but upon the facts of a particular case, and whether these are interpreted by the courts as having *a substantial effect upon competition.*

Illustrative is the case of the Thomson Mfg. Co. This firm, along with its principal competitor, followed the practice of leasing rivet setting machines in combination with rivet sales. For a small rental fee, the lessee was provided with a costly machine, under the condition that all rivets be purchased from the machine owner. It was shown that the rivets were priced about 10 per cent higher than in the open market, this diffe-rential compensating the manufacturer for the use of the machine and the maintenance services that were also provided. Evidence of an adverse effect upon competition was presented by the Federal Trade Commission in that rivet manufacturers who did not provide machines had been largely excluded from this field. The court ruled that "the practical effect is to preclude the use of supplies of a competitor and thus substantially lessen competition."

13

Department Stores

In practically all major cities, the focal point of the central business district consists of two or more substantial stores. Such establishments are of special interest because of the vast number of customers served by them, unusual size, broad range of merchandise offerings, community leadership, and market dominance in certain lines of goods. They are, furthermore, one of our most mature forms of retailing institutions, constantly in the public eye through various forms of publicity.

DEFINITION

Department stores are retail organizations which carry several lines of merchandise such as women's ready-to-wear and accessories, men's and boys' clothing, piece goods, small wares, and home furnishings and which are organized into separate departments for the purpose of promotion, service, accounting, and control. Departmental organization distinguishes them from the general store.

A more important distinction is their common emphasis upon shopping goods. Department stores are distinguished from specialty, single-line, and other departmentized stores by the wide range of merchandise handled; and from most variety stores, by the wider price range of their merchandise. A widely held conception is that a department store is a large organization. In conformance with this view, the Bureau of the Census limits this classification to otherwise qualifying individual establishments that have twenty-five or more employees.

HISTORY

The department store in the United States is primarily a product of the period since the Civil War. The East, with its concentrated population, was the area of largest department store development until the last quarter of the nineteenth century, when rapid improvement in transporta- tion facilities and the growth of cities led to the establishment of large numbers of department stores in other sections of the country. As the department store is a product of urban conditions, its development paralleled the growth of cities. Use of advertising in extending trade areas, ordering by telephone, development of delivery systems, and increased style elements in merchandise are additional factors accounting for the growth and multiplication of department stores.

Many department stores developed from dry goods stores, a few descended from general stores, and some had their beginning in men's or women's clothing stores. A few represent consolidations of single-line stores. The origin of a particular department store has some significance, since it may materially affect its later patronage. For example, those which had their origin as men's clothing stores frequently enjoy a larger patronage in men's wear than those developing from dry goods stores, resulting from a well-established reputation in its original line and because other lines are built around the original nucleus.

IMPORTANCE

In the Census of Business for 1958, 3,157 establishments were classified as department stores. This group, representing only about one-fifth of 1 per cent of all retail stores, accounted for more than $13 billion of sales, or 6.7 per cent of total retail trade. It is not surprising, therefore, to learn that several department stores have been able to achieve annual sales considerably in excess of $100 million and a substantial number exceed $50 million. Employment within this store classification amounts to about one out of every ten paid employees in all retail stores.

Following World War II, department stores declined in relative sales volume importance. While their total volume in 1958 was much greater than in any previous Census of Business year, their share of total retail sales of 6.7 per cent was somewhat lower than the figure of 7.3 percent in 1948 and much lower than the level of about 9 per cent which prevailed in the 1930's. The principal reason for this relative decline is that consumer expenditures for types of merchandise commonly handled in department stores have not kept pace with certain other categories of expenditures in retail stores, notably those connected with the automobile and its operation. Between 1954 and 1958, however, department stores increased their share of the total retail market slightly, from 6.3 to 6.7 per cent, with this improvement undoubtedly reflecting both geographic (branch store) and merchandise line expansion.

If the comparison of department store sales performance is confined to the so-called "department store market" (i.e., lines of merchandise commonly sold by department stores and in which department stores account for a significant share of total consumer expenditures), such institutions are much more prominent. From 1929 to 1955 they rather consistently accounted for about 22 to 24 per cent of total sales in this "department store market," but in the 1955-60 period, their share of it dropped moderately to about 20 per cent.

From other viewpoints, department stores are of institutional significance far beyond their importance as measured by sales. Such stores are high-prestige institutions which attract shopping traffic to central business districts and to major suburban centers. With their specialized personnel and financial strength, they are able to innovate and experiment. They are, accordingly, frequently recognized as leaders setting the general tone of retailing in the community.

CLASSIFICATIONS AND SPECIAL CHARACTERISTICS

The department store field includes a variety of kinds of institutions when classified by ownership, method of operation, or clientele. Also, a number of unique features characterize department store retailing to a greater extent than other types of stores.

Ownership and Operational Types

When department stores are classified on the basis of ownership and operation, several distinct groups are recognized. First are the *independents that have no ownership affiliation with other department stores.* In 1958 the stores in this group represented about 20 per cent of all department stores and accounted for about 14 per cent of total department store sales volume. This represents a substantial drop in the relative importance of this category which is explained by construction of branches by some former single unit stores, acquisition of some large independent stores by ownership groups, and greater relative expansion of chain organizations.

In the multiunit category, which accounts for 80 per cent of department store establishments and 86 per cent of their sales, several distinct types may be differentiated. *Department stores operated by regular retail chains* are centrally owned and supervised through central or district offices. Illustrative are the larger stores of Sears, Roebuck and Company, the J. C. Penney Company, and Montgomery Ward and Company. Much of the buying is done by central office executives who, as a rule, make all resource contacts. Individual stores usually must conform to standardized company merchandising, service, and operating policies, and they tend to have somewhat similar physical appearance and layout.

Some of the larger and newer stores operated by variety store chains and "discount store" organizations meet the definition requirements of department stores and fall in this group. Chains of more than 100 stores account for nearly one-half of all department store establishments but only for about one-third of department store sales. Stores in this classification, for the most part, are operated in a much different manner than those in other classes and have a greater resemblance to regular corporate chains.

Ownership groups are a second type of multiunit organization. While technically qualifying as chains on the basis of ownership, they differ from regular chains in several ways. These groups, unlike regular chains, have usually expanded their interests by purchasing established independent stores which, in most cases, have retained their original identity, personality, operating personnel, executives, and operating policies. The degree of central control varies but the general manager of an individual store usually has much more freedom than managers in regular chains. Illustrative of ownership groups is Federated Department Stores, Inc.

A third multiunit type consists of *branches* operated by many independent stores as well as by some of the stores in ownership groups. Branches may be distinguished from the units of regular chains in that they are satellites of a large store and are usually administered by the operating executives of that so-called main or parent store rather than by central office executives. While a few companies have operated branches for a number of decades, branches are essentially a modern development t—one that reflects accelerated decentralization in the retail trade structure of metropolitan areas.

An important limitation of the classification just presented is that all stores within the various multiunit types are not "department stores." Many smaller stores operated by regular chains such as Sears, Roebuck and Company do not carry a sufficient range of departmentized merchandise to be so considered. The same is true of many stores in certain ownership groups. Some of them, including many department store branches, are more properly considered as departmentized specialty stores.

Customer Appeal

In larger cities it is especially difficult for a department store to make a strong appeal to all socioeconomic classes. Thus, in communities with a variety of department stores, each one tends to have a personality or character which makes a more definite appeal to some group, even though the clientele of most or all of them overlaps to some extent. Some stores emphasize quality and fashion leadership in elegant surroundings which are consistent with merchandise offerings in the higher price ranges. Such stores are in strong competition with high-class specialty stores and make their main appeal to the higher socioeconomic groups. Other stores concentrate primarily on medium-high- and lower-priced merchandise, to appeal largely to the great middle-class group. Great increases have occurred in the size of the socalled middle-income class and in the volume of purchasing power at its command. For this reason, many department stores appealing to this group have experienced notable expansion. A third group of department stores places major emphasis upon lower price lines of merchandise, with the objective of appealing to those in the lower-income strata, or to other families for whom price is the paramount purchasing consideration. Many so-called "discount" department stores are clearly in this category.

In order to broaden their customer appeal, most medium-sized and large department stores in the independent and ownership group classes have a "basement store" which is organized separately from the main store departments. By handling merchandise in lower price lines, featuring frequent bargain sales, purchasing and offering considerable distress or job-lot merchandise, and sometimes by offering a much more limited range of services and breadth of assortment, basement divisions compete aggressively with various forms of price-appeal and limited-service stores.

Kinds of Merchandise Sold

Department stores carry a wide range of merchandise, including shopping, specialty, and convenience goods. Women's and children's ready-to-wear occupies a prominent place and dry goods departments are important. Convenience goods are, in the main, those purchased by women, and specialty items are also largely those which appeal to the housewife, such as household appliances and equipment. Shopping goods are the most important class. The sale of women's ready-to-wear and accessories and of piece goods and household textiles is of greater relative importance in smaller stores. The largest department stores place more emphasis on the sale of home furnishings, and miscellaneous lines, such as toys, sporting goods, cameras, and on restaurant service.

Although department stores sell men's clothing and furnishings, a large percentage of these items is bought by women who select such goods for other family members.

Leased Departments

The practice of leasing certain departments to outside operators is common in department stores, and it is not at all unusual for more than 10 per cent of the total number of departments to be leased. Some lessees are independent business men and others are chains that operate numerous similar departments. Among merchandise departments most commonly leased are millinery, shoes, jewelry, sewing machines, and automotive accessories. Service departments such as beauty salon, jewelry repair, and photographic studio are also frequently leased.

The usual arrangement is for the leasing organization to buy all merchandise for the leased department, provide salespeople, and operate the department as part of the store. Usually the public does not know that the leased department involves separate ownership and management. The store supplies space, light, heat, credit, and delivery service, and in return receives a definite percentage (usually 10 to 20 per cent) of sales or some stipulated sum.

A number of circumstances have contributed to the leasing of departments. Often the lessee has specialized knowledge or skills which would be difficult to duplicate among store personnel. Some leasing organizations, especially large chain operators, have superior market contacts and access to preferred sources of supply, thereby affording the store more desirable merchandise assortments than could be provided through its own merchandising staff. Departments are also often leased when the cost of sending store buyers to remote wholesale markets would be prohibitive.

Departmentized Specialty Store

The departmentized specialty store sells men's or women's ready-towear, or both, and a full line of accessories. Its relatively large size makes it possible to departmentize its operations and to organize it like a department store. It differs from a regular department store principally because it does not sell furniture or home furnishings and usually handles no piece goods or domestics. A number of such stores exist in all principal cities and they are usually located in the same part of the shopping districts as department stores, since both institutions compete for much of the same trade.

Due to the great similarly between regular department stores and departmentized specialty stores, the following discussion may be regarded as characteristic of both classes of establishments, with proper qualifications for the somewhat more limited range of merchandise carried by the departmentized specialty store.

ANALYSIS OF COMPETITIVE POSITION

The competitive position of department stores can be evaluated through a consideration of their strengths and weaknesses in comparison with those of competing types of retailing institutions.

Advantages

The competitive advantages of department stores are of two classes: those enjoyed because of status as large-scale retailers, and those which are peculiar to department stores as a specific type of large-scale retailing.

Distinctive Advantages

One advantage of distinctive institutional character is the very *wide range of merchandise sold.* Many of our largest stores have 150 or more merchandise departments, and even among the smallest department stores the number of separate departments is rarely less than 25. This facilitates consumer shopping in that the ability to buy a large variety of goods in one place is a time-saver and in other ways appeals strongly to consumers. Moreover, effective promotion of some lines of goods stimulates the sale of other related and dissimilar lines, due to the store traffic thus generated. Another special advantage consists of benefits derived from a *wide range of customer services.* In addition to delivery, liberal adjustments, and several forms of consumer credit, which are not particularly distinctive, most department stores offer a variety of unique services including fashion shows, maintenance of lounges and rest rooms, children's play rooms, nurseries, telephones, and libraries.

Some even offer rooms where women's organizations may hold meetings, or provide space for displays by local art clubs. These services build good will and prestige and bring many customers into the store. This variety of services, whether connected with the sale of goods or offered for the convenience and enjoyment of shoppers, exerts a strong appeal. A third distinctive advantage consists of the *highly public, expositionlike character* of department stores. Everyone feels free to enter and roam about at will even when no purchase is contemplated. Department stores attempt to capitalize on the traffic thus generated by continually creating an atmosphere of buying excitement. This is done by layout planning, attractive displays, use of demonstrations, and special effects created at various seasons as at Christmas, the Easter season or at schoolopening time.

Peculiar Advantages of Size

While the advantages of division of labour, departmentization, buying power, financial strength, integration, prestige, and experimentation and research have already been discussed in the treatment of large-scale retailing, some of these take an unusual form in the department store and deserve additional comment. The department store type of *division of labour* differs considerably from that ordinarily found in a chain organization, unless of course the chain is composed of department stores. Because of the size of the individual establishment, a complex organization is the general rule. Selling specialists number about one-half of total employees in medium-sized stores and only about one-third in the largest stores. By such specialization, salespeople can develop a high degree of product knowledge and selling skill. The remainder of the organization provides for stock clerks, merchandising experts, advertising and display specialists, credit personnel, accountants and clericals, personnel specialists, training supervisors, morale managers, warehouse employees, janitors, elevator operators, tailors, carpenters, watchmen, detectives, researchers, truck drivers, appliance installation experts, comparison shoppers, and so on. In fact, almost every kind of skill may be found within department stores. Individual units operated by chains, on the other hand, are not necessarily large, and the performance of multifarious activities is often the responsibility of a single individual.

The department store also differs from many chains with respect to *risk distribution.* While risks are distributed geographically in the multiunit types of department stores, they are also widely dispersed by virtue of varying types of merchandise sold. For example, a loss in the shoe department may be offset by a particularly favorable showing in women's coats.

While all large-scale retailers can engage in *extensive advertising,* department stores tend to dominate the advertising in local newspapers. Because of the large amount of space used, competitive institutions find it difficult to make a comparable impact upon the public. Many such stores also play an active role in community affairs, and because of the large sums expended for advertising, obtain much "free" publicity for these activities.

Disadvantages

Some of the most important disadvantages of department stores have already been indicated because they are primarily attributable to size of enterprise. As large-scale retailers, such stores suffer to some extent from lack of personal contact between top management and consumers and from complex supervisory procedure in the organization structure.

In addition, some limitations are rather distinctively characteristic of department stores. One of the most serious of these is *a high operating expense ratio.* Small, medium-sized, and large department stores all incur operating expenses which are typically about 33 or 34 per cent of sales. Contradictory as it may seem, the very services from which department stores derive a competitive advantage are also partly responsible for high costs of doing business. Costs are also high because of the complexity of organization structure and the accompanying high overhead costs of supervision, systems, and recording believed necessary to control operations. All expenses typically experienced by such stores must, of course, be recovered from sales, and this limits freedom in maintaining prices that are competitive with limited-service stores.

Since *customer returns* are reflected in a high operating cost ratio, they may be viewed as another disadvantage. In the largest stores, for every $1,000 of merchandise purchased by customers, nearly $90 worth is returned to the store or must for some reason be *credited* to customers' accounts. Because of liberal policies with respect to adjustments, many customers abuse the privilege. Some women complete their shopping after taking several items home "on approval." While some of these returns are unavoidable and some others are due to poor salesmanship or overselling, many of them cannot be explained on such grounds. A large part of this returned merchandise can be sold only at marked-down prices and some not at all.

Another problem relates to *markdowns.* A large portion of the merchandise is never sold at its original retail prices but must be reduced for clearance. Markdowns are not unique among department stores, for they exist in all forms of retailing. They are of greater magnitude in department stores, partly because most such institutions have policies requiring that complete assortments be carried through the peak of each selling season. On a storewide basis, the amount of reductions from original retail prices is about 6 per cent of sales. In other words, for every $1,000 of net sales the store has taken about $60 in price reductions. In some departments, such as women's better dresses, the ratio is usually three times this amount. In large measure this is attributed to the fact that much initial pricing of high-fashion lines is experimental until the trend of demand becomes evident. The pricing process is therefore complicated by the necessity of providing some additional margin to allow for anticipated price reductions. Furthermore, the consumer's anticipation of clearance sales leads to a fairly common reluctance to purchase merchandise at original prices. The high expense ratio and the need for allowing a sufficient margin to cover markdowns necessitates an average original markup of about 38 to 40 per cent of original prices in most regular department stores. This markup is higher than that required by many types of competitive, limited-service, price-appeal establishments. To overcome such a disadvan-tage, the department store must do an unusually outstanding merchandising job, anticipating consumer wants and bringing in desired offerings in broad assortments in advance of competitors who operate on a lower margin.

Downtown department stores suffer from *traffic congestion* and lack of parking facilities. It is time-consuming and often expensive for the consumer to reach the store. Because of the larger proportion of people now living in suburban areas and the increased demands upon the time of women, many of whom are employed, there is a growing trend to shop in specialty stores in outlying shopping districts.

Finally, though the location of merchandise may be clearly indicated, the very size of many department stores makes for *confusion* in shopping and for the preference on the part of many consumers to patronize smaller, more specialized establishments. The constant shifting of departments aggravates the situation. Again, the same kind of merchandise is often carried in several different departments in widely scattered locations with the result that consumers must do a large amount of in-store traveling in order to view the establishment's complete assortment. While store executives justify this rather common practice on the basis of needing separate departments for the purpose of catering to different income or style-interest groups of customers, it is nevertheless a practice that is resented by many consumers who wish to see all that the store has to offer.

NEWER ASPECTS OF DEPARTMENT STORE COMPETITION

Until about the late 1940's most department stores found that their competitive orbit was limited substantially, although not altogether, to other department stores and shopping goods stores in the apparel and home furnishings classifications. Since that time many changes have brought the department store into more strenuous rivalry with other types of institutions.

Variety-Department Stores

The variety store trade had its origin in 1879 when F. W. Woolworth opened his historic "Great Five-Cent Store." Success of this institutional innovation led to rapid multiplication of Woolworth stores and imitation of his methods of operation by founders of other variety chains. Early variety stores met certain social and economic needs of the era. Department stores at that time appealed primarily to medium- and high-income classes, but low-income families of industrial and agricultural workers did not feel at home in them. Variety stores were a new source of a wide range of merchandise, priced within specific limits which appealed to the minimum disposable income of such families. From the early days of the limited-price variety store trade until the late 1930's, expansion consisted primarily of opening additional stores. By 1940 ten major variety chains were operating 4,956 stores as compared with 93 in 1900 and 1,706 in 1920. In spite of great environmental changes over six decades of variety trade history, practically all companies adhered rigidly to major policies and practices inaugurated by Woolworth. These included:

- A clearly specified maximum price limit, even though it had been advanced gradually from time to time in most companies;
- Maximum open display and customer examination of merchandise;
- Limited customer service with operations on a cash-
- Clear identification as a distinctive class of institution carried to the extent of use, by most variety chains, of highly similar red and gold store signs, almost identical store fixtures and layouts, and practically interchangeable merchandise offerings;
- Dependence upon high-traffic locations, rather than advertising and promotion, as a means of attracting customers.

In the post- World War II era, and to an accelerated extent in the late 1950's, executives in the trade realized that the rigidity of several generations had unrealistically limited their potential market. Among the environmental changes which had rendered many traditional policies obsolete were rising levels of consumer income, population growth in suburban areas, development of planned shopping centers, increased acceptance and use of consumer credit, and aggravated interindustry competition in the sale of traditional variety store items, as illustrated by nonfood sections in supermarkets and extensive general merchandise offerings in chain drug stores. These changes eventually forced a number of innovations which were not unique in retailing but were revolutionary developments within the limited-price variety store field. The major change was abandonment of traditional policies of limited price ranges. Three forms of *trading-up* may be distinguished:

- Evolutionary trading-up, or gradual increases in offerings of higher unit value in traditional lines, to expand the range of quality or breadth of assortment for items such as school supplies, cosmetics, or costume jewelry;
- Revolutionary trading-up by adding substantially higher-priced items in traditional lines, as illustrated by $14.95 floor lamps and $29.95 power tools in existing housewares or hardware departments;
- Diversification of merchandise by adding entirely new categories such as furniture and major items of outerwear apparel.

Planned shopping centers afforded new and practically unlimited opportunities for additional stores which, because of merchandise item and line expansion, became much larger. In the late 1940's and early 1950's the typical new variety store was one of about 10,000 square feet, but by 1960 new establishments in larger centers were commonly in the range of 30,000 to 50,000 square feet, and some 7 per cent of new store openings were in planned centers.

Increased emphasis on the sale of high-unit value and bulky items brought about the need for additional customer services like instalment credit and charge account facilities, arrangements for delivery, and "lay-away" plans. More stress on shopping goods also stimulated variety store advertising in newspapers and other local media. In recognition of such changes, some chains adopted the term *variety-department store or junior department store* as being more descriptive than the historic designation *limited-price variety store.*

The rapidity of these innovations brought with them many serious operational problems, including pricing techniques, markdown control, and stock control procedures for fashion items; material handling problems for bulky items; and personnel development challenges incident to drastic changes in size of establishments and functions performed. The cumulative effect, however, is that the newer type of variety-department store is more sharply in direct competition with regular department stores and other types of general merchandise stores including discount houses. A pattern of adjustment will undoubtedly continue and traditional variety store companies will almost certainly undergo further transformation, as suggested by a 1961 announcement that F. W. Woolworth Co. planned to start a new separate division for the purpose of opening and operating large new discount stores under the name "Woolco."

Other New Competition

Most of the other newer forms of department store competition are discussed elsewhere in this text; hence it is adequate merely to enumerate them at this juncture. Of substantial concern are various types of discount houses which operate in most urban areas, featuring branded merchandise at significant reductions from retail list prices. Second, with the growth of population in suburban markets, many department stores lost patronage to smaller stores located in new outlying shopping centers. Third, to a varying degree in different parts of the country, supermarket companies have expanded their activities in nonfood lines, with some aggressively merchandising selected classes of apparel and durable household goods, as well as various kinds of convenience nonfood items which are sold in practically all supermarkets. Fourth, catalog or mail order retailers have expanded their facilities, providing additional outlets for accepting orders, and offer rapid delivery service through the facilities of local retail merchants' delivery organizations.

Response of Department Stores

Some tradition-bound regular department stores have tended to ignore the newer forms of competition in the hope that their fashionminded and service-seeking customers would remain loyal. The more progressive firms have tended to respond vigorously in various ways and with considerable effectiveness. To cope with discount stores, some department stores have held frequent or continuous warehouse sales at which appliances and other items are sold at greatly reduced prices under conditions of limited customer service. Discount house competition has also forced a re-examination of the department store operating cost structure. During the 1950's most large department stores embarked upon elaborate programs of expense control and cost reduction.

This often involved a survey of traditional services to determine which are used by only a small percentage of the consuming public and, for that reason, might be eliminated or placed on a self-sustaining basis by specific charges for them. Many department stores have also reduced costs by placing a large number of merchandise lines on a self-service basis, thereby cutting payroll expense in relation to sales in some cases.

Some organizations reevaluated their pricing policies, and decided to meet discount house prices on all items. In many cases, such a decision has been implemented by greatly expanded comparison shopping of competitive prices in all types of outlets, adjustment of store selling prices as frequently as needed to meet market situations, and aggressive advertising of a policy of refusing to be undersold.

The challenge of suburban retailing had been met by wide-scale construction of branch stores which now dominate many regional shopping centers. Many of the early post-World War II branch stores were small and caused serious operational and customer relations problems due to the difficulty of projecting the image of a major downtown store in an outlying unit which was only a small fraction of the size of the main store. More recently, branch stores have been constructed on a more elaborate scale, bringing to the suburban shopper a fuller range of department store merchandise and services, even though the number of departments and breadth of assortments are still necessarily somewhat more restricted than in parent stores. Many newer branches have a complete basement store operation, to make a strong appeal to consumers who are most price conscious, and a few department stores have specialized branches which carry only basement store merchandise.

Some of the newer branches of department stores are operated as discount stores. In 1961 several leading ownership groups of department stores announced specific plans for engaging in discount retailing in a major way, in some cases by setting up special divisions to operate such stores under separate identity, management, and control (e.g., Allied Stores Corp.), and in other instances by incorporating discounting merchandising strategy within well-established stores for those departments handling more standardized types of goods as well as in new discount stores (e.g., May

Department Stores Co.) In spite of suburban retailing trends, it has become apparent that major central business district stores hold an attraction for many consumers, particularly for items of low purchasing frequency, that cannot be rivaled in any but the very largest planned suburban shopping centers. Consequently, millions of dollars have been invested in modernization of downtown establishments. Department store executives have been among the most active civic promoters for revitalization of central business districts. This movement has become of such great national significance that the National Retail Merchants Association has a "downtown development committee" to aid local groups of department store merchants in such programs.

Hrovision of downtown parking facilities and additional night openings in central business districts are among other related competitive methods. To cater to consumers who wish to buy without visiting the shopping district, many department stores have expanded their telephone and mail order selling services. This has been particularly pronounced during the Christmas merchandising season, when it is common to issue large, wellillustrated catalogs in which most departments are represented. With a view to obtaining more consistent patronage from a somewhat broader segment of the public, new and more flexible forms of credit services have been inaugurated. Another outstanding development has been increased attention to research in merchandising, which has resulted in better executive training along the line of offering assortments which are more in harmony with the buying wants of customers.

Future of Department Stores

Department stores have certain inherent competitive advantages and are a well-established part of our retailing structure. Over the period 1955-60 they have accounted for about 20 per cent of the total market sales in the kind of goods commonly sold in such stores. This suggests that they are a mature type of institution, already serving all segments of the consuming public that wish to buy from them. For this reason, it is not expected that they will increase their share of the market for department store types of merchandise. Indeed, it is apparent that they will have to struggle to hold their own in the face of newer forms of competitive activity. The initial success of various responsive measures discussed in the preceding section suggests, however, sufficient flexibility to maintain their position. An important reason for optimism is that the top management staff of our major department stores includes much of the best merchandising talent in the United States. Still another reason is the great financial strength of most such organizations, which permits them to engage in costly experiments and in long-range research activity.

Indeed, experimental efforts involving the operation of discount stores in 1961 suggests that department store companies are likely to become leaders in that field of merchandising.In relation to the total economy, it may be recalled that department stores have experienced a declining position. If high and increasing levels of consumer income extend over a span of several decades, it is likely that department stores will continue to occupy a more limited place in the total retail trade structure unless they are effective in expanding their merchandise offerings in lines of goods and services now extensively sold in such stores. Even if that cannot be done, they can expect a larger and larger absolute volume of business if they can only maintain their present share of the market for department store types of merchandise.

14

Supermarkets, Shopping Centers, Discount Houses

Three notable and relatively recent institutional developments in retailing have been the increased influence of supermarket merchandising methods, the rapid expansion of planned shopping centers, and the birth and attainment of an aura of respectability by discount houses. Each of these developments has made an important contribution and exerts a real influence on channels of distribution, competition, and on our way and standard of living.

SUPERMARKETS

Supermarkets have revolutionized the distribution of food. Their phenomenal success in the grocery trade has also had a persuasive influence upon the marketing of consumer goods of all classes. Supermarket merchandising techniques have been applied to some extent throughout almost all segments of the retail trade structure.

What Is a Supermarket?

The term *supermarket* is very loosely used in marketing discussions. In general the concept conveyed is that of a very large, departmentized retail store dealing in dry groceries, produce, meats, baked goods, and dairy products. Such a store usually handles certain drugs, toilet goods, hardware, houseware items, and a variety of other classes of merchandise. Emphasis is placed on large volume of sales, mass appeal, complete assortments, and price. Up to about 1937 super-markets were usually located outside the downtown or neighborhood areas, in a factory or a barnlike structure which had formerly been used for industrial or recreational purposes. Such a concept has been greatly modified because almost all the supermarkets constructed since that time have been of an altogether different type. Supermarkets are now to be found in all types of retailing locations; better buildings are used than in the earlier years; more emphasis is placed on display, service and assortments, and less on price. In view of the nature of these developments a useful and inclusive definition of a supermarket is that it is a large, departmentized, retail establishment offering a relatively broad and complete stock of dry groceries, fresh meat, perishable produce, and dairy products, supplemented by a variety of convenience, nonfood merchandise and operated primarily on a self-service basis.

Importance

Any quantitative evaluation of supermarkets depends upon the precise criteria selected for classification purposes. The Bureau of the Census has refrained from defining the term *supermarket* owing to lack of agreement within the food trade and among marketing authorities as to precise definition. Unfortunately, the Bureau of the Census is the only organization in a position to make complete enumerations for the whole country. Other organizations, such as the national trade association, the Super Market Institute, collect statistics from members, but no such reporting agency obtains figures from all stores that might be classed as supermarkets.

The most serious problem encountered in attempting a statement regarding quantitative importance is that almost all definitions have included a minimal annual sales volume requirement which has varied, according to the viewpoint of the defining authority, from as low as $100,000 to as much as $1 million. This is disheartening when attempts are made to effect historical comparisons. Because of changes in the price level—which for grocery store items increased by 147 per cent over the period from 1940 to 1959—a store classified as a supermarket in one year might not be so classified in another, even though the physical volume of business had not changed significantly. In most trade sources some criterion of minimum sales volume size has been used, although changed from time to time to reflect major changes in the level of prices. The criteria, while arbitrary, are undoubtedly reasonably representative of stores commonly regarded as supermarkets. Supermarkets accounted for some 70 per cent of grocery store sales in 1959—a share of market nearly three times that which they enjoyed in 1940. The number of stores classified as supermarkets grew from 6,200

History of Supermarkets

There are random early examples of very large food stores, such as Tiedke's in Toledo, Ohio, certain public market stores, and the L-type or drive-in markets which originated in California in 1918. During the 1920's the Ford Motor Company operated several commissary stores of unusual sales volume size. Their operations reflected some attributes of supermarkets, such as limited service and fast turnover, but they were not set up on the basis of self-service, a characteristic that was later to become one of the distinguishing aspects of supermarkets. The first true self-service supermarket did not appear until the early 1930's when "King" Cullen opened his first market in an abandoned Long Island garage with empty ginger-ale cases for display tables. The first "Big Bear" market was opened near Newark, New Jersey, in

December, 1932, and in one year sold $3.6 million in goods. The supermarket at once became the sensation of the food industry and a problem to manufacturers, wholesalers, and chain and independent retailers alike.

The depression-born supermarket was stimulated by the severity of the economic crisis. Operators were able to occupy huge buildings for low rent, to obtain merchandise in large quantities from distressed sources. They had an almost inexhaustible market, consisting of consumers with depleted purchasing power. Being anxious to stretch every dollar, they responded readily to the appeal of low prices. There was little need for a convenient location, fancy fixtures, displays, or service. Hence some of these early markets incurred operating expenses of as little as 6 or 8 per cent of sales and were able to operate satisfactorily with a gross margin of profit in the range of 9 to 12 per cent of sales, which was considerably lower than the average gross profit in the then typical chain or independent counter-type store where clerks waited upon customers and where, especially in the case of independents, many orders were delivered and a large proportion of sales was made on a credit basis. These early supermarkets reduced by about one-half the margins prevailing in the food industry and, as a consequence, brought great turmoil into the market.

The first supermarkets were opened by independent merchants. Large grocery chains did not follow their lead until it became clear that something more than selling food from empty boxes and in an abandoned barn was involved. When the validity of the principles upon which the supermarket is based became clearly established, chains entered into active competition with pioneer independents and today this type of store is of outstanding importance in their operations. The chains, and successful independents as well, soon began to build stores upon modern lines, using fixtures, lights, and other specially designed equipment.

Chain store organizations now dominate the supermarket industry for two reasons. First, many original independent supermarket operators were highly successful and became multiunit organizations as profits from the first units were reinvested in new locations. In all parts of the country are to be found important local chains which can be traced to the birth of the supermarket as a retailing institution. Second, the large, well-established chains were quick to adapt to this new method of merchandising as soon as its soundness became apparent. Since 1933 the operations of the older and larger chains have been characterized by the policy of closing down small units and replacing them with larger and fewer stores of the supermarket type.

It must not be inferred, however, that supermarkets today are altogether of the chain variety, as there is a considerable number of independent markets of this type, many with annual sales over $2 million. According to one trade study, independent supermarkets and superettes —medium-sized stores that have adopted supermarket methods to a high degree—accounted for more than one-fourth of the total number of independent food stores and more than 90 per cent of their sales volume. Many of these are affiliated with some type of voluntary chain organization.

Merchandising Strategy

During the earlier years of the supermarket industry, when grocery trade competition was mostly between supermarkets and counter-type traditional grocery stores, rather than among supermarkets themselves, certain fundamental policies rather clearly differentiated supermarkets from their older rivals. First, self-service, though used prior thereto on occasion, has been a characteristic of supermarkets since their inception. Second, due to the absence of personal selling, emphasis was largely upon national brands rather than upon unknown or private brands which were commonly "pushed" by clerks in service stores.

Third, price appeal was a pervasive promotional attribute, both in the case of special promotions and in the emphasis on "everyday low prices." Fourth, the typical supermarket carried a very wide range of merchandise, commonly five to ten times the number of individual items found in ordinary grocery stores. A fifth characteristic, high average sale, arose out of the large number of merchandising items, mass display and quantity pricing, a tendency for week-end rather than everyday shopping, increased use of the automobile for shopping trips, and better facilities for home storage of food, particularly items requiring refrigeration. An additional attraction was the provision of automobile parking facilities, often in amounts equal to three to four times the total area of the store.

Dynamics in Supermarket Operation

The basic character of supermarket merchandising strategy was well established, in terms of the features outlined above, prior to the 1940's. The supermarket business has, however, continued to be one of the most dynamic of any in our retailing structure. Operators in this field have been hard pressed to keep abreast of new developments and to adapt their businesses to changing competitive and environmental conditions. Nevertheless, they have manifested an amazing ability to cope with problems of continuing innovation, adjusting their operations to the changing requirements of customer preferences.

Size of Store

In 1949 the "ideal" size of a supermarket was deemed to be about 11,700 square feet of total floor space, but by 1956 it had grown to 20,000 square feet, an increase of more than 70 per cent. In the later 1950's the *average* size of *new* stores leveled off at about 20,000 square feet, perhaps indicating that supermarkets are now about as large as they will become. Stores of larger size require a larger than average trading area to support economical operation and competitive conditions are such that it is difficult to find sites where a supermarket does not have to compete with at least several similar stores. There is, however, considerable variation from the *average* size, with many supermarkets in excess of 30,000 square feet and some larger than 50,000.

Hours

Store hours have been adjusted to provide greater opportunity for family shopping. Between 1951 and 1960 the proportion of supermarkets open every evening increased from 27 to 66 per cent, and those open on Sunday increased from 9 to 22 per cent.

Store Refinements

Many types of store refinements have become common in newer supermarkets. By way of contrast with the barnlike atmosphere of the early 1930's, many contemporary planners incorporate elaborate facilities, including "Kiddie Korrals," rest rooms, better lighting, striking colour combinations, murals, automatic doors, parcel conveyors, in-store music, air conditioning, and a variety of other customer-pleasing devices.

Extension of Self-Service

While self-service in the grocery department has been an attribute of supermarkets since their beginning, the trend has been to extend this method of merchandising to all departments. In 1950, 41 per cent of the supermarkets operated meat departments on a complete self-service basis and 47 per cent of the produce departments were of this nature. By 1960, these percentages had increased, respectively, to 87 per cent and 64 per cent; moreover, most stores without complete self-service in these departments were at least partially on that basis.

Growth in Merchandise Items

While supermarkets have traditionally carried many more items than other grocery stores, the increase in the number of items handled by the typical supermarket is startling. In 1950 the average supermarket carried 2,000 items, but by 1960 this had increased to 6,000, with the middle one-half of the stores reporting between 5,000 and 7,500 items. This growth is partially explained by a larger number of nonfood items, but is attributed primarily to a steady stream of new products developed by manufacturers in traditional grocery store categories.

More and more of the housewife's work in the area of food preparation has been shifted to the manufacturer of food products, thus contributing to an increase in the number of available items. In the case of frozen foods, technological innovations opened the way for a wide variety of food items previously unthinkable. To a substantial extent, the stream of new items has both contributed to and resulted from a "splintering" of former product classifications into numerous. Within each of the new product classes, supermarkets have found it necessary to make merchandising decisions regarding a number of different available brands with several package sizes or types for each.

Nonfood Merchandising

Early supermarkets specialized in selling groceries, produce, and meats, although certain nonfood household items such as paper products and soaps have traditionally been part of the grocery department. Following World War II, the picture changed radically as many companies added new classifications of goods not formerly sold in supermarkets. Sales in so-called "nonfood lines" (i.e., those not traditionally included in grocery departments) grew from almost nothing in the mid-1940's to 3.4 per cent of supermarket sales in 1954 and to 5 per cent in 1957. In 1958 and 1959, however, such sales remained stable at 5 per cent, indicating that the rate of increase was no more rapid than the growth in total supermarket sales.

This apparent stability can be misleading. Actually, the increase in the dollar volume of sales of nonfood items has been substantial, owing to the fact that the number of supermarkets and their share of total grocery store sales has grown markedly. According to trade estimates in 1961, supermarkets were accounting for some 50 per cent of sales of leading health and beauty items, about 13 per cent of total phonograph record sales, and about 20 per cent of total newsstand magazine sales. The number of nonfood lines commonly stocked in supermarkets has continuously increased, as has also the proportion of supermarkets stocking each such line. Within most such lines, however, assortments are usually quite limited, with merchandising emphasis confined to products of high consumer purchase frequency and to the most popular brands.

Hybrid Stores

In the late 1950's and early 1960's, some supermarket companies diversified substantially through the operation of so-called "hybrid" stores of some 40,000 to 60,000 square feet, of which about one half is devoted to general merchandise, similar to the offerings of a modern variety-department store. A notable example is the Grand Union Company, an eastern chain of some 440 supermarkets, which by 1960 had opened some 17 such hybrid grocery—general merchandise stores, identified as "Grand Way Discount Centers." Success of these establishments plus scattered examples of similar ventures by other supermarket chains provoked considerable speculation about the possibility of the supermarket eventually becoming a complete one-stop shopping centre within itself. The outlook for such a development is not promising, for two major reasons. First, it takes at least several times as many families to support a given sales area devoted to general merchandise as it does to support a food store of comparable size, owing to the much greater relative importance of food expenditures in the typical family budget. Thus, a hybrid store of the kind described above must draw families from a much larger trading area than required to support an ordinary supermarket. Second, the hybrid supermarket must compete aggressively for general merchandise business with strongly entrenched competitors, such as variety stores, department stores, discount houses, and many kinds of single-line stores.

Supermarkets have been somewhat concerned about a tendency of certain discount houses to add large grocery departments to attract more patrons to their general merchandise departments, and to some extent ventures into general merchandise retailing by supermarkets have been regarded as defensive measures. Certainly some supermarket organizations will build large hybrid stores, and the number of them will increase. In view of the reasons explained above, it seems evident, however, that the large hybrid store will be the more exceptional case and that the typical supermarket will continue to be predominantly a food store.

Promotional Practices

As the number of supermarkets has grown, and as most supermarket companies have demonstrated increasing willingness to meet the lowest competitive prices prevailing in their area, price in itself has become somewhat less important as a patronage-attracting feature. Emphasis has tended to shift to various promotional strategies which tend to induce the consumer to purchase from a given store on a continuing basis. The use of trading stamps, grew from 13 per cent of supermarkets in 1953, to 40 per cent in 1955, and to 67 per cent in 1959. The cost of using trading stamps is commonly about 1.5 to 1.8 per cent of store sales volume, but is regarded as a competitive necessity in metropolitan areas where such stamps have wide consumer acceptance and where their distribution is widespread. Regular continuous premium plans other than trading stamps were used by 8 per cent of the supermarkets in 1959.

Efficiency Programs

Supermarkets have made extensive application of scientific work simplification programs and have made great strides in the use of mechanized equipment in receiving and handling merchandise, prepackaging of meat and fresh produce, price-marking, and check-out stand operation. As a consequence, great strides have been made in the productivity of store employees. Over the period 1951-56, when retail food store prices were relatively constant, sales per full-time store employee equivalent increased from $29,700 to $43,400. This is an increase of 46 per cent in sales per employee, a record which, it is believed, cannot be matched by any other type of store. Since 1956, however, sales per employee have remained virtually stable, indicating that efficiency measures and forms of mechanization have been carried about as far as is practical under existing conditions.

Expenses of Operation

As a consequence of some of the above factors, especially those pertaining to merchandise line expansion, trading stamps, and increased customer facilities, and because of rising wage rates, operating expenses and gross margins in supermarkets have tended to increase. In 1955 operating expenses amounted to 14.72 per cent of sales, but increased to 15.96 per cent in 1957, and to 16.27 per cent in 1959—a marked contrast with the 6 to 8 per cent achieved by some supermarkets in the early 1930's. Nevertheless, the supermarket continues to be one of the most economical forms of retailing.

Future of the Supermarket in the Grocery Trade

In the early years of supermarket merchandising in the food field, this form of retailing grew rapidly, at the expense of the relative market position of traditional clerk-service-type food stores. By the late 1950's it was apparent that supermarkets were rapidly approaching a more stable relative market position. In 1940 there was about one supermarket to 5,700 families, but by 1960 the ratio was one for 2,300 families. Practically all consumers who wish to buy in this type of store now have the opportunity to do so. Supermarket chains are now hard pressed to find desirable locations for new establishments because supermarkets are to be found in most market areas where the population potential is adequate to support a large volume store.

The major competition for supermarkets is now with other supermarkets rather than with smaller stores, and the smaller stores that remain use supermarket merchandising methods to a high degree. This suggests that supermarket expansion in food sales will, in the future, be at a less rapid rate, more in line with increases in population and buying income. As a point of saturation is approached, the supermarket will be able to increase its share of total consumer expenditures only by continuing to expand activities in nonfood merchandising. The opportunity for doing this on a large scale does not seem particularly encouraging because of the manner in which retailers in other lines have adapted their operations to supermarket merchandising strategy. Nevertheless, it is expected that the supermarket industry will be one of continued growth and development, merely because of the long-run market increases attributable to population expansion and rising incomes. As population grows, especially in suburban market areas, many new, large, and ultra-modern supermarkets will be opened to serve the needs of people in these areas.

General Impact of Supermarket Merchandising Methods

Merchandising methods developed in the supermarket industry have provided a strong attraction for the modern consumer for a variety of reasons. First, self-service methods are commonly associated with the ability to purchase at lower prices. Second, well-designed impersonal store layouts enable consumers to shop quickly, which seems to be in character with the pace of contemporary living; still, it is also conducive to relaxed, "look around" shopping, and so is in harmony with another aspect of modern times. Third, the opportunity to serve one's self relieves the consumer from some distrust of salespeople, particularly when people wish to avoid "high-pressure" salesmanship. Another thesis sometimes advanced to explain the popularity of self-service is that this type of buying provides the consumer with the opportunity to engage in a creative, absorbing, problem-solving type of activity which may be contrasted with being dependent upon the aid of a salesman.

The way in which the consumer has responded to the various appeals of supermarket merchandising strategy has resulted in imitative modifications of operating practices which are visually evident among newer or modernized stores in almost all lines of retailing.

In department stores the prevailing tendency has been to avoid the "limited-service" connotations of "self-service" operation, but many such stores have approached supermarket merchandising strategy by increasing the extent of open display and by utilizing conspicuous "transaction processing stations." These are, in reality, a modification of the supermarket check-out counter, and are often identified with signs such as "Bring Your Own Selection Here for Quick Service." Applications of this type of merchandising have been most common in departments that handle easy-to-select types of items, such as greeting cards, notions, house wares, books, and toys. However, some leading department store organizations have engaged in self-service merchandising on an extensive scale, particularly in many of the newer branch stores, and more especially in those engaging in discount retailing to the greatest extent.

Most of the newer stores operated by major variety and drugstore chains are of unusually large size, utilize open display fixtures that expose merchandise items in the majority of the classifications, and have a number of regular check-out counters concentrated at the front of the stores in a manner almost identical to that of the grocery supermarket. The layout of new or modernized hardware and automotive accessory stores reflects a similar trend, with emphasis upon self-selection and a greater diversification of visually displayed merchandise than characterized such stores in the past.

Modern discount houses utilize supermarket methods to a high degree and have sometimes been described as general merchandise supermarkets. Even in the apparel field, the supermarket has had considerable influence. The Robert Hall chain of clothing stores has grown from a relatively small to a nationally known organization by utilizing, to a high degree, self service methods. Many other apparel retailers have made similar adaptations in their methods. Even in the shoe field, a limited number of stores are operated on a self-service basis, to the extent of allowing consumers to do their own fitting and taking their merchandise to the check-out stand. So extensive has been the influence that many establishments in nonfood lines are publicized as "supermarket" drugstores, hardware stores, nurseries, or even lumber yards.

Many supermarket adaptations have been experimental and have failed because the need for some type of personal selling assistance was overwhelming, at least for some merchandise items or for some customers who prefer personal assistance. Successful innovations in nonfood stores have usually rested upon a new approach to the handling of the retail sales transaction. Under traditional clerk-service forms of retailing, the consumer is totally dependent upon the service of a regular salesperson for all phases of the transaction. The influence of supermarket merchandising has been essentially that of dividing sales transactions into two components—first, the merchandise selection aspect and, second, the recording aspect. The first can be handled *either* by the consumer through the process of self-selection *or* by the salesperson who assists the consumer with personal selling advice. The recording phase is handled at some kind of a centralized check-out counter or transaction processing station which is equipped for this purpose and manned by specialized personnel.

The majority of retailers who have attempted well-planned modifications of their operations by utilizing supermarket merchandising strategy have derived substantial advantages. The prevailing tendency has been for sales to increase when clerk-service stores are converted to a self selection basis. This is attributed to several factors. First, the influence of store modernization which is in harmony with contemporary consumer buying habits undoubtedly plays a major role. Second, many more merchandise items are exposed to consumer contact and it is widely accepted that consumers buy more on impulse from open displays than they do in clerk-service stores. Third, personal selling efficiency tends to improve, because this type of selling is largely confined to merchandise classifications in which the consumer actually requires buying assistance.

Self-service methods have often had a favorable influence upon store profits. In part, this is attributable to a larger volume of sales per establishment. It is also due to a smaller amount of employee time per transaction or greater volume of sales per employee. This results from the fact that people tend to help themselves in the case of familiar "easy-to-choose" items. Trained salespeople are thus able to concentrate their efforts on higher unit value transactions where assistance is required because of the technical character of goods, or because of special compounding or fitting problems, as in the case of appliances in hardware stores, prescriptions in drugstores, and suits in men's clothing and furnishings establishments. As a result of these factors, many retailers have found that they can handle a considerably larger volume of sales in an establishment of given size without adding to the number of employees required to care for the greater number of transactions involved.

Stores adapting to supermarket self-service methods have encountered various new operational problems, one of which is the planning of assortments in relation to available display space. Under clerk-service arrangements, items can be added without the same kind of planning, since the salesperson presumably knows the stock and can bring forth those items which he believes will meet the expressed needs of the customer. Under self-service techniques, however, all items must be visibly displayed for customer selection.

Since there are rather rigid restrictions on the possible number of "item facings" on given display fixtures, more serious planning attention must be given to the size of inventory, the number of items contained in it, the sales potential of items, and the allocation of display space in relation to sales and profit potential of items. Just as items may vary in their price or income elasticity of demand, they may also vary in their *display elasticity of demand.* Since merchants often have more control over allocation of display space than they do over item pricing, the concept of display elasticity of demand becomes of great importance when supermarket merchandising techniques are used. As applied to manufacturers, the concept shifts channel relationships from emphasis upon obtaining personal selling support to securing preferred display locations in stores and to getting more "item facings" on display fixtures.

PLANNED SHOPPING CENTERS

Planned shopping centers are not retailing institutions in the ordinary sense, but rather spatial arrangements of stores which have been grouped to provide a balanced shopping attraction to the area served. Each store is a tenant in common with others with respect to certain shared facilities as parking and shopping malls, and usually participates in various kinds of group promotional efforts. Thus, planned shopping centers are a type of enterprise in which tenants have joined interests with developers and with other stores to an unusual degree, giving rise to the need for considering such centers as a form of enterprise, not merely as a collection of individual stores.

Distinctive Characteristics

All major cities have a number of secondary business districts which have evolved gradually over a long period of years as a consequence of many individual location decisions made by a wide variety of business firms. Planned shopping centers of the modern variety differ from these uncontrolled business districts in a number of respects. All of the land and buildings in a planned centre is typically owned by the developing organization which gives it an unusual measure of control over architectural, parking, store arrangement, service, and other facilities. Second, a balanced grouping of different kinds of stores and service establishments is provided for the purpose of affording a one-stop kind of shopping. Third, the greater part of the available ground space is used for free automobile parking. Ratios of parking space to store selling area are commonly about 3 or 4 to 1. Fourth, such centers are developed according to an over-all plan prepared with the help of architects, market analysts, traffic engineers, and other specialists prior to initial construction of the first rentable units in a new centre.

Types of Planned Centers

Planned centers are of several types, distinguished according to size, nature of tenants, and trading area served. At one extreme are *neighborhood centers* usually consisting of several to a dozen or more stores of the convenience goods and service type. Most such centers have less than 50,000 feet in total store area. At the other extreme are *regional centers* which may have 50 to 100 stores, including one or more department store units, a number of almost all kinds of shopping goods stores, several variety store chains and supermarkets, and a group of convenience goods stores and service establishments. Such centers are usually developed on tracts of land in excess of 40 acres, commonly provide parking for 4,000 or more automobiles, have some 500,000 or more square feet in store area, and may draw customers from a trading area of as much as some 20 minutes' driving-time radius.

Ownership Interests

Different types of ownership interests have been involved in the development of planned shopping centers. One class consists of residential real estate developers who provide for shopping centre facilities as part of the master plan for large suburban subdivisions. A second class consists of a number of organizations that specialize in building and operating centers. Some of these organizations employ a large staff of market analysts, real estate appraisers, architects and designers, and administrative personnel. One of the best known is the Don M. Casto Company of Columbus, Ohio, which has developed, owns, manages, and promotes some 30 large planned shopping centers and many small ones located in ten different metropolitan areas and in a number of small cities. A third type of ownership interest is represented by regular retailing companies that develop shopping centers in which they wish to become major tenants. Examples in the department store field include the J. L. Hudson Company of Detroit which developed famous regional shopping centers in that city; the Allied Stores Corporation, builders of Bergen Mall, near Paramus, New Jersey; and the R. H. Macy & Co., Inc., developers of the Garden State Plaza Shopping Centre, also near Paramus in the New York metropolitan area. Several other examples are to be found in the food field where certain chains have formed subsidiary real estate corporations to develop centers in which the chain will have the opportunity to be the exclusive or dominant supermarket tenant.

Growth of Shopping Centers

The decade following World War II afforded a favorable environment for shopping centre growth. During the war years, new home construction and commercial building had been practically at a standstill. After the war, new family formation increased markedly, and the birth rate soared, thus stimulating population growth, which was primarily concentrated in suburban areas. Such new areas, being relatively devoid of established retailing facilities, afforded a natural opportunity for the new type of centre.

A second major factor consists of the more widespread ownership and greater usage of the automobile. In 1920 there were only 20 million privately owned automobiles in the United States but there were 52 million by 1955. This gave rise to serious problems of congestion and created parking difficulties in the central business districts. Longer distances to be traveled from newer residential areas to such districts discouraged frequent visits by suburbanites. Increased utilization of automobiles also adversely affected many outlying neighborhood business districts, since it made the consumer more independent and more willing to travel appreciable distances for even ordinary items needed for daily living. Thus the planned shopping centre, with its large free parking areas, presented a patronage appeal that was in harmony with contemporary living.

Another major factor is to be found in changed consumer buying habits. As a result of mass market advertising, consumers became better informed about the availability of merchandise items. Because women are busier, either at work or in a variety of social pursuits, there is greater willingness to shop from the somewhat limited assortments available in suburban shopping centers, especially when the advantages of convenience, informality, and ease of parking are set in contrast with conditions associated with trips to central business districts.

Because of the factors just enumerated, the number of planned shopping centers grew from a mere handful in the late 1940's to some 4,000 in operation in 1960. These centers in 1960 contained about 500 million square feet of store area—an amount which is adequate, based on ratios of sales per square foot used for planning purposes, to sell $35 billion annually, or about 11 per cent of total retail sales. Shopping centre store capacity by lines of trade varies considerably, being relatively much higher, for example, for types such as supermarkets and variety stores, which are to be found in nearly all centers, than is the case for establishments which are not commonly an important ingredient of such centers. Most such centers, however, have a sales volume below planned capacity and could appreciably increase sales without adding to floor space.

Competitive Position of Shopping Centre Stores

The controlled type of centre, especially the larger ones, holds for its tenants a number of *advantages.* Some of these are obvious from the foregoing description of characteristics and reasons for growth. One is the convenience of adequate free parking. A second consists of the balanced shopping attraction which affords the consumer an opportunity for a one stop buying expedition.

Third, the uniform architectural treatment is generally attractive. Fourth, all stores located in such centers are, at this early stage of development, newer and more modern than those located in competitive types of locations. Fifth, individual stores benefit from aggressive promotion of the centre as a whole, at least in contrast with more limited community efforts typically associated with unplanned business districts. Sixth, most planned shopping centers provide a greater number of night openings, which has been especially attractive from the standpoint of family shopping.

Impact on Character of Retailing Structure

From the foregoing discussion it is readily apparent that the planned shopping centre has had a significant impact on the character of retailing, particularly with reference to the distribution of trade among various types of store locations, especially as related to a diminishing share of total retail business transacted by stores located in central business districts. In addition, two common types of tenant selection policies have tended to govern the composition of planned centers and, owing to their growth, have influenced the changing competitive positions of certain types of retailers.

The first type of policy relates to preferential treatment accorded to large-scale retailers, especially chains. After a centre is planned and leases have been obtained, financing is by means of long-term mortgages involving millions of dollars. Such mortgages are usually handled by large insurance companies which approach the problem from the viewpoint of an investor of policyholders' funds. Such a financing organization often requires that the amount of rental income assured from the leases of large well-established firms be adequate to cover all fixed charges (mortgage amortization, interest, taxes, etc.). In practice, this usually requires that the developer lease about 70 per cent of the total centre space to firms with a net worth of more than $1 million and with high composite credit ratings.

Since large chains and major department stores are about the only types of potential tenants with this amount of net worth, independent merchants and small multiunit organizations are practically excluded from the first 70 per cent or so of the space which is leased in a large proportion of planned Shopping centers. Thus, financing arrangements have tended to favour the relative growth of large multiunit firms. A second factor is that shopping centre leases often contain provisions which place restrictions upon the kind and amount of competition within the centre.

Such provisions are many and varied but one of special inter have resulted in a highly competitive era for planned shopping centers. Whereas early centers enjoyed an almost unchallenged opportunity to serve new and rapidly growing suburban areas, many of them are now in aggressive competition with other nearby centers. Multiplication of centers in some cities has greatly curtailed the trading area that can be served advantageously by any individual centre and has limited opportunities for new developers. In most large cities, the point has been reached where a new planned centre can be properly developed and promoted only as a result of successful competition with rival centers. From the standpoint of future development, the need is evident for greater emphasis upon sound market analysis, the best architectural planning, a truly distinctive group of outstanding retail tenants, and the provision of various kinds of attractive community services and entertainment facilities.

DISCOUNT HOUSES

A significant institutional development of the post- World War II era has been the expansion of "cut-price" retailing. Some of the major forms of discount selling, the principal explanations for it, its influences upon the nature of competition within retailing, and its impact upon distribution channels are examined in this section.

Discount Selling Versus Discount Houses

The business press of the 1950's carried many articles on the subject of "discount retailing." Some writers have regarded such retailing as a new phenomenon while others have referred to it as a continuation of the ancient art of price cutting. Estimates regarding the quantitative significance of discount retailing have varied over a wide range. Agreement is general, however, that discounting or cut-price retailing has been growing and accounts for a substantial share of total retail sales. Part of the confusion on this subject arises out of the failure to distinguish between various forms of "discount selling" which are rather widely practiced by regular retailers on a discriminatory basis and "discount houses" that consistently offer all or most of the merchandise items in their stock at prices below so-called list or regular prices. Consumers believe that they are buying at a discount under a variety of circumstances as when they:

- Negotiate a lower price by bargaining or higgling with a retailer;
- Obtain special privileges by membership in some organization or affiliation with some group;
- Buy from an establishment which actually is, or is represented to be, a wholesale place of business;
- Purchase from a store which, as a matter of policy, consistently sells below regular or "fair trade" prices.

Discount selling has been practiced, at least to some extent, by many kinds of retailers over decades. Some gasoline service stations offer certain favored customers discounts of two or three cents per gallon from posted prices. Practically all automobile sales that involve trade-ins have been "negotiated" for many years, with the effect that the skillful and persistent bargainer obtains a "better deal" than many other purchasers. In some furniture and appliance stores, customers who manifest resistance to posted prices are turned over to another salesman who presents a more attractive offer. Drugstores commonly give "professional discounts" to physicians, especially to those who favour the store with prescription references. Many retail stores, as well as wholesale and manufacturing companies, sell to their own employees according to some discount policy.

Types of Discount Houses

Most discussions of discount selling have not been concerned so much with the aforementioned types of examples of occasional discriminatory selling on the part of regular stores as with a surge in the volume of business accounted for by establishments generally recognized as a regular source of discount prices. A number of such "discount houses" existed at least as early as 1930's. Most of the earlier types were located in outof-the-way places and were not widely publicized. Several major types of discount houses may be distinguished.

Open Showrooms

Particularly in the home furnishings field, there are open showrooms, operated by manufacturers and wholesale middlemen, for the purpose of maintaining centralized displays for small dealers and decorators who cannot maintain full stocks in their own establishments. While it has been conventional to admit consumers only upon introduction from a retailer, many such establishments have willingly done business with anyone who visited them. Consumers buying from such showrooms usually believe, sometimes without justification, that substantial price concessions are obtained.

Brokerage Buying Arrangements

Certain appliance repairmen, upholsterers and other types of service establishments with access to wholesale sources of supply have rendered buying services to their regular customers and others. Usually they have no stocks of merchandise but may agree to purchase specified items for consumers at cost plus some brokerage or buying fee of about 10 per cent of cost. In some cases the amount of this type of brokerage buying has become such a dominant character of the business that it becomes known as a discount house.

Closed-door Discount Houses

Certain large discount houses sell only to consumers who purchase a membership. The "privilege" of joining is usually restricted to certain classes of consumers, such as government employees, members of labour unions, or people with a recognized professional status. Since admission to the merchandising facilities is open only to "card-holding members," such establishments are known as *closed-door discounters.* Some such organizations operated in the 1930's, usually on a small scale as judged by size of facilities. They often did not carry much of an inventory, but ordered merchandise for customers who made buying decisions on the basis of displays of sample items or catalogs. In the late 1950's and early 1960's this type of discount house assumed a new character and expanded rapidly. While still operating on the basis of a closed-door philosophy, thus giving the members a feeling of being "in" on something from which others are excluded, facilities have grown to stores of substantial size, often occupying as much as 100,000 square feet. These stores are usually recognizable by an abbreviated name such as FAME, GEX, GEM, or BEX which usually signifies the name of the organization and suggests the character of those eligible for membership (e.g., GEX—Government Employees' Exchange).

While the membership requirement suggests the flavour of a consumers' cooperative, these organizations are private enterprises operated for profit. Many of them consist largely of a collection of leased departments, similar to arrangements common in department stores, but where each lessee agrees to operate under the cut-price philosophy of the organization and to maintain certain standards of merchandising and service. Such stores are usually to be found in "solo" or "lone-wolf" locations, along major traffic arteries in large metropolitan areas. Some 16 companies, with about 40 outlets in 1960, are members of the National Association of Consumer Organizations, a closed-door trade association formed in 1957 for the purpose of exchanging information. At least 40 additional such outlets were known to be in operation in 1960 and most such companies had announced plans for the immediate construction of more stores.

Regular Discount Stores

The more common conception of a discount house is a large modern retail store which is open to the general consuming public, incorporates aspects of supermarket merchandising strategy to a high degree, prices all merchandise at a relatively low markup above cost, carries large stocks, renders only limited types of consumer services and usually on the basis of a specific extra charge, advertises regularly, occupies a good retail store location well exposed to consumer traffic, and can be distinguished from regular retailers only by its consistent emphasis upon "discount prices" and its self-designation as a *discount store.*Most such stores are units of discount chains. Some of them became well known in the late 1940's and early 1950's due to rapid expansion by the successful discounting of appliances and other types of durable goods.

Growth of Discount Houses

A number of factors have contributed to the growth of discount stores. A redistribution of purchasing power has undoubtedly had some effect. the lower and middle income groups experienced the greatest increases in real family buying income and this brought many new families into the market for various kinds of durable goods. Many of these families were not accustomed to the wide range of services offered by department stores, furniture stores, and regular appliance dealers and were willing to purchase in the somewhat less attractive and more limitedservice atmosphere of the discount house. Second, there is some relationship between the impact of supermarket merchandising methods and discount house operation. Increasing emphasis throughout the economy upon such methods contributed to greater willingness on the part of the consumer to arrive at purchase decisions without the usual services of a retail salesperson. Consumer confidence in heavily advertised brands of appliances and furniture removed some feeling of dependence upon the integrity of the retailer and made consumers more willing to purchase on a self-selection basis in almost any type of outlet.

Third, and undoubtedly of greatest importance, is the discount house's consistent appeal of substantial price savings. This was made possible, in part, by a merchandising strategy geared to the requirements of *mass market* rather than *limited market* retailing, especially in the case of the more modern promotional type of discount house. This can be understood by comparing certain characteristics of appliance marketing in the periods prior to and following World War II. The postwar era was characterized by great increases in the capacity for manufacturing, accomplished largely through more automatic methods of producing goods in highly mechanized new factories.

Durable goods poured forth from these factories in quantities that can only be described as staggering by prewar standards. They flowed, nevertheless, into a distributive system that possessed essentially the same attributes it had in the earlier years. It consisted chiefly of a very large number of retail stores, most of which continued to appeal to limited segments of the total market, and in which a relatively large amount of personal selling and service effort was required for the consummation of the ordinary transaction. Retailer margins that had become traditional in the prewar economy were, for the most part, perpetuated in the postwar market, thus providing an umbrella of list prices under which the large-volume, limited-service organization could operate success-fully at discounts.

Part of the discount house's success in underselling regular merchants is explained by its ability to operate profitably at lower expense by dispensing with some usual retail store functions. Another factor in expense reduction is that the more modern types of discount houses attempt to maximize profit by selling a large volume of items at a low percent-to-sales margin, thereby achieving high ratios of sales per dollar of inventory investment, per square foot of store space, and per employee. Through such service limitation and operating economies, large discount houses have been able to save as much as one-half of the operating expense ratio traditionally incurred by regular or full-service retailers in the department store, furniture, home furnishings, and apparel trades. This had made it possible for discount houses to offer discounts ranging from about 12 or 13 per cent of regular list price on low-margin items to about 20 per cent on higher margin goods. Many discount houses have publicized savings amounting to much higher percentages of list prices, and these, if they exist, cannot be explained by any operating cost advantages. Several additional factors help to explain the basis for the price appeal of the discount house. One is that many discount houses have been able to obtain discriminatory prices and other probably unearned benefits from their suppliers. In the appliance trade, manufacturers have traditionally sold to large-scale home builders at prices substantially below those prevailing in regular channels of distribution. Some merchandise, ostensibly sold originally to the "builder market," has been diverted, ending up on the floors of large discount houses at retail prices lower than the wholesale cost to the regular dealer. Some discount houses have also been able to obtain other concessions from manufacturers, including advertising allowances and so-called "push money" for retail salesmen, which may not have been offered to regular retailers on proportionally equal terms.

Impact and Future of Discount Houses

It is unquestioned that discount houses have had a substantial effect upon modern retailing. Their importance in terms of sales volume is a matter of conjecture, as estimates have varied widely owing to problems of classification. According to one report, 1960 sales of regular and "closed door" discount houses were estimated at $5 billion. This is less than 3 per cent of total retail sales volume. The competition impact of discount houses is not, however, equal throughout the retail trade structure, and has been particularly pronounced among the various types of general merchandise stores. In the late 1940's and the early 1950's, discount operators were commonly referred to as parasites, bootleggers, or described in even more uncomplimentary terms.

In the later 1950's they had attained a semblance of more general respectability. Goaded by the success of some discount houses, other retailers have been forced to reconsider their position, to enter into more forceful and dynamic selling methods to stimulate people to buy, and to pare selling and other operating costs to meet such price competition. By 1960, it was not uncommon to find aggressive department stores, automotive accessory chains, appliance dealers, drug chains, and general merchandise departments of supermarkets regularly featuring "discount prices" of the type found in regular discount houses, thus diminishing somewhat the importance of price as a distinctive attribute of the discount house. Moreover, as previously noted in Chaps. 9 and 10, various well-established department store and other general merchandise chains (e.g., Allied Stores Corp., May Department Stores Co., F. W. Woolworth Co.) embarked upon programs in 1961 for constructing new specialized outlets of the discount house type, thereby enlarging the scope of their customer appeal and extending the variety of kinds of companies engaged in discount merchandising.

The character of discount houses has been transformed. Many of the earlier types offered only limited assortments of merchandise, often of a distress character or of discontinued models; sold from poor physical facilities; provided practically no customer services; and were generally held in low esteem, even by many of their patrons. In order to reach a wider market, many of them have had to seek better locations; enlarge or modernize their facilities; and add various kinds of widely demanded services, such as installation, repair, delivery, and instalment credit facilities. Their success in winning customer patronage made them more desirable outlets, with the result that they are actively sought as customers by many major brand name manufacturers.

As a consequence of these factors, the larger discount houses have become more or less accepted as a limited service type of departmentized store with well-established relationships with regular sources of supply for practically all classes of merchandise that they choose to handle. At the same time, many of their competitors who have adapted their operations to compete more effectively have made it difficult to distinguish clearly between discount houses and other price appeal stores. A major effect of discount house competition has been an expansion in the market for many kinds of goods formerly sold selectively to limited segments of the market. It appears probable that a permanently lower level of gross margins on some types of goods has been brought about as a result of the pressures from this type of competition.

15

Nonstore Retailing

Thus far, the discussion of retailing has been concerned with *stores*, previously defined as establishments which are open to and frequented by the general consuming public. A small but significant proportion of retail trade is accounted for by *nonstore* retail *establishments*. These are distinguished from stores by the fact that the customer does not make his purchases at the establishment operated by the retailing organization.

The principal types of nonstore retailing establishments are mail order houses, house-to-house selling organizations, and operators of vending machines. In 1958 such nonstore retailers operated 74,679 establishments which came within the scope of Census of Business coverage and these accounted for 2.8 per cent of the sales of all retail establishments. Each of these *methods* of retail selling is of greater importance than indicated by Census data, because some manufacturers, agricultural producers, and regular store retailers utilize nonstore techniques to some degree, but are not classified in the nonstore category since their *primary* business is not that of operating a nonstore retailing enterprise.

MAIL ORDER AND CATALOG RETAILING

The number of firms operating exclusively on a mail order basis is relatively small, but this method of operation is sufficiently widespread to justify detailed consideration. Moreover, it represents a distinctive way of doing business and illustrates the effect of changing conditions upon retailing institutions.

Types of Organizations

Four distinct types of organizations sell by mail. The most important are the general merchandise mail order houses which sell a great variety of consumer and farmer goods, carrying more items than are sold by any department store. Such companies are primarily retail institutions. They purchase the majority of their goods from manufacturers, although the two biggest companies in this field— Sears, Roebuck & Company and Montgomery Ward & Company—both control the manufacturing of many private brand items. A second type consists of specialty retailers. Kinds of business in which specialty mail order operations by retailers is of some signficance include books, home furnishings, apparel and apparel accessories, food, and automotive accessories. Manufacturers who sell by mail constitute the third type of mail order institution. Some such producers have found that their particular products can be sold directly to the consumer by mail without the use of wholesalers or retailers. The fourth type of mail order retailing is carried on by certain department and other large stores which accept orders by mail. Primarily confined to orders for merchandise currently advertised, this type of selling is a supplement to the receipt of orders over the telephone.

History of Mail Order Retailing

Mail order selling arose in a number of ways. Montgomery Ward & Company was founded in 1872 by a former clerk in Chicago who had also worked as a traveling salesman. The Patrons of Husbandry (the Grange) had established a number of cooperative stores and needed a wholesale connection. Mr. Ward saw the opportunity and started the business which still bears his name. The Grange stores were not generally successful so Mr. Ward's business was expanded into a mail order house to take advantage of good will among former members of the cooperative stores.

Sears, Roebuck & Company, the largest mail order firm, grew out of the efforts of Mr. Sears, a small-town station agent in Minnesota, to sell watches which had been shipped to his station on approval but rejected. The success of this venture led to a watch and jewelry mail order house in Minneapolis which was later moved to Chicago. The present largescale enterprise has grown from this small part..

Other general mail order houses had varied beginnings. Many have expanded from ordinary retail stores. Others started as specialty mail order houses and gradually expanded until they handled a more general line of merchandise. Probably the most important reason for the success of the mail order houses in the early stages of their development is to be found in the failure of country merchants to adjust to changing conditions. In the post—Civil War period the country general store was a dominant institution. Throughout the West and South, farmers and small-town residents raised their standards of living after the period of reconstruction. Cash farm income became larger and farmers became interested in the kinds of things bought by city people. Rural and small-town merchants, however, did not appreciate such changes and continued to stock only staple merchandise which had sold well for many years. Even if such merchants had realized the significance of environmental change, the limitations of their small, local markets would have made it impossible for them to rival the assortments of the evolving mail order institution.

Another factor contributing to the development of mail order retailing was the growth of rail transportation. This made it possible to place orders by mail and to deliver merchandise to scattered areas at reasonable cost and at relatively certain dates. The spectacular and consistent development of mail order retailing began, however, with the establishment of rural free delivery service. Farmers as a class began to subscribe for city daily papers. They were thus reached by style news and by information on various changing methods of life which before had come to their attention only indirectly. Later, the moving pictures and the rotogravure supplements of the newspapers exercised their effect in creating demand for many articles not previously included in the rural standard of living. Mail order retailing offered an opportunity for the purchase of these goods. Developments in catalog making made it possible to advertise goods effectively and to supply realistic photographs. Establishment of the parcel post system in 1913 made it possible to ship small packages more economically. Another factor in the growth of mail order houses was the recognition that this method of selling could take advantage of the economies of large-scale retailing. The larger mail order companies engaged in programs of diversification as the country became more urbanized and opened many retail establishments of the department store type. Such stores now account for the majority of the business of both Sears' and Ward's, but mail order or catalog retailing continues to be a very large segment of their total sales volume.

Present Status of Mail Order Establishments

In 1958 there were 2,550 retail mail order establishments, of which 1,502 had paid employees and 1,048 were small units operated exclusively by proprietors and family members. Aggregate sales volume of these establishments amounted to $20 billions, or about 1 per cent of the sales of all retail establishments. There has been practically no change in the relative sales volume importance of mail order establishments over the period 1929-58. While the 2,550 mail order establishments operated in many lines of trade, more than 75 per cent of their sales was reported by only 35 large establishments handling a complete line of department store merchandise. More than one-half of these establishments are operated by two companies—Sears' and Ward's—thus indicating high concentration in this field.

Competitive Position of General Catalog Houses

The general merchandise mail order organizations have, in the main, the advantages and disadvantages of other large-scale retail enterprises. Due to the peculiar nature of their business, certain special conditions affect their competitive situation.

Advantages

As compared with single-line and general stores in the rural districts, mail order houses offer a more complete and varied line of merchandise. Their location in the larger cities gives a certain amount of prestige to their merchandise, especially in style goods. Prices, at least for many articles, are somewhat lower than those charged for corresponding articles in the rural communities.

Buying from a catalog is perhaps quicker and easier for rural people than going to stores in somewhat distant cities, and such shopping can be done at any time of day or evening that is most convenient. Convenience, moreover, is a strong appeal among urban customers who patronize catalog order offices or telephone order facilities maintained by leading mail order companies in large cities. Absence of pressure to buy, avoidance of the confusion of crowded stores, informative statements concerning products, guaranties, and a liberal returned-goods policy are other attractions. Because sales are made in all sections of the country and to different classes of consumers, sales are not greatly affected by local industrial depressions, as are those of local merchants.

Some general advantages enjoyed by all mail order vendors grow out of certain operating economies. Warehouses are located in parts of the city where rent is much lower than that which must be paid by the ordinary retailer. Expensive fixtures are unnecessary, for only equipment of the warehouse type is required. It is unnecessary to employ retail salespeople, for the catalog descriptions plus the reputation of the firm and price appeals effect sales. Hence, employees of the clerical and shipping department type are used and their work is scheduled to permit an efficient utilization of time—something difficult to accomplish in retail stores which must be staffed in accordance with daily and hourly variations in consumer traffic.

Disadvantages

Selling by catalogs is limited by the impossibility of examining merchandise in advance of purchase. For shoes, gloves, or clothing, it may be difficult for the buyer to secure the right articles without trying them on for size and fit. Many consumers hesitate to order products where size, colour, style, or texture are significant in choice making. An important limitation is inflexibility of the merchandising programme. Semi-annual catalogs published by Sears' and Ward's comprise between 1,000 and 2,000 pages. Plans must be made well in advance of the season as to the detailed composition of the line of goods and the manner in which they are to be featured and illustrated.

More important, prices must be determined months before catalogs are distributed, and the firm usually must live with its pricing decisions throughout the catalog season. While the catalogs contain statements that prices are subject to change without notice, and even though special sale catalogs are issued, the companies do not have the pricing flexibility of other forms of retailing. They cannot mark down individual items of merchandise as the rate of sale becomes too slow or as costs decline; neither can they raise prices on individual items as demand increases or as wholesale costs rise. New items can be added or dropped only when new catalogs are prepared.

Dynamic Adjustments in Catalog Retailing

The inception and period of rapid early development of mail order retailing was associated with the concept of a new merchandising service to the nonurban population. In modern times, with contemporary conditions of communication, transportation, and urbanization, it is indeed remarkable that catalog retailing (as measured by Census of Business data for the period 1929-58) has been able to hold a stable share of total retail sales, thus growing at the same rate as all of retailing. This is attributed to certain dynamic, and in some cases distinctive, methods and policies adopted by the general catalog houses—in large measure for the purpose of capitalizing upon their advantages, minimizing their limitations, and adjusting to changing consumer preferences.

Sales promotion activities are efficiently organized. Mailing lists are prepared with care and efforts are made to keep them up to date. Careful tests are made of the success of different types of copy and appeals. Experienced copy writers know the language and the appeals which are most useful in reaching their clientele. In order to overcome the reluctance of buyers to purchase articles which they cannot see before the order is placed, mail order houses give a very liberal guaranty, covering as a rule both quality and price.

If the purchaser is dissatisfied with the commodity, it may be returned at the expense of the seller, and the purchase price is promptly refunded. The general catalog houses have a special brand problem. To attract business, as they do in part, on a price-appeal basis, they must purchase from suppliers at lowest prices. For this reason such houses do not generally carry very many nationally advertised, branded articles. They prefer to sell unbranded commodities or those which carry their own brand. It is usually necessary to brand the specialties which they sell, in order to identify them and give them a certain distinction. Hence it is common for catalog houses to purchase such articles as vacuum sweepers, gasoline engines, washing machines, farm implements, cosmetics and drugs from suppliers who manufacture to the specifications of the catalog firm and who attach to the goods the private brand of the mail order company.

In order to reach a larger number of potential customers, the major firms have opened a large number of catalog order offices which are located in storerooms in hundreds of small cities and in many suburban shopping centers of large cities. No merchandise is available for sale over the counter in these establishments, but selected items and swatch and sample books are displayed for examination. Employees assist customers to make out and transmit orders. Many such order offices have teletype communication with a regional warehouse which services the area. Orders received prior to a certain time each day can be delivered to the customer's home on the following day in most cities, thus rivaling the speed of delivery service available from local stores. Similar catalog departments are also found in the regular retail stores operated by mail order companies. In the typical Sears' store, the catalog order desk is usually the largest sales volume department.

Some catalog companies have expanded their customer contact points by establishing order stations in retail establishments operated by other companies. Certain small-town and cross-roads stores have displayed the general merchandise catalogs of some companies for a number of years, and accept and process orders on a commission basis. More recently some variety chains and supermarket organizations have made similar arrangements with mail order firms. For example, in 1960, Ward's established catalog order stations in certain New York state supermarkets of Loblaw, Inc., thus giving Ward's sales outlets in areas where it had no retail stores, and providing the Loblaw organization with a 100,000 item increase in its offering of nonfood merchandise lines. Another feature is the operation of telephone order offices. While confined to larger cities in which there is a considerable potential volume of daily business, this development is one of increasing significance, accounting in 1960 for more than 30 per cent of all catalog sales volume at Sears'. The catalog customer can sit in her home, order by number from the catalog, have her order dispatched by teletype as explained above in connection with catalog order offices, and receive next-day delivery in many large cities.

As a consequence of such innovations, the historic *mail order business* has evolved into a more modern conception of *general catalog retailing*, characterized by efforts to bring to the consumer wanted merchandise at various points of sales contact, using means of communication and delivery which are appropriate to contemporary conditions.

Catalog Selling by Store Retailers and Manufacturers

Mail order selling is used to some extent by specialty retailers and by certain manufacturers who sell direct to the consumer. It is also used in the direct marketing of some farm products with a special appeal, such as Smoked Virginia Hams, smoked turkeys, and gift packages of fruit.

Such sellers usually do not have elaborate catalogs, but secure orders by advertising in newspapers and magazines, on radio and television broadcasts, and by direct mail addressed to the homes of consumers. Goods so ordered are shipped by parcel post, express, truck, or ordinary freight.

This type of selling brings many kinds of goods to the attention of a broad market. Items so sold are often of a novel or unusual character and are not available in local stores, especially in smaller communities. Some merchandise is sold direct to consumers by manufacturers who stress a price appeal. While specialty mail order retailing is relatively expensive, since it usually involves substantial advertising and handling and shipping costs, many consumers are nevertheless influenced by an appeal which suggests that they save money by purchasing direct rather than from a retail store.

Appeals of "lower prices," "greater values," or "substantial savings," have been used by most of the major book and record club companies that have a membership which is contacted by mail. Such savings are customarily offered in terms of "free" or "bonus" books, awarded when the member actually purchases a predetermined number of books at regular prices, in accordance with a membership agreement. Bonuses offered in this manner are largely due to low purchase prices negotiated with publishers when contracting for large numbers of copies and not to economies of selling and distributing to individual consumers on a mail order basis. Manufacturers and retailers who sell a narrow line of goods by the mail order method are subject to most of the disadvantages enumerated above in connection with general catalog houses. In addition, they usually lack the prestige enjoyed by a large nationally known organization. Hence, such selling is relatively unimportant, and there are no reasons to believe that it will ever be of much significance in other than a very narrow range of merchandise items.

Catalog selling is also an important form of supplementary promotional effort among many regular *store retailers,* especially large department stores and departmentized specialty stores, who have a ready-made mailing list consisting of their regular charge account customers. This is especially significant for the promotion of gift merchandise during the Christmas shopping season.

HOUSE-TO-HOUSE RETAILING

According to common: usage, the term *house-to-house selling* includes almost any type of retailing that involves contacting the consumer at his residence (or sometimes at his place of work) rather than in a retail store.

Types

Several variations of house-to-house retailing are common. First, some manufacturers and retailers actually canvass on a house-to-house basis. Often solicitation is confined to residential areas or types of families which, in the experience of the individual company, have proved the most fruitful source of business. In some cases, sales coverage is haphazard because solicitation is confined largely to friends, neighbors, or other individuals who have personal contacts with the salespeople of a "house-to-house" selling organization. Some house-to-house salesmen are employees of the manufacturer who uses this method of direct distribution; others are independent dealers who buy merchandise from the manufacturer and resell as merchant middlemen, often handling the products of several organizations.

Second, some companies use what is known as the party plan. Salesmen arrange to have a housewife give a party in her home, at which merchandise is demonstrated to a group of the hostess' friends. The hostess receives merchandise prizes, awarded on the basis of the amount purchased by those attending and, in some cases, also on the basis of the number of those attending who agree to serve as hostesses for similar parties. A variation of this method is a "club" plan, according to which a consumer is awarded prizes or granted discount buying privileges by getting new customers to join the "club." The "club," of course, is the group of customers served by the selling organization and one joins by making purchases. These approaches involve something of the chain letter technique, in that each new customer is expected to obtain a number of additional new customers for the company.

Third, many companies sell to the consumer at his home on the basis of advance prospecting information. Home calls may be preceded by telephone solicitation in which women with pleasing telephone personalities are employed to call large numbers of consumers. Names of those who manifest some degree of interest are turned over to skilled salesmen who call on the consumer at home. Prospect information is also obtained in response to offers made in newspaper, car card, or other forms of advertising.

One or more of the above forms of selling are used by a large number of well-known manufacturing or distributing companies, including Avon Products, Inc. (cosmetics), Beauty Counselors, Inc. (cosmetics), Electrolux Corporation (vacuum cleaners), Fashion Frocks, Inc. (women's apparel), Fuller Brush Company (brushes, cosmetics, and household items), The Process Company (greeting cards), Real Silk Hosiery Mills, Inc. (hosiery and apparel), and Stanley Home Products, Inc. (brushes and household cleaning aids). Such methods are also widely used on a national basis in selling reference books, encyclopedias, and magazine subscriptions. Some local retailers and small manufacturers use the same approaches in selling a wide range of items, especially in the home furnishings or home improvement categories.

A fourth method coming within the general coverage of "house-to-house" selling consists of route delivery service of perishable food items. Milk is commonly delivered to the consumer's home by a driver-salesman. In most cities some baking companies (e.g., Omar, Inc.) sell direct through route salesmen. Since this method involves frequent and continuing contacts with regular customers who are purchasing in this manner largely because of convenience, it is somewhat apart from the other methods enumerated above. Most of the following discussion is only partially applicable to the operations of such route companies.

Importance of House-to-House Selling

House-to-house selling is the most important form of nonstore retailing. According to 1958 Census of Business data, some 64,000 direct selling "organizations" accounted for about $2.6 billion of sales, or about 1.3 per cent of total sales of retail establishments. This is believed to be less than one-half of the volume of retail sales made by this method, because the Census does not enumerate as house-to-house organizations those companies which operate a house-to-house salesforce out of a manufacturing, wholesaling, or service establishment whose principal activity is something other than retail trade in tangible goods, nor the house-to-house selling activities of regular retail stores, nor the sales of self-employed canvassers operating on a restricted part-time basis and reporting annual receipts of less than $2,500.

The Census figure of some 64,000 "organizations" is somewhat misleading, as it includes all selfemployed salesmen operating as dealers, provided annual sales of more than $2,500 are reported. Actually, there are some 180 members of the National Association of Direct Selling Companies, which is probably more indicative of the number of companies regularly distributing their products or services on a house-to-house basis. It has been estimated that some one and a half million salespeople are engaged in direct selling, about 850,000 men and 650,000 women, with a majority working on a part-time or supplementary income basis.

Reasons for Use

Certain manufacturers and retailers use house-to-house selling primarily because of their ability to build a large volume of business through concentrated and specialized personal selling techniques. Trained in the art of high-pressure salesmanship, the house-to-house man gets results whether it be a small item or one involving several hundred dollars. If the salesman can interest the consumer in his offering and can, by carefully planned selling phrases, suggest that nothing like it can be had locally or that its price is very attractive, the sale is a natural outcome.

Manufacturers are interested in house-to-house distribution in some cases because an attractive margin is available but more often because they can get volume only by this method. If several hundred specialized salesmen can be recruited, trained, and assigned to territories and if the product is worthy, sales may be expected. The problem of interesting wholesalers or retailers in stocking the product and of getting their salesmen to present it to buyers through displays or face-to-face selling is avoided. It is not necessary to use extensive advertising, for personal sales effort is substituted for advertising except in the case of a few large firms who sell in all parts of the country and have found that advertising helps the salesman to gain admission and to secure an audience.

House-to-house selling is attractive to some organizations because sales costs are flexible, varying directly with volume. Salesmen are compensated, in the great majority of cases, altogether on the basis of commissions. Thus there is no expense for selling except for sales actually made.

Limitations and Disadvantages

Lack of consumer confidence in the salesman, his firm, and his product is an important limitation to house-to-house selling. There are just enough fraudulent schemes to cause careful buyers to be wary. Better Business Bureaus have done much to limit the work of fraudulent sellers and in doing so have assisted legitimate firms.

The housewife's inconvenience or annoyance at taking time from household tasks to listen to the salesman is a disadvantage of this method of selling. To overcome the reluctance of housewives even to answer the doorbell, some companies have adopted a variety of plans to pave the way for calls, such as leaving a card saying the salesman will return at a stated time with a useful gift, or leaving an attractive catalog at the housewife's door a day or two in advance of the salesman's visit. In spite of these plans, house-to-house selling is self-limiting because it can grow only at the expense of increasing demands upon the time of the consumer.

Another disadvantage consists of the sales management problem of recruiting, training, and supervising large numbers of salesmen or socalled agents. Usually they are of the type who need constant stimulation and close supervision, and contacts with them must be maintained frequently.

When the sale is by description only or even by sample, the salesman is handicapped, for many buyers have a definite preference for goods which can be inspected at a local store. Moreover, when an order is given to a canvasser, sufficient interest must be created to last until the delivery can be made some days later. Often desire has cooled by that time, and the order is rejected, even at the cost of forfeiting the partial payment made to the salesman.

Many cities have enacted ordinances regulating or forbidding house-to-house selling, canvassing, or soliciting of business, and thus protecting local merchants from this type of competition. The first such ordinance, which forbade this type of selling or business solicitation, except with the permission or upon the invitation of the householder, was enacted in Green River, Wyoming, in 1933; hence all comparable enactments by municipalities have become known as "Green River" ordinances. Such prohibitions tended to increase in the 1950's following a Supreme Court decision upholding their constitutionality. For the most part, however, they have been enacted in small towns and suburban communities near major metropolitan areas. While constituting a problem, the coverage of such laws has not been sufficiently widespread to limit materially house-to-house selling on a national basis.

An important limitation is the high cost of this method of distribution. Some consumers believe that they save by buying from house-tohouse salesmen, especially when dealing with a manufacturer's salesman or agent. Experience has proved, however, that direct-selling manufacturers do not eliminate any of the retail middleman's functions but, in fact, usually incur higher costs than manufacturers who distribute through normal channels. Commissions paid to house-to-house salesmen are within the range of about 25 to 40 per cent and are often higher than the total gross margin realized by store retailers handling similar commodities. In addition, high costs of shipment or delivery are incured on items of low unit value. Unless the consumer pays in advance, there are C.O.D. ("collect-on-delivery") charges to be considered. Even among regular retailers who use house-to-house selling as a supplement to store selling, as is often done in the furniture and appliance trades, commissions paid to "outside" salesmen are usually about twice as large as those paid to salesmen who work in the store. Because of the various problems and limitations involved in this method of distribution, it is not likely that it will ever become a larger part of total retail trade. The method is confined largely to types of items where sales volume can be expanded greatly by highly concentrated personal selling effort and to situations in which an unusually wide gross margin may be obtained so that the high costs of this method of distribution can be covered.

VENDING MACHINES

Distribution of goods through automatic vending machines is a third distinctive form of nonstore retailing. By vending is meant the selling of goods through an automatic machine which releases an item of merchandise upon insertion of a coin or coins by the consumer, thus completing the transaction without the aid of a salesperson.

Historical Development

Crude forms of vending machines were in operation in Europe and in the United States in the nineteenth century. Early machines were restricted largely to the sale of candy, nuts, gum, tobacco products, and postage stamps. During the early part of the twentieth century, there was a great expansion in the United States in bulk vending (i.e., machines which measure out a portion of some unpackaged items such as nuts or candy), especially, "penny sale" machines. In the late 1920's and in the 1930's, new types of machines were designed to vend 5-cent confections, bottled soft drinks, and packages of cigarettes. The development of cigarette vending machines and their acceptance by the consuming public is widely heralded as the inception of the modern era of automatic merchandising. Cigarettes were the first class of commodities retailing for more than five cents and sold on a wide basis through vending machines.

Present Status

Outside of the tobacco, soft drink, and candy trades, vending did not attract much attention until the late 1940's, when experimental attempts were made to merchandise a wide variety of items on an automatic basis, some of which proved relatively successful. In 1958, according to the Census of Business, there were some 3,524 "merchandise vending machine operators," with sales of $842 millions, or about 0.4 per cent of the sales of all retail establishments. These are middlemen who specialize in the operation of vending machines that primarily dispense merchandise rather than provide services. Trade estimates indicate that the total volume of vending machine sales is much greater than reported by the Census. In 1958 a trade source reported sales of $2.1 billion and in 1959, $2,4 billion. Differences between

Census data and trade estimates are explained by three factors. First, some wholesalers operate retail vending machines as an adjunct to their wholesaling business, especially retail cigarette vending by tobacco jobbers.

Second, many machines are owned or are serviced by local processors or manufacturers. Bottled soft drinks, ice, and milk are among the commodities often distributed through vending machines by the manufacturer rather than by a vending machine retailer. Third, many vending machines are owned and serviced by very small operators who engage in this activity only as a sideline and thus do not meet Census requirements for classification as a business establishment within the vending machine trade. While vending machines account for only a small part of total retail trade, they are extremely important in the sale of certain commodities. Of total vending machine merchandise sales, about 44 per cent consists of sales of cigarettes, about 22 per cent of cold and hot bottled and cup drinks, and about 14 per cent of candy and gum. All other products collectively constituted less than 20 per cent of the total vending machine market in 1959.

Vending Machine Operators

The vending machine firm is a rather distinctive form of enterprise in that its operations are carried on in locations owned by businesses or institutions. While there are a few large vending firms, it is predominantly a field of small operators. Some are strictly family businesses, and most of the others have only a few employees. The trend, however, has been toward a smaller number of companies of larger individual sales volume size. A few companies are exceptionally large, particularly Automatic Canteen Co., which operates nationally, and Automatic Retailers of America (ARA), which operates in a number of states.

Like other retailers, vending machine operators buy merchandise and maintain an inventory. Even though most firms are small and deal only in convenience items, it is common for them to purchase direct from manufacturers. Their business is so specialized by merchandise lines that direct buying arrangements are often feasible.

Vending machine locations are organized into routes which are served on schedule. Route men clean machines, replenish inventory, remove and audit sales receipts, and make any minor adjustments that may be necessary. Some operators have specialized service men to handle emergency calls whenever a mechanical failure occurs.

A major and distinctive problem of the operator is that of soliciting location-owners to obtain the right to place a vending machine on their premises. One type of location consists of regular retail stores, which use vending machines as a supplement to their personal selling service. Other locations include almost any kind of site at which a large number of people congregate or pass by with regularity. Examples of the more desirable types of nonstore locations include industrial plants, airports, amusement centers, apartment buildings, armed service installations, bus terminals, hospitals, office buildings, railroad stations, turnpike restaurants and service stations, schools, and theatre lobbies.

Machines are sometimes sold or leased to the owner of the location but, more commonly, the vending machine operator retains ownership and pays the location-owner a rental fee, usually determined as a percentage commission or a special amount per unit of product sold. Thus, to a considerable degree, the usual operational arrangement is analogous to that of a leased department.

Evaluation

Vending machines are used, in some instances, in regular stores where retailers wish to avoid certain "nuisance problems." Soft drink, candy, and cigarette sales are usually of low unit value and therefore relatively expensive to process by personal selling effort. Also, such items are often pilfered by customers or consumed by store employees who do not bother to pay for them, with resulting inventory loss. Such problems are often avoided by the use of vending machines.

Vending machines have enlarged the opportunity for marketing many items by offering them for sale at places where, and at times when, it would not be feasible to provide regular store selling service. Many items sold through vending machines are purchased for immediate consumption; hence, the quantities marketed are to a substantial measure dependent upon the vending machine as a distribution method. There has been a tendency to sell through vending machines more items in the so-called "take-home" market. Ice, ice cream, and milk have been vended profitably in many cities from nonstore locations which are accessible twenty-four hours a day, seven days a week.

One of the most rapidly growing markets for vended products consists of industrial plants where increasing interest has been devoted to machines as dispensers of foods. In some factories, vending machines supplement regular cafeteria food service by providing hot and cold beverages, sandwiches, and desserts, at a variety of in-plant locations. In many small plants that cannot provide regular in-plant food service, the vending machine has become an attractive supplement to the traditional lunch-pail. The vending industry experienced a very favorable rate of sales growth in the period subsequent to World War II—a factor which has stimulated much discussion about this method of distribution, and one which has prompted all sorts of judgments as to its future.

Opportunities for vending machine retailing have been limited by several circumstances. First, notable success has been achieved only in the case of products possessing certain accepted "vending characteristics." These include small size, high, frequency of purchase by the average consumer, and purchase on a strictly convenience basis. Attempts to merchandise shopping goods through vending machines have not been successful, except in highly specialized situations. Second, even though vending machine sales are effected without the aid of a salesperson, vending is still a relatively expensive form of distribution. It can be carried on profitably only at locations where a reasonable volume of regular sales can be expected. Machines in common use involve substantial investments of capital, which must be recovered by adequate depreciation charges. Servicing of the machines by route men is time-consuming and costly.

In addition, the vending machine operator must cover the overhead costs of his business and pay the location-owner a fairly substantial proportion of the total receipts for rent. Vending could not have attained its present state of development if consumers were not willing, at least in many cases, to pay some premium over regular retail store prices for the added convenience of buying at nonstore locations and at odd hours.Third, vending machines have been limited historically by the use of coins, which factor restricted their application to types of items that can be bought with change carried by the average consumer. In 1960, however, new types of equipment were introduced with "bill-changing" sections.

Such machines are capable of accepting currency of various denominations, rejecting counterfeits, and returning correct change to the customer. While the eventual influence of such equipment is highly speculative, it does remove one traditional restriction in the use of vending machines as a marketing device.In summary, it is apparent that vending is a relatively high-cost method of distribution, that gross margins on goods vended must ordinarily be higher than on goods sold in large volume through ordinary retail store methods, and that vending is limited substantially to convenience goods items which may be purchased by the consumer at almost any place without advance planning. Vending is likely to remain a small factor in the total retail sales pictures, since machines for selling traditional vendible commodities are already available in nearly all types of feasible locations. New types of bill-changers, however, open additional opportunities for experimentation with products of higher unit value and suggest possibilities for rapid growth in vending, even though it is likely to remain a very small part of total retailing.

16

Currency Adjustment and Balance of Payments

GAINS FROM INTERNATIONAL TRADE

More and more, we live in an interdependent world in which countries are not self-sufficient, but they trade with each other according to their comparative advantage. Exports and imports of goods and services and financial transactions have increased drastically since World War II.

The direct or indirect benefits of international trade and finance come primarily from the enlargement of the market and the specialization and more efficient employment of productive resources, as well as technological advances. Each country has certain advantages, compared to other countries, that can be better exploited through foreign trade. When a country is able to supply another country with a cheaper commodity, it would be better for the latter country to import this commodity and concentrate instead on the production of other commodities in which it has some advantage. In this case, the first country has what is called an absolute cost advantage over the second country. This might be due to better climatic conditions, more advantageous soil and subsoil resources, cheaper labour or other factors of production, or better technology.

What matters most, though, is not the absolute but the relative cost. One country that may be able to produce two commodities, say jute and wheat, more cheaply than another country has an absolute advantage in both commodities. But if the production of jute is comparatively cheaper than wheatmore the first country can still benefit from trade by specializing in the production of jute and exchange some of it for the other country's wheat. And the second country will be better off by specializing in the production of wheat and exchanging some of it for jute. In this case, the first country has a comparative advantage in jute over wheat and an absolute advantage in both jute and wheat. Likewise, the opportunity cost of jute is equal to the amount of wheat to be given up to release resources for the production of a unit of jute.

The Multiplier Effect and Absorption

Additional investment (*dI*) in the economy would increase income (*dY*) by a multiple amount and the multiplier (*k* = *dY*/*dI*) depends on the marginal propensity to consume (*MPC*), that is, k = 1/1 – MPC = 1/MPS where MPS stands for the marginal propensity to save. For example, if MPC is 0.8 or the MPS 0.2, then k = 1/0.2 = 5, that is, each additional $1.00 invested would increase national income by $5.00, assuming no leakage in the spending rounds. In an open economy, the leakage of spending outside the economy into imports (*M*) is making the multiplier smaller depending on the marginal propensity to import (*MPM*). That is,

$$k = 1/ (MPS + MPM)$$

Thus, assuming MPM = 0.2 and using the above example, we have,

$$k = 1/ (0.2 + 0.2) = 1/0.4 = 2.5,$$

which is smaller than that without imports. The same thing would occur from additional government spending or exports, which increase the multiplier. National production (or gross domestic product, *GDP*) may be different than national expenditures for consumption (C), investment (*I*), and government spending (*G*). That is, total domestic output, or what an economy produces, may be different than total domestic expenditures (demand), or what it absorbs (*A*). The difference is net exports, that is, exports of goods and services (*X*) minus imports of goods and services (*M*). Then, total output is equal to total expenditures, or

$$GDP = C + I + G + (X - M)$$

As absorption, A, is equal to C + I + G, then GDP = A + X – M and GDP – A = X – M. If absorption or total domestic spending exceeds total domestic production, then the difference will be covered by imports. Depending on the elasticity of exports, a devaluation, ceteris paribus, is expected to increase exports if there is unemployment in the economy; but if there is full employment, the result would be inflation.

The Use of Geometry

The gains from foreign trade. Before international trade, country 1 produces and consumes at point A, where the indifference or consumers' preference curve meets the production possibility curve. After trade with other countries, production moves to point B as the country specializes in the production of commodity X for which it has a comparative advantage, that is, a comparative cost advantage. A straight line tangent to the production possibility curve at point B and the shift of the indifference curve I to indifference curve II indicate the gains of society from foreign trade from A to D. As a result, the country exports BC of commodity X and imports CD of Y.

Likewise, country 2 with a comparative advantage in the production of commodity Y would specialize in the production of commodity Y, exporting B_2 C_2 of Y and importing C_2 D_2 of X. In a broad sense, a country has a comparative advantage in the production of a commodity if the exports of this country's commodity, as a percentage of total exports, is higher than its imports of this commodity. For example, the U.S. chemical exports are 12 per cent of total exports and imports are 6 per cent of total imports, the United States has a comparative advantage in chemicals, whereas Japan has a comparative advantage in cars with exports of more than 20 per cent of total and imports of only 3 per cent of total, respectively Two countries with identical production possibility curves but different indifference curves (tastes). Before foreign trade, country 1 produces and consumes at point A and country 2 at point A_2. With foreign trade, the first country specializes in the production of commodity Y, where it has a comparative advantage, producing at point B, whereas country 2 specializes in the production of commodity X, producing also at point B. A straight line tangent to the production possibility curve at point B shows the higher consumption levels through the shift of the indifference curves from I to II for country 1 and from I_2 to II_2 for country 2. Both countries enjoy higher consumption at points D and D_2, respectively, because of trade between them. Country 1 exports BC of Y and imports CD of X, whereas country 2 exports BC_2 of X and imports C_2 D_2 of Y.

Two countries with the same taste, as the common indifference curve I indicates. The tangency of this curve on the production possibility curves at points A and B shows production and consumption of countries 1 and 2, respectively, before foreign trade. After trade, country 1 specializes in the production of commodity X, producing at point A_2, whereas country 2 specializes in the production of commodity Y, producing at point B_2, which are determined by a straight line tangent to the production possibility curves of country 1 and country 2, respectively. Both countries consume at point D on a higher indifference curve I_2, and country 1 exports A_2 C of X and imports CD of Y, whereas country 2 exports C2 B_2 of Y and imports C_2 D of X..

With foreign trade, the quantity of supply increases from Q_2, determined by the equilibrium of domestic demand and supply, to Q_3. Domestic demand is Q_1, total supply is Q_3, and the difference $Q_1 - Q_3$ is absorbed by exports, whereas additional production due to free trade is $Q_2 - Q_3$.

TERMS OF TRADE AND CURRENCY DEVALUATION

In general terms, the ratio of export prices to import prices is called the terms of trade. A distinction can be made between commodity or net-barter terms of trade, measured by the ratio of the export price index to import price index *(Px/Pm)100*; gross barter terms of trade, measured by the ratio of physical quantity index of exports to that of imports or *(Qx/Qm)100*; and income terms of trade, which can be derived by multiplying the price index of exports by the quantity index of exports and dividing by the price index of imports or *(Px·Qx)/Pm*. Finally, by multiplying net-barter by gross-barter terms of trade, the current-account terms of trade is derived or *(Px·Qx)/ (Pm·Qm)* × *100*. The last expression is important because it incorporates both prices and quantities of exports and imports and, therefore, indicates whether a country has a deficit or a surplus in its trade balance. Thus, if the index of a current-account terms of trade is lower than 100, this means that total export proceeds are less than total import payments. Inversely, if it is higher than 100, the country is better off; at 100 there are no net gains or losses for the country from foreign trade. When productivity of exports (*Rx*) is also considered, we can measure the single factorial terms of trade *(Px/Pm)Rx*. When the productivity of both exports and imports *(Rx/Rm)* is considered, we have the double factorial terms of trade, that is *(Px/Pm) (Rx/Rm) × 100.*

The reciprocal demands between two countries establish the terms of trade, which are affected by domestic costs. This principle can be explained with the help of what Alfred Marshall called the reciprocal demand curves, or offer curves. Thus, the offer curve of country X (say the United States) indicates how much steel the country demands from another country Y (say Japan) in exchange for wheat at different prevailing prices and vice versa for country Y.

Such offer curves can be used also for bundles of exportable goods in exchange for bundles of importable goods. After successive trade transactions between the two countries, the two offer curves meet at the equilibrium point E, where the amounts of wheat offered and steel demanded by country X equal the amounts of steel offered and wheat demanded by country Y; that is, where the reciprocal demands of the two countries are equal. The price ratio, which is measured by the slope of the ray 0A, shows the terms of trade. A change in the supply or demand against country X and in favour of country Y is reflected by the shift in Y's offer curve to a new position (Y2), establishing a new price ratio, 0B; that is, new terms of trade more favourable for Y and less favourable for X. Thus, at the price ratio 0A, one ton of steel was exchanged with one ton of wheat, whereas at 0B, the same one ton of steel is exchanged with more wheat (1.3 tons). This means that X's terms of trade deteriorated by 30 per cent in favour of Y.

Exports and imports react to exchange rate changes. Net exports, that is, exports minus imports, are expected to rise when the currency of a country depreciates and to fall when it appreciates, after a time lag. As the price of a currency, in terms of other currencies, rises, export prices increase and prices of imports fall. As a result, the volume of exports declines and that of imports rises, or the gross-barter (quantity) terms of trade decline. Ceteris paribus, this has a contractionary effect on domestic output and employment. This is so, because with a currency depreciation (devaluation) exports rise and imports fall, thereby improving the balance of trade and the economy of the country in question, and vice versa with a currency appreciation. An appreciation of the currency of country Y (Japanese yen) would shift its offer curve to Y_2 and the slope 0A to 0B, in which one ton of steel would be exchanged with 1.3 tons of wheat. Therefore, through the currency appreciation, the gross-barter or quantity terms of trade improves for country Y and deteriorates for country X, which is exchanging more of its product (wheat) for the same amount of steel.

The opposite is expected to occur with currency depreciation, as the prices of exports would be lower for other countries, without an equivalent currency depreciation, and foreign demand for exportable goods would increase. This would lead to deterioration of the net-barter or price terms of trade, but to the improvement of the gross-barter or quantity terms of trade. Therefore, the net effect on the balance of trade would depend on which index, the price index or the quantity index, would be higher, and this would be shown by the current-account terms of trade. The exchange rate depreciation (devaluation) is affected by the price elasticity of imports and exports. In order to pay for imports, foreign exchange is needed, which can be obtained by exports. The size of the devaluation of a currency depends on the price elasticity of demand for imports (*Epm*), which is determined by the percentage change in the quantity (*Q*) of imports (*m*) demanded over the percentage change in price (*P*) of imports, or, Epm = (dQm/Qm)/ (dPm/Pm)

Likewise, price elasticity of exports is equal to the percentage change in the quantity of supplied exports over the percentage change in price. In the case of devaluation of a currency, expectations are that the balance of trade would improve, depending on the international demand elasticity. Thus, if the price elasticity of demand for imports is 1.2, Epm nd that for exports is 0.7, Epx then a devaluation of the currency of the country by 20 per cent would improve the balance of trade by 38 per cent.

If the summation of the elasticities of imports and exports is higher than 1, ceteris paribus, there would be improvement in the balance of trade. In our example, Epm + Epx = 1.2 + 0.7 = 1.9. If this summation is equal to 1, there would be no change, but if it is less than 1, there would be deterioration in the balance of trade. For example, if the elasticity of imports is 0.4 and that of exports 0.5, then Epm + Epx = 0.4 + 0.5 = 0.9, and the balance of trade would be worse off.

Usually, the summation of the international demand elasticities is higher than 1, thereby ensuring improvement in the balance of trade following a devaluation or depreciation of a currency. This is so because a devaluation or depreciation of a currency means higher prices for imports and lower prices for exports, and therefore less imports and more exports, thereby improving the balance of trade of the country. Moreover, the income elasticity of imports (*Eym*) is determined by the percentage change in the quantity of imports demanded over the percentage change in national income (*Y*), or,

$$Eym = (dQm/Qm)/\ (dY/Y)$$

Also, income elasticity of exports is equal to the percentage change in the quantity of supplied exports over the percentage change in national income.

DETERMINATION OF EXCHANGE RATES

Exchange rates, that is, prices of a currency in terms of other currencies, may be fixed or flexible. In the case of a fixed exchange rate, the central bank of a country determines the price of its currency versus the currencies of other countries. With flexible exchange rates, the price of a currency in terms of other currencies is determined by free market supply and demand. The price of the dollar in terms of euros, the new currency introduced by the European Union.

The equilibrium point (E), where the familiar down sloping demand (D) curve meets the upsloping supply (S) curve, indicates the price of the dollar in euros and the quantity of dollars demanded and offered at this price. If the price is higher than the equilibrium price, there would be more dollars supplied than demanded; that is a surplus of dollars. When the price is lower than the equilibrium price, there would be a shortage of dollars.

Ceteris paribus, in the case of surplus, there would be a pressure for lower prices, whereas in the case of shortage, there would be a pressure for higher prices, back to the equilibrium point. Globalization driven mainly by information technology and impressive financial development is revolutionizing production, constantly expanding markets, changing social conditions, and intensifying the interdependence of nations. In this type of globocracy and internetocracy, globocapitalism is subordinating politics and resulting in what Marx and Engels predicted more than a century ago, withering the state away, but voluntarily, not through the dictatorship of the proletariat.

With the liberalization of capital in a growing borderless world, huge amounts of money circle the planet instantly, replacing the use of letters of credit and other previous financial instruments. Nevertheless, there are arguments, mainly by Professor John Gray, that globalization, based on laissez-faire capitalism and Thatcherism, is a utopian idea, an Enlightenment thinking, which erodes social cohesion and imposes cultural imperialism that vests on British-American power.

It is an unstable, inequitable, and immoral neoliberal system, destroying the welfare state, traditional societies in emerging nations, and families everywhere. Varieties of capitalism and national variations, with state spending to avoid stagflation and high inequality, which prevails largely in Latin America and even in the United States, should be the economic goal, according to these arguments, because, in an analogy to Aristophanes and Gresham's law, under globalization, "bad capitalism drives out good." It seems that, in spite of the disadvantages of globalization and neoliberalism, global-capitalism would prevail in the twenty-first century, because welfarism and state intervention lead to inefficiency and laziness.

The rise in the middle class and the spread of ownership in shares, as many countries follow the U.S. system in which over 50 per cent of Americans have investments in stocks, supports the argument of Joseph Schumpeter of the trend towards the system of people's capitalism or in practical terms "shareholder capitalism."

The evolution of the international monetary system went through a number of stages, from the use of different goods as money to the gold standard period, the interwar instability, and the Bretton Woods fixed exchange rates. The postwar trade deficits in many countries led to the dollar shortage up to the late 1950s, but severe competition from abroad turned the United States from a surplus to a deficit country and to a substantial gold drain from the U.S. reserves resulting in the post-1973 floating exchange rates.

The growing capital mobility made pegging exchange rates, that is, the price of a currency following the value of another hard currency, such as the dollar, difficult to maintain. The implication is that floating rates are expanding all over the world. Through arbitrage, equalization of spot and forward exchange rates can take place almost instantly, whereas foreign exchange options are rapidly growing worldwide.

Although international trade is, in principle, no different from domestic trade, the use of different currencies and different laws and regulations distinguish global from domestic trade and finances and require separate analysis. Some important international currency symbols are shown below.

Country	**Currency**	**Symbol**
Brazil	Real	R1
Australia	Dollar	A$
Canada	Dollar	C$
European Union	Euro	€
France	Franc	FF
Germany	Mark	DM
Greece	Drachma	Dr
India	Rupee	Rs
Japan	Yen	Y
Mexico	Peso	Ps
Saudi Arabia	Riyal	SR
Singapore	Dollar	S$
South Africa	Rand	R
Switzerland	Franc	SF
United Kingdom	Pound	£
United States	Dollar	$

The equilibrium (E1) of supply of and demand for dollars ($), in terms of yen, at a price of 80 yen per dollar and quantity 6 (say billion dollars). In case of shift in the demand curve from D1 to D2, the new exchange rate would be 100 yen per dollar and the quantity $8 (billion). This would be the result of an increase in the price of the dollar, through a depreciation of the yen. If the

U.S. Federal Reserve Bank (Fed) decided to reduce the price of the dollar, it can supply dollars to the market, thereby restoring the initial price. Changes in exchange rates affect foreign trade. Thus, as a result of the rising exchange rate (appreciation) of the dollar, above the rate of inflation, in the early 1980s, net exports (exports minus imports) fell sharply. The opposite occurred when the dollar began to fall after 1985 and net exports began to improve, but with a time lag of more than a year.

BALANCE OF PAYMENTS AND FOREIGN EXCHANGE

An accounting statement showing the transactions of the United States with all the other countries for a period of time. Positive figures (credit) show items that bring gains in foreign exchange. Negative figures (debit) indicate items that bring losses in foreign exchange. The U.S. balance of trade, that is, exports minus imports of merchandise, was negative since 1975, reaching a record deficit of $168.8 billion in 1998, some $64 billion with Japan and $ 56.9 billion with China. The balance of current accounts, which includes the balance of goods, services and investment income as well as unilateral transfers, reached a record deficit of $233 U.S. billion dollars in 1998. The previous record deficit was that in 1987 of $168 billion. Even higher current account deficits are predicted in the near future.

Ceteris paribus, under flexible exchange rates, the depreciation of a country's currency restores the trade equilibrium and eventually the balance of payments of the country in question. Countries with fixed exchange rates will face problems of excess supply and overvaluation of their currencies, then running balance-of-trade deficits. Once their reserves of foreign exchanges are depleted, their currencies, sooner or later, would be depreciated to correct the trade imbalance. The main reason of depreciation of a currency is inflation, which may be due to excess demand over supply, which may be the result of an increase in spending and in money supply (demand-pull inflation), or to higher costs due to an increase in wages and other costs (cost-push inflation). Demand-pull and cost-push inflation as a result of the shifts in the demand and supply curves, respectively. Moreover, inflation may be the result of structural rigidities and inflexibility in production, imports and income distribution (structural inflation), mainly in emerging nations.

The effects of a devaluation or depreciation upon the balance of trade of a country. As a result, the prices of imports of the country in question increase and those of exports decline. With inelastic demands, quantity for imports changes little, as does quantity for exports. Therefore, the balance of trade deficit and the demand for foreign currencies could increase for some time, as a result of the devaluation or depreciation, before improving later through long-run increases in the elasticity, as the J-curve shows. Indicates the equilibrium price after trade. Country 1 exports commodity Y and country 2 imports Y until the equilibrium price is reached in the middle graph. The relationship of foreign trade and national income. Investments (I) and exports

(X) act as injections in the economy, increasing national income (Y), whereas savings (S) and imports (M) are considered as leakages. When S + M = I + X, then we have the equilibrium level of income. An increase in exports (X2) leads to a new equilibrium of income (Y2 2).

The relationship of balance of payments and foreign exchange. Suppose that U.S. buyers demand more European products. Ceteris paribus, this would lead to a deficit in the U.S. trade balance and a lower price of the dollar in terms of euros, from 1.2 to 1.0, as the supply curve would shift to S2. Assuming the same demand curve, the new equilibrium would be at point b at a price 1.0 and quantity 8, that is, a lower amount of euros per dollar and more dollars offered than at the previous equilibrium. Therefore, under flexible exchange rates, the depreciation of the dollar restores equilibrium to the foreign exchange market at point b.

PROBLEMS OF PROTECTIONISM AND THE WORLD TRADE ORGANIZATION

From time to time, protectionist measures, in the form of quotas, tariffs, or capital movements, are imposed by a number of governments around the world, which inhibit free trade and investment. Restrictions on imports of steel, cars, textiles, dairy products, fruits, and a host of other products, as well as on financial instruments and multinational companies, were and still are imposed by a number of developed and developing countries. For example, the United States wants to limit annual steel imports, mainly from Japan, Brazil, South Korea, India, Italy, France, Indonesia, and Russia, to about 29 million tons because unfairly they sell in the United States market at prices less than the cost. It is argued that protection may be needed for infant industries, mainly in developing countries. Alexander Hamilton, the first Secretary of the Treasury of the United States (1791), and Frederick List, a German political refugee in the United States, urged the use of tariffs to foster growth in U.S. manufacturing. Via internal economies of scale and cost reduction, as well as external economies, through backward and forward linkages with other industries, industrialization would improve. Moreover, through industrial protection, diversification in the domestic economy would be achieved, and overspecialization in agricultural or mining products in poor countries, which are easily exposed to cyclical fluctuations, would be avoided. However, it is doubtful if protection would be removed when the "infants" become "adults" able to compete in open markets.

Policymakers can move closer to the competitive ideal and maximize social welfare, reaching Pareto's optimum, by removing distortions to this ideal, thereby achieving the first-best solution. However, this may be difficult in practice because of the eventual side effects of such a policy. For example, removal or reduction of a tax on gasoline may increase the satisfaction of one group but reduce the welfare of society as a whole by increasing air pollution. If the adverse side effects of the first-best solution are excessive, then the second-best policy may be applicable through the introduction of another distortion to reduce or offset the effects of existing distortions, as for example, the shift from a gasoline tax reduction to an income tax reduction, as long as expected gains are greater than losses to society.

Similar evaluations of second-best policies can be made in the formations of common markets, regarding inner group benefits versus the rest of the world. In order to reduce protectionism and encourage free international trade, the General Agreement on Tariffs and Trade (GATT) came into existence in Geneva on January 1, 1948. Its main functions were to organize conferences for nondiscriminatory tariff reduction, enforce international agreements regarding prohibitive barriers (quotas, export subsidies, and the like), and to help improve the position of the poor member nations. Under the auspices of GATT, extensive negotiations for tariff reduction produced good results during the Kennedy Round (1962–1967) for industrial countries, but limited results for developing countries. Such reductions were sizable (up to 50 per cent), mainly for raw material and manufacturing goods. The Trade Expansion Act, which the U.S. Congress passed in 1961, authorizing the President to make across the board tariff cuts, influenced, to a large extent, the negotiations of the Kennedy Round. Because poor countries received little attention in their appeal for more trade and no aid, by the GATT, which was considered as the "rich countries' club," they supported the creation of the United Nations Conference for Trade and Development (UNCTAD). The main conferences of UNCTAD in Geneva in 1964 (attended by 122 countries), in New Delhi in 1968, in Nairobi in 1976, and so on, made suggestions to help poor nations improve exchange reserves and increase imports of capital goods. In order to end unfair trade practices mainly by Japan and to meet the European complaints as well as to reduce the pressure for import quotas by Congress, mainly in textiles, steel and agricultural products, the Nixon administration called for a new round of GATT negotiations. As a result, the Tokyo Round produced results similar to the Kennedy Round, cutting tariffs on manufacturing products by 36 per cent, on the average. The meeting of GATT members at Punda del Este, Uruguay, in 1986–1993, known as the Uruguay Round, produced new measures for trade liberalization through cuts in tariffs and subsidies, as well as for protection in intellectual property and elimination of dumping.

Particular attention was given to the interests of the developing countries, mainly Brazil and India, and the encouragement of foreign investment. In 1993, it was agreed by all member nations to reduce the subsidized agricultural exports by 21 per cent over six years, whereas restrictions on rice imports in South Korea and Japan were eliminated. The United States, Australia, and Canada, as large exporters of farm products, want to liberalize trade of such products and they object to the EU Common Agricultural Policy (CAP). The World Trade Organization (WTO), which replaced GATT in 1995, extended its authority to agricultural products and services, whereas a vote of two thirds of members was enough to settle trade disputes rather than a unanimous vote as under GATT.In the meeting of the member nations in Seattle, United States, in November 1999, and in Washington in April 2000, developing countries complained against the industrialized countries that rich nations get benefits from the trade rules at their expense. They proposed to reintroduce subsidies that are needed to protect their native industries and to weaken antidumping measures that protect mainly U.S. producers from cheap imports.

Also, they proposed to delay the enforcement of intellectual property rights (copyrights, patents, trademarks), to shorten the ten-year restriction on imports by rich countries, and to avoid policies that harm the environment. Furthermore, it is argued that infant industries need protection until they become competitive through economies of scale and experience. Representatives of developing countries, environmentalists, and labour unionists argue that globalization and the WTO ignore core labour issues and environmental standards. As the argument goes, by reducing tariffs and supporting greater openness, the WTO encourages investment in countries with low wages, without the protection of the environment. Such problems would have more importance after China's membership in the WTO. Because of the rebellion by developing nations, the riots, and the infighting among the 135 member countries, the WTO conference in Seattle collapsed.

The argument of poor nations, mainly Brazil, India, and Egypt, was that Washington had tried to benefit the United Steelworkers, Boeing, Amazon.com, and other industries in this conference at their expense, whereas Europe and Japan emphasized their disputes over agriculture and steel. Nevertheless, open global markets foster the movement of capital, products, and people around the world. Moreover, free trade spurs competition, lowers prices, increases average wages, and improves the quality of life. However, globalization may increase inequality, which is poisoning democracy. Some countries unfairly subsidize exports to infiltrate and increase their shares in foreign markets. Japan did that for exports of steel and other products in the United States. Such policy forced the U.S. government not to allow the sale of Japanese steel at a lower price than that of American steel ("trigger price mechanism") and to establish quotas for the number of imported Japanese cars. Lately, the U.S. Department of Commerce complained that NEC and Fujitsu, both Japanese super-computer makers, sold their products on the American markets at prices well below fair values, thereby harming Silicon Graphics, a U.S. competitor. For that reason, and as a result of the International Trade Commission ruling, the United States imposed duties to compensate for the related damage.

EFFECTS OF CUSTOMS DUTIES

Although tariffs and other restrictions are in the domain of international economics, their growing importance for domestic fiscal and financial policies requires a brief review here. In taxed imports, through tariffs or customs duties, foreign suppliers have to sell their products at lower net prices, affecting domestic policies on subsidies, employment, and bankruptcies. The burden of product taxes is thus shifted to foreigners. Such a shifting runs counter to the international equity principle, according to which each country should pay its own taxes. However, other countries whose products are taxed use the principle of retaliation and impose their own taxes on products they import. The results of such protectionist policies are higher prices and lower quantities of products exchanged. Similar changes in prices may take place through taxes on exports, which burden foreign consumers.

Countries that enjoy monopolies or oligopolies in natural resources or products and dominate export markets may impose export taxes, thereby increasing the cost of exports. Again, the foreign consumers will pay more, free trade will be restricted, and conflicts among countries may arise, unless such policies are in harmony through mutual understanding or international agreements among the governments concerned. The government can use customs duties to collect revenue and, at the same time, to protect domestic production and employment, especially in infant industries. The amount of revenue from tariffs and the degree of protection depend on the elasticities of supply and demand for the commodity imported. The higher the elasticity of demand for imports, the more the decrease in the quantity of imports and the less the revenue from custom duties. The same holds true for the elasticity of supply. The supply and demand for a commodity that is partly produced domestically and partly imported (AG) to cover total demand. When a tariff per unit is introduced, total demand would be reduced, domestic production would be increased, and imports would be reduced to EF. The government would collect total revenue BCFE (revenue effect), that is, (EB) × (EF). The triangle ABE measures the benefits of tariffs to the producers (protective effect); the triangle CGF measures the sacrifice to the consumers (consumer effect) because of higher prices due to tariffs. Domestic producers produce more output by AB, and consumers demand less output by CG as a result of tariffs. The result is a payment of subsidies to domestic producers, which can be considered as an income transfer from the consumers to the producers of the import-competing good considered.

Some governments provide budget subsidies for certain products that can be unloaded to other countries at prices below the cost of production (dumping). To retaliate, other nations use antidumping and countervailing duty measures. Such subsidies and antidumping policies restrict free and fair trade among nations and increase the possibilities of protectionism, in addition to budgetary expenditure needed to pay for subsidiaries. Among the products subsidized are textiles, electronics, and primarily steel. Steelmakers in the United States complain against Japan and the EU and ask for quota restrictions; the Japanese complain against South Korea; EU steelmakers complain against Romania and Brazil; and those in developing countries, against industrial countries, accusing them of trying to keep the "new boys"—the Third World producers off the world markets.

To avoid protectionism and trade wars, many steelmakers and other producers ask for multilateral agreements among interested nations similar to that of cotton textiles in the 1960s, which allow developed countries to restrict textile imports from developing countries. However, steel users and primarily automakers and construction industries object to such agreements, which protect inefficient domestic manufacturers and push up prices. For the government, though, such agreements lead to less unemployment and more tax revenue.

An unwise policy of protectionism in the 1930s exacerbated the Great Depression of that period. Throughout the 1920s, U.S. exports increased, as did private loans to finance such exports to other countries. After the crash of 1929, average tariffs were raised to 40 per cent. Foreign firms could not sell their products to the United States and could not collect dollars to pay their loans. The tariffs of the 1930s walled out competition and walled in inefficiency. They cut back imports, but they reduced exports as well. The result of the beggar-thy-neighbour policy of protectionism reduced world industrial production by about 30 per cent and increased unemployment by more than 25 per cent, whereas world trade in manufactured goods declined by more than 40 per cent and overall government revenue from tariffs was reduced.

For some commodities, effective tariffs are relatively high in the United States, mainly for clothing, fabrics, milk, cheese, butter, cigars, cigarettes, plant, vegetables, olive oil, and other primarily agricultural products. Similar and even higher tariffs prevail in Japan and the EU countries. Tariff reductions and improvements in trade with the poor nations would also allow reduction in U.S. aid, which is a burden on the budget, and stop the cry of the poor nations for "trade, no aid."

Recently, the United States and the European Union had a "banana war" because the Europeans refused to open their markets to bananas produced mainly in central American countries and shipped by Chiquita Brands International and Dole Food, two American companies. In retaliation, the United States announced 100 per cent tariffs on some European products, such as cashmere sweaters, Mont Blanc pens, tapered candles, and bath products. The Europeans argue that the companies are American and influence politicians through generous contributions to both Democrats and Republicans, but the bananas are produced elsewhere. However, the World Trade Organization ruled that Europe has to abide and negotiate a settlement in order to avoid retaliation.

LETTERS OF CREDIT AND BANKERS' ACCEPTANCES

In order to reduce foreign trade risks, exporters want assurances that they will receive payment for the products they sell. Normally, an importer applies to a commercial bank for a letter of credit (LOC) in which the bank guarantees payment to the exporter, at a specific time, with the presentation of required documents, mainly the bill of lading. The LOC may be revocable, that is, it can be changed by the parties or, usually, irrevocable, in which case it cannot be changed without the consent of the parties. Also, the LOC may be revolving, when it is used for many shipments for a period of time, or may be a standby LOC, when the bank, with a fee by the exporter, promises to pay the exporter in case the importer defaults. To facilitate trade financing and minimize currency risks, banks or other firms may buy invoices from exporters at a discount, collecting the invoices from the importers (factoring). Moreover, the exporters can sell the promissory notes, endorsed by importers' banks, to forfeiting banks with a discount.

These financial (forfeiting) devices are used by banks and other institutions to finance exports to emerging nations. Also, barter trade or counter trade can take place among traders of different countries to conserve foreign exchange and avoid tariffs and other restrictions. Bankers' acceptance is a time draft an exporter draws and presents, together with the shipment documents, to a bank for acceptance. The bank that accepts the draft usually pays the exporter before maturity at a discount and may rediscount it with the Federal Reserve Bank at the prevailing discount rate. At maturity, the bank will pay the holder of the draft the face value of the draft received from the importer a day earlier. Bankers' acceptances are used mainly for large amounts of trade between different countries, for which the importer pays a fee, usually 1.5 per cent of the draft value.

Index